SHAKESPEARE PROBLEMS

Edited by J. DOVER WILSON

VIII. NEW READINGS IN SHAKESPEARE

VOLUME II

NEW READINGS IN SHAKESPEARE

by
C. J. SISSON

VOLUME TWO
THE HISTORIES
THE TRAGEDIES

CAMBRIDGE
AT THE UNIVERSITY PRESS
1956

PUBLISHED BY
THE SYNDICS OF THE CAMBRIDGE UNIVERSITY PRESS

London Office: Bentley House, N.W. 1
American Branch: New York

Agents for Canada, India, and Pakistan: Macmillan

Printed in Great Britain at the University Press, Cambridge
(Brooke Crutchlev, University Printer)

CONTENTS

ILLUSTRATIONS

THE HISTORIES

KING JOHN

ACT 1

1.54 *Cordelion*[1]

If we are to correct *Cordelion* to *Cœur-de-Lion*, as even in some recent texts, we are going against a frequent Elizabethan form of the name, an anglicized version of it. It is as much a sophistication as the reading *Brittany* for the Folio and Elizabethan *Britain*. These were the forms used by Shakespeare, and they should be preserved.

1.236–7 *Sir* Robert *could doe well, marrie to confesse*
   Could get me Sir Robert *could not doe it;*

New Cambridge, following Vaughan's variation upon Pope, reads:

  Sir Robert could do well—marry, to confess—
  Could he get me. Sir Robert could not do it;

Alexander reads:

  Sir Robert could do: well—marry, to confess—
  Could he get me? Sir Robert could not do it.

I accept Pope's insertion of *he* in l. 237, but I propose a radically different reading which is in accordance with the Folio punctuation, seems to me to be more in character, and gives a better sense. The parenthesis seems to me out of place in this highly unapologetic Bastard.

 READ: *Sir Robert could do well; marry to confess*
   He could get me, Sir Robert could not do it.

(I now prefer this reading to my original *Could he get me,*) The omitted initial *he* might well have been in the form of *a*, and the more easily missed therefore. There is a marked

---

[1] Citations are from the text of the First Folio, the basic text.

emphasis on *me* which contrasts 'do well' with 'get *me*', and almost justifies italics. 'Sir Robert could play his part well enough in getting a son; but if put on his oath to say that he could beget *me*, he could not do it.'

'Confess' is often used in evidence in Elizabethan English to mean 'agree', not necessarily a guilty admission.

1.256–7 *Heauen lay not my transgression to my charge,*
   That art the issue of my deere offence

Rowe, following F 4, emended *That art* to *Thou art*, in order to make sense of the first line, and so Kittredge and Alexander read. But *New Cambridge*, following Staunton, emends the second *my* in l. 256 to *thy*, and leaves l. 257 as in Folio. I have no doubt that the thought and feeling of the speech point to the latter emendation, and that the compositor merely repeated the *my* from *my transgression*, a more plausible error than to misread *That* for *Thou*.

Lady Faulconbridge could not well pray for absolution from her own sin. But she could well pray that her guilt should not fall upon her son too, that the sin of the mother should not be visited upon her child, a thought that haunted Elizabethans, familiar as they were with the Bible, as it haunted Shakespeare's Henry the Fifth before Agincourt, and Constance in this play (2.1.179).

READ: *to thy charge,*

ACT 2

1.104–7 *That* Geffrey *was thy elder brother borne,*
   And this his sonne, England *was* Geffreys *right,*
   And this is Geffreyes *in the name of God:*
   How comes it then that thou art call'd a King,

New Cambridge reads:

       [he points to Angiers
   And this is Geffrey's in the name of God:
   How comes it then that thou art called a king,

I suggest the following reading:

And this is Geffrey's [points to Arthur]. *In the name of God,*
How comes it then that thou art called a king,

'Geffrey', says King Philip to John, 'was thy elder brother, and this (Arthur) is his son. England was Geffrey's by right, and this (Arthur) is the representative of Geffrey's rights.'

1.144 *As great* Alcides *shooes vpon an Asse:*

Theobald confidently read *shows*, i.e. 'as great Alcides' (robe) would show upon an ass', and *New Cambridge* follows, with Kittredge and Alexander. The emendation is of course attractive, and brings in Hercules' lion's skin to join Richard's worn by Austria. But it cannot be argued that the emendation is necessary, only that it is plausible, with the spelling *show* for *shoe*. But one wonders why a compositor, with *shows* before him (*show* was more rarely spelled *shoe* than the converse) should read and set up *shooes*. The ass, as Malone points out, has hoofs as well as a back. And Steevens cites a number of references to Hercules' shoes, which were perhaps better known even than his robe in popular imagery. I find the reading forced, moreover. One might have expected:

As great Alcides' on an ass's back.

My only hesitancy comes from the line following:

But Asse, Ile take that burthen from your backe,

The insult of calling a man an ass was, however, mostly linked up with a reference to its hoofs. The insult seems sufficient, and in the Bastard's vein. And the Folio reading should stand, in the absence of manifest corruption, which cannot be alleged.

READ: *As great Alcides' shoes upon an ass.*

1.152 England *and* Ireland, Angiers, Toraine, Maine,

It is common to emend *Angiers* to *Anjou*, even though admitting that Shakespeare confused *Angiers* with *Anjou*. This is unashamed 'improvement', and cannot be justified, though all recent editors accept the emendation. Holinshed also uses Anjou and Angiers with equal indifference.

1.215 *Comfort yours Citties eies, your winking gates:*

Capell suggested *Confronts*, with general acceptance, as in *New Cambridge*. I prefer, however, Rowe's *Confront*, with the plural subject of *preparation* and *proceeding*, an easy misreading by the compositor, whose final *s* in *yours* is a mere slip.

1.432–4 *Such as she is, in beautie, vertue, birth,*
         Is the yong Dolphin euery way compleat,
         If not compleat of, say he is not shee,

Hanmer meets the difficulty of l. 434 by reading *O say* for *of, say*. *New Cambridge* suggests, but does not read, *all, say*. Kittredge reads, *I say* for *of, say*. Corruption is manifest to all except Alexander, who reads the line as in Folio, but preceded by a dash.

I suggest *completed* for *compleat of*, with some graphic plausibility. The sense would then be an anticipation of later lines in the speech. 'If he is not completed—and he will not be completed till he is joined with Blanche—he will be less complete than Blanche now is.' 'Completed' has the sense both of perfection and of wanting nothing.

READ: *If not completed, say he is not she;*

1.438 *Left to be finished by such as shee,*

I see no justification for the emendation of the Folio *such as she* to *such a she*, which 'Dr Thirlby prescribed' and Theobald and *New Cambridge* accepted.

1.487 *For* Angiers, *and faire* Toraine Maine, Poyctiers,

New Cambridge and others correct *Angiers* to *Anjou*
here as above, 1.152, and elsewhere, but leave *Poictiers*. To
be logical, they should surely correct all Shakespeare's
geography, and read also *Poitou* for *Poyctiers*. I prefer to
read with Shakespeare *Angiers* and *Poictiers*, and *Anjou*
where he reads so, as in l. 528 below. These readings are
not compositors' errors.

ACT 3

1.155-6 *But as we, vnder heauen, are supreame head,*
         So vnder him that great supremacy

It is well known that the censorship interfered with oaths
and blasphemy in the hands of Sir Henry Herbert, and that
'gingerbread' expletives were substituted in the Folio in
many places for the less inhibited originals. It seems to me
that where the evidence is reasonably clear we may
properly restore these originals to the text. In this instance
the *Book of Common Prayer*, with other documents, and
the use of *him* in l. 156 corroborate Collier's *God*.

READ: *But as we, under God, are supreme head,*
       So under Him that great supremacy

1.258-9 *France, thou maist hold a serpent by the tongue,*
         A cased Lion by the mortall paw,

Theobald read *chaféd* for *cased*, and recent editors follow.
Dover Wilson assumes the compositor's omission of the *h*
of *chafed*, and the corrector's alteration of *cafed* to *cased*,
an elaborate process, to justify the reading. It seems more
natural for Shakespeare here to be taking an image from
experience. The one place where one is likely to take a lion
by the paw is in a Zoo, and accidents are frequent to this
day from such foolhardiness. The Lions in the Tower were
one of London's sights in Shakespeare's day, and there was
a white lion kept in the Bear Garden. On all grounds I

therefore suggest *caged*, which Dover Wilson records also as a suggestion of Moore Smith's, though he reports him as thinking of a man shut up in a cage with a lion. I do not, however, pretend to explain how the misreading arose in the press.

READ: *A caged lion*

3.1–2 *So shall it be: your Grace shall stay behinde*
So strongly guarded:

Lettsom proposed *More* for the second *So*, which *New Cambridge* accepts. Kittredge and Alexander retain *So*. The second *So* was perhaps caught up from above. I am disposed to be assured that there is corruption, though for a somewhat different reason. I suggest the reading *And* for the second *So*, with a certain emphasis in the word. A particular form of ampersand as an abbreviation for *And*, in frequent use, could readily be misread as *So*, and this is what may have happened.

READ: *And strongly guarded.*

3.39 *Sound on into the drowzie race of night:*

The early editors accepted *race* as giving sense, 'mankind at night', but read *one* for *on*, 'sounding one o'clock.' In the nineteenth century, *race* only was found unsatisfactory, and Collier proposed *ear*, accepted by most editors now, including *New Cambridge* and Kittredge. Alexander however retains *race*, which he here glosses as 'course'(presumably the space through which Night passes in her course). I find it difficult to accept either defence of the Folio *race*. But I find more difficulty with the explanation offered by Dover Wilson for the presumed Folio misreading of *race* for *eare*. This involves a foul *e* box, resulting in *eare* being set up as *care*, and the corrector transposing *c* and *r*, thus arriving at *race*, a rather far-fetched theory. I cannot see why a corrector should change an unintelligible *care* to a more unintelligible *race*.

I offer the emendation of *face* for *race*, with the suggestion that the *r* in the Folio *race* is possibly a broken *f*,
though we may be driven to 'foul case' as an alternative
explanation. Dr McManaway, when consulted, examined
ten copies of the Folio at the Folger Library, and reported
the *r* to be worn or broken in some copies but fairly clear
in others. In the two copies that I have examined myself
the foot of the letter is abnormal to my eyes. But re-
examination, upon Dr McManaway's report, left me more
doubtful. Dr Pafford upon minute inspection of the
University of London copy found the letter defective but
was satisfied that it is an *r*, though not impossible as a
broken *f*. The Second Folio reads *race*. The reading, however, gives a good sense and a vivid image. King John's
later words in the speech refer to eyes, ears, and tongue,
a wider image than ears only,

> Without eyes, ears, and harmful sound of words,

in his contrast of day with night. (It is hardly consonant
with the image of a *course* of Night, by the way.) I feel
bound to report a parallel phrase which supports the
reading *ear*, and which does not seem to have been cited:

> I have heard
> Two emulous Philomels beate the eare o' th' night.
> (*The Two Noble Kinsmen*, v. 3. 141–2.)

But I see no plausible explanation of the compositor's
misreading *eare* as *race*, a difficulty which Dover Wilson
clearly feels acutely.

READ: *Sound on into the drowsy face of night;*

3.52 *brooded watchfull day,*

Pope read *broad-eyed* for *brooded*, followed by *New
Cambridge* but not by other recent editors. I do not follow
the advantage of such a change, or the objection to the
Folio reading. *brooded* and *watchful* go admirably together
and are almost synonymous except for the image implicit in

brooded. The contrast is with *drowsy night* above. *Brooding* is not 'in melancholic absorption' here, but 'jealously vigilant'. (Chapman's *broad-eyed* is rather different from the Greek 'broad-seeing'.) And it is very difficult to justify such a misprint on any plausible grounds.

READ: *brooded*

3.65–6 Iohn. *Death.*
       Hub. *My Lord.*
       Iohn. *A Graue.*
       Hub. *He shall not liue.*

Editors all read *My Lord?* It is a small point, but of much significance in the acting and interpretation, and the Folio *My Lord.* seems to me right. The trend of John's thought has become clear to Hubert already. His *My Lord* is not an exclamation or surprised question. It is submissive, understanding, and decisive, and follows naturally what has gone before. Certainly, there is no necessity to alter the Folio, thus read, or to assume that punctuation is always negligible.

4.182 *Strong reasons makes strange actions:*

For *strange* F2 reads *strong*, and most editors follow, though not Malone or Kittredge, i.e. not 'all modern editors', as Dover Wilson reports. I agree with Malone that the emendation in F2 is officious. That such an error was easy to make is not evidence that it was in fact made. Why should the First Folio compositor have made it, having read the first *strong* correctly, unless he were setting up as editor and disapproving the repetition? *strange actions* makes perfectly good sense, and seems to me a much more effective phrase here than the repeated *strong*. It refers back, moreover, to Pandulph's words just before:

            'Tis *wonderful*
    What may be wrought out of their discontent,

READ: *Strong reasons make strange actions.*

ACT 4

2.42–3 *And more, more strong, then lesser is my feare*
         I shall indue you with:

Tyrwhitt's emendation of *then* to *when* has been resisted in some modern editions. Kittredge, for example, reads

And more, more strong (then lesser is my fear),

New Cambridge and Alexander, however, return to *when*, though it can hardly be justified except as a pure error. I suggest a reading which is plausible graphically and which gives plain sense also. It was easy to misread *the* as *thẽ* (then).

READ: *And more, more strong, the lesser is my fear,*
         I shall indue you with.

As Dover Wilson rightly observes, John is speaking of Arthur, who is his 'fear', and of Arthur's coming death, after which he can explain more freely. This reading, in fact, gives the same sense as the *New Cambridge* emendation from Tyrwhitt.

2.117 *Where is my Mothers eare?*

There is debate upon the actual initial letter in the Folio text of the last word here. Most editors consider the letter to be a broken *c*, and read *care*. The Second Folio, certainly, read *eare*. It seems to me, as to the Cambridge editors, to be possibly a damaged *e*, and I read *ear*. Opinions may perhaps be affected by stylistic objection to *ear* in the light of John's later words, 'And she not hear of it?', as tautological. But there is good authority for this kind of writing: 'He that hath ears to hear, let him hear.' And there is stronger evidence in the Messenger's direct reply to John's 'Where is my Mother's ear?':

My liege, her ear
Is stopped with dust.

ear seems to me natural and logical, and *care* forced and unlikely in the context. The typographical evidence is at any rate open to debate.

3.15–17   *The Count* Meloone, *a Noble Lord of France,*
          Whose priuate with me of the Dolphines loue,
          Is much more generall, then these lines import.

Most recent editors find these lines explicable, on the basis of interpreting *private* to mean 'private report', and the deletion of the comma in l. 16. But I agree with Dover Wilson that the word can hardly bear this sense. There is no authority, or likelihood, given the known general sense of *private* as a noun, for this interpretation. Emendation seems necessary. Dover Wilson, while reading *private with me* in *New Cambridge*, in a note suggests *warrant* (*wr^t*) read as *with*, and *me* added by a corrector.

I suggest *notice* for *with me*, a misreading that could readily occur with the pattern of writing. *not* is read *w^t*, and *ice* as *me*. *private notice* gives exactly the sense that editors read into *private* alone. The compositor was misled by an obvious nexus of thought, 'The Count, who is private with me of the Dolphin's love', and thought that 'The Count, . . ., is much more general than these lines import', continued the sense. As indeed it does, and it would be a good interpretation but for the fact that it is not an answer to Pembroke's question, and assumes his knowledge of Melun.

READ: *Whose private notice of the Dauphin's love*

ACT 5

2.64 *And euen there, methinkes an Angell spake,*

New Cambridge gives a stage-direction, [*a trumpet sounds,* to give sense to *an Angell spake.* But surely this obscures the true sense of the words. 'I spoke like an angel; see, there is the Legate, who speaks for heaven, and will speak as I did.' This is approximately Malone's explanation, which I prefer to Johnson's. Certainly there is no need for emendation, e.g. of *spake* to *speaks*, or for suspecting a pun upon *nobles* and *angels*.

6.12–13   *thou, & endles night,*
               Haue done me shame:

   The early editors accepted *eyeless* for *endles*, one of Theobald's flashes of genius, and it has been little questioned. *Endless*, of course, gives sense of a kind, but it is so irrelevant an epithet here that we are justified in concluding, on stylistic grounds, that there is corruption. It is not death, or the endlessness of night, that is in Hubert's thought. It is the deeds of a 'Black, fearful, comfortless, and horrible' night, an 'eyeless' night ('a sightless night', as Shakespeare says in *Lucrece*), that did Hubert shame. The compositor's misreading of *eyeless* as the more familiar *endless* is easily explicable, as Walker and Dover Wilson saw, on the basis of the spelling *eieless* for *eyeless*.
   READ: *eyeless night*

7.15–16   *Death hauing praide vpon the outward parts*
           Leaues them inuisible,

   It is generally agreed that *invisible* makes no sense here, though *New Cambridge* and Alexander retain the Folio reading, Alexander without special glossing. Dover Wilson in a note suggests *invasible*, while leaving *invisible* in his text. Attempts have been made to defend the Folio text by interpreting *invisible* as qualifying *Death*, meaning in effect *invisibly* or imperceptibly, which seems hardly relevant here. Hanmer read *insensible*, followed by Kittredge, with little plausibility. Steevens suggested *invincible*, as an adjective referring to *Death*.

I suggest *unusable*, which may at first appear somewhat desperate but is entirely plausible graphically and makes very good sense. 'Death completes the paralysis of the body by sickness, and then turns upon the last fortress of being, the mind.'

READ: *Leaves them unusable*,

KING RICHARD THE SECOND

DRAMATIS PERSONAE

It is surely right to include *Glendower, a Welsh Captain* among the *dramatis personae*, and not to leave him name-less. (See note on Act 2, Sc. 4, *Stage-direction*, below.)

ACT 1

1.97 *Fetch from false Mowbray*[1]

What is known as the White Quarto (Q.W.) reads *Fetcht*, and Folio *Fetch'd*. Most editors read *Fetch*. On the whole, *Fetched* seems preferable, in spite of the authority of Q1. Bolingbroke is rehearsing past misdeeds, and 'he did plot' in l. 100 suggests *Fetched* in the past tense as more consonant in sequence, as also in sense, for the treasons of eighteen years ago can hardly now *fetch* 'their first head and spring'.

READ: *Fetched from false Mowbray*

1.186 *Coosin, throw vp your gage,*

Folio reads *throw downe*, and many editors follow, though *New Cambridge*, Kittredge and Alexander follow Quarto with *throw up*, i.e. 'throw up to the upper stage'. It may seem dangerous as a piece of business to make the King lean down to catch a thrown gage, and even undigni-fied for a subject to throw anything for his King to catch. The insistence throughout, in constant repetition, is upon *throwing down* for subsequent presentation to the King as guardian of the gages, probably picked up by the Lord Marshal. The previous order, 'Give me his gage', is addressed to Mowbray, not to Bolingbroke.

READ: *throw down your gage;*

[1] Citations are from the First Quarto, the basic text.

1.195 *Stage-direction.*

Folio marks an exit for Gaunt. None is marked in Quarto or in *New Cambridge*. The exit is fully motived, for Bolingbroke has refused to obey Gaunt. It is also necessary, for Gaunt's re-entry on the different scene following. Kittredge and Alexander concur.

READ: [Exit *Gaunt.*

2.70 *heare*

Some copies of Quarto read *cheere*, followed by Malone. Folio adds its authority to that of later pulls of the Quarto, in which *cheer* is corrected to *hear*, giving a better sense and undoubtedly the original text. A similar misprint involving confusion between *h* and *ch* occurs in *A Midsummer Night's Dream* 2.1.101, on which see note on Vol. I, p. 126. My own former apparent adhesion to *cheer* was the result of an oversight in the preparation of copy. The sense is manifestly better with *hear*, for the Duchess is describing the desolateness of Plashy, 'empty lodgings, unfurnished walls, unpeopled offices, untrodden stones', and surely *silence* everywhere. There is again the direct sequence of 'what shall good old York there *see*...and what *hear* there'.

READ: *And what hear there*

3.20 *To God, my King, and my succeeding issue,*

Folio reads *his* for the second *my*. *New Cambridge* and Alexander read *my*. But it is a very forced interpretation that makes Mowbray here swear his loyalty to God, to the King, and to his own successors in his own title, a very odd oath. It is irrelevant that Richard has no 'issue'. Every King has successors in his throne. Moreover Bolingbroke was suspect on this point, as Mowbray was not. It is the usual oath that swears loyalty to God, to the King, and to his heirs and successors. There is no true parallel between this and the subsequent 'my God, my King, and me'.

Line 20 defines Mowbray's oath of loyalty, l. 24 the objects
of Bolingbroke's treachery. It is most reasonable to assume
that the compositor's *my* was attracted by the preceding *my*
of *my King*, and that the Folio reading is a true correction.

READ: *and his succeeding issue,*

3.129–38 *And for we thinke...kinreds bloud;*

Dover Wilson's note in *New Cambridge* suggests that
this passage reveals the printing of both of two versions,
a first draft and a revised, instead of the revised version
only. He is fortified in this by the omission of ll. 129–33
in the Folio text. But Dover Wilson very fairly indicates
that the deletion of ll. 134–8 would have the same effect,
and his own text in *New Cambridge* makes no deletion in
fact. I prefer to believe that the deletion in Folio is a
genuine 'cut', along with other cuts in the Folio text, and
not a textual correction. I see no difficulty in accepting the
whole passage as it stands in Quarto as Shakespeare's
definitive copy. 'Peace, now slumbering in our country's
cradle, roused up by drums and trumpets, might be
frightened from our quiet country.' There is no difficulty
in the change of construction involved in

> Which so roused up...
> Might from our quiet confines fright fair peace,

READ: as in Q.

4.23 *Our selfe and Bushie,*

Folio adds *heere* Bagot *and* Greene, and the 1634
Quarto *Bagot here and Greene*, which most editors follow.
New Cambridge reads as in Quarto, in a broken line. I
think it probable that the *here* of Folio was editorial and
metrical, but that Bagot *and* Greene formed part of
Richard's speech to Aumerle, Bagot and Green being
present with him.

READ: *Ourself, and Bushy, Bagot and Green,*

4.52 *Stage-direction.* Enter Bushie with newes.

Folio here reads: Enter Bushy.

> Bushy, *what newes?*

New Cambridge rightly points out the plausibility of confusion between *w^t* (with) and *w^t* (what), in this evident
confusion of dialogue with stage-direction in the Quarto
text. Most editors read as in Folio. But it seems safer to
follow the material of the Quarto, which affords a stage-
direction, *Enter* Bushy, and a line of speech, *What news?*
The Folio reading is surely editorial.

READ, as in *New Cambridge*:   Enter *Bushy.*

> *What news?*

ACT 2

1.18 *As praises of whose taste the wise are found*

The text of this line, corrupt itself, was further corrupted
by later Quartos and consequently by Folio, beginning with
state for *taste*, and ending with the Folio

> *As praises of his state: then there are sound*

The Second Folio returned to *found.* Collier suggested
fond for *found* in the First Quarto text, and this emendation
has been established and is accepted by recent editors, *New
Cambridge*, Kittredge and Alexander. *found* is taken as a
misreading of *fond,* possibly spelled *fonnd,* and the line to
mean 'sounds such as praises which even the wise relish',
i.e. even Richard himself. This offers difficulty, as Dover
Wilson feels, inclining him to Lettsom's *unwise* for *wise,*
and consequently to leaving the text here marked with an
obelus.

A further difficulty is the destruction of a rhyme, *found,*
sound, by the substitution of *fond.* It might seem that the

corruption may rather be in *praises* than in *found*. I suggest *praisers* for *praises*. There is a clear parallel to this confusion in Hand D, *Sir Thomas More*, l. 127, where the manuscript reads *flandes* for *Flanders*. The line then takes on an entirely different sense, much more apt and significant in the context of York's criticism of Richard, 'flattering sounds, for example flatterers, with whose taste for adulation prudent men are found to join in chorus'. It is wisdom or policy to share this fashion for adulation, which infects the whole Court.

READ: *As praisers of whose taste the wise are found,*

1.19 *to whose venome sound*

Folio also reads *venom*, and all editors follow. I suggest, however, that the Quarto compositor misread *d* as *e*, and that his copy read *venomd*, a more natural formation of the phrase and image. It is true that later on he spells *venom* as *venome* (2.1.157). In *Lucrece* 850 *venome* may well be *venomd* also.

READ: *venomed*

1.70 *For young hot colts being ragde, do rage the more.*

New Cambridge reads *ragged*, a 'ragged colt' being 'unbroken'. Other editors read *rag'd*, the Folio version. But neither reading satisfies the apparent antithesis implicit in the line, nor makes really good sense. If *raged*, then it is pointless to say that a horse, if deliberately tormented, will rage the more for being *raged*. If *ragged*, it may be asked why *the more*. Again it is too obvious, and weak. I suggest a corruption in the Quarto compositor's reading of his copy, of *raged* for *raynd*. *reined* gives full antithetical effect, and is entirely apt in the context. 'The more you try to rein in or control a young spirited colt, the more he is likely to kick over the traces or to bolt.' And so Ritson read.

READ: *For young hot colts being reined do rage the more.*

1.280 [*The son of Richard Earl of Arundel,*]

This line is not to be found in Quarto or Folio. It was supplied by Malone, as in *New Cambridge*, to bring Shakespeare's text into line with the facts as given in Holinshed, or nearly so, and to relate the presumably missing l. 280 thus supplied with l. 281 following. The two errors involved in two lines of the original texts, the identity of the prisoner of the Duke of Exeter, and the family relations of the Archbishop of Canterbury, are too much for probability, even if we allow Shakespeare great discretion in following his source. Alexander follows Quarto. But the true alternative to Malone's insertion is to indicate a lacuna, as Kittredge does, if we accept, as I think we must, that the compositor omitted a line.

1.284 *Francis Coines;*

Folio reads *Quoint*, followed by most editors. Holinshed gives the form *Coint*, which Dover Wilson adopts, with good reason. Folio gives the correct form of the name, but in a spelling characteristic of its decade. I find, for example, 'twenty-four pound of ready *quoyne*' in a will of 1624 (J. Pountis. P.C.C. 64 *Byrde*) meaning 'ready coin'. We may reasonably accept the Folio form in the Quarto spelling, i.e. *Coint*.

2.3 *life-harming*

Q.W. reads *halfe-harming*, Folio *selfe-harming*, both puzzling, except that Folio is apparently an attempt to make sense out of the later Quarto reading. There is no need to depart from Q 1.

2.11–12   *my inward soule,*
        With nothing trembles, at something it grieues,

So both Quarto and Folio read the line (Folio without comma after *soul*), and editors universally emend it. Pope suggested a radical emendation, followed by *New Cambridge*:

> *With nothing trembles, yet at something grieves,*

This assumes that the compositor read *yt* (it) for *yᵗ* (yet), having omitted it, and then inserted it in the wrong place, a difficult theory. Most editors are less drastic and are content with re-punctuation, e.g. Kittredge:

> *With nothing trembles. At something it grieves,*

But there is no clear need for emendation. The line as it stands is quite comprehensible, idiomatic, and in sequence with the trend of the speech, with an emphasis in the speaking on *something*.

READ: *my inward soul*
> *With nothing trembles, at something it grieves,*

2.110 *Thus disorderly thrust into my hands,*

   New Cambridge reads *thrust disorderly*, against the evidence of all Quartos and Folio, and as suggested by Steevens. Kittredge concurs. It is a mere metrical interference with the authoritative text, and is unjustifiable, especially as it injures the sense, which is not *thus thrust*, but *thus disorderly*.

3.80 *And fright our natiue peace with selfeborne armes?*

   Many editors read *self-born*, meaning domestic or home-grown, in civil war. *New Cambridge* and Alexander rightly retain *self-borne*. But Dover Wilson's interpretation as 'borne in one's own interest' seems to offer difficulty. Surely the phrase simply means 'arms borne by the natives of the country itself (not by invading foreigners)'.

Sc. 4 *Stage-direction.* **Enter erle of Salisbury and a Welch captaine.**

Folio reads: Enter Salisbury, and a Captaine.

There is no doubt that the Welsh Captain is Owen Glendower, and that this marks Glendower's first entry upon Shakespeare's historical stage. It is clear in Holinshed that this is so, in the passage from which this scene was drawn, and that Shakespeare knew his name when he wrote it. He is mentioned by name by Bolingbroke in 3.1.43. It is, moreover, abundantly plain that this is a first sketch for the fuller, later, portrait of Glendower in *1 Henry IV*, for his speech is concerned with portents and omens at the death of a King, as at his own birth in the later play. It seems entirely reasonable to include Owen Glendower in the *dramatis personae* of this play, and to name him here.

R E A D : Enter *Salisbury* and *Glendower*, a Welsh Captain.

ACT 3

2.29–31 *The meanes that heauens yeeld must be imbrac't*
And not neglected. Else heauen would,
And we will not, heauens offer, we refuse,

Lines 29–32 are omitted in Folio. Pollard suggested that the reason was their obscurity and the need to insert *if* in l. 30 to make sense. *New Cambridge*, Kittredge, and Alexander concur, and read:

> *And not neglected; else, if heaven would,*
> *And we will not, heaven's offer we refuse,*

But the obscurity of the Quarto text rests only in the punctuation of one line, and re-punctuation of l. 31 yields perfect sense, the sense more laboriously expressed in the emended version. The sole virtue of an inserted *if* here is metrical.

READ: *The means that heavens yield must be embraced*
And not neglected. Else heaven would,
And we will not. Heaven's offer we refuse,

Much turns upon *Else.* 'We must accept heaven's help. If we do not (*else*) the position is that we are saying no to heaven's yes.'

2.40 *In murthers and in outrage bouldy here,*

The apparently obvious emendation here, *bloody*, is supported by a later Quarto and by Folio. The transposition of *l* in *bouldy* yields *bloudy*. But Kittredge, *New Cambridge*, and Alexander all read *boldly*, which is surely more apt here, where the sense demands an adverb rather than an adjective. The error of the compositor is at least equally plausible, the omission of an *l* in *bouldly*.

READ: *boldly*

2.84 *Awake thou coward Maiesty thou sleepest.*

Folio reads *sluggard*. Dover Wilson notes that some editors think this 'more Shakespearian', but rightly reads *coward* as in Quarto. The word follows close upon Richard's previous words, 'Have I not reason to look pale and dead?' *pale* and *pale-faced* are attributes of fear and cowardice, not sluggishness, at any rate in Shakespeare.

READ: *coward*

3.17 *Lest you mistake the heauens are ouer our heads.*

Rowe improved what Folio accepted, and read *Lest you mistake: the heavens*, as does *New Cambridge*, as giving better sense. But it may well seem to give a far weaker and flatter sense (though Kittredge and Alexander support it in their texts), and in any case one cannot ignore punctuation entirely in textual criticism. The text as it stands, indeed, offers two senses, both cogent and forcible. The more obvious one is 'Lest you ignore the fact that the heavens are above us', but I think it more probable that the sense is,

'Lest you go against divine will, against the heavens which
are above us', with the omission of the relative pronoun so
frequent in Shakespeare and in Elizabethan English.

READ: *Lest you mistake the heavens are over our heads.*

3.99–100   *and bedew*
Her pastors grasse with faithfull English bloud.

Capell and Theobald improved *pastor's* to *pastures'* and
pasture's respectively, and editors now follow one or the
other. There is no need whatever to emend a reading
which stands in all early texts and gives a better sense than
that accepted by editors. It is Richard speaking, who is
almost obsessed with images of his royal function, here the
image of the shepherd or pastor, England his grass-land,
and its people his sheep. *pastures'* or *pasture's* seems
equally forced and awkward in comparison. We must not
be misled by modern associations of *pastor* exclusively with
ministers of religion.

READ: *Her pastor's grass*

3.119 *This sweares he, as he is princesse iust,*

Q.W. read *a prince* for *princesse*, and Folio improved by
inserting *is*, thus giving the reading *he is a Prince, is iust*,
which all recent editors follow. This reading seems
awkward and artificial, and it is the result of early editorial
labours, which took us part way only in the later Quarto,
and led into error in Folio. It seems highly probable that
the Quarto compositor found *prince ę iust* in his copy and
that he misread the *ę* as *es* and read *princes*, spelling it
princesse of course. But it was an ampersand, in the form
that closely resembles the *s:es* sign, giving *a prince & just*.
So read, the line becomes natural and rhythmical, and leads
up to the following line,

And as I am a gentleman I credit him.

READ: *This swears he, as he is a prince and just,*

3.121 *Northumberland, say thus, the King returnes,*

The reading which appears to be universally accepted is

Northumberland, say thus the King returns—

or its equivalent in punctuation. The Quarto comma after *thus* is ignored. It may seem that *thus* is hardly relevant in this sense in the context, and Richard's speech loses effect with this reading. Northumberland is something like a herald, charged to repeat the King's words. Part of Richard's message is that he, the King, has returned. It is, once more, in his vein to put it so. The rest of the message follows.

READ: *Northumberland, say thus. The King returns:*

This reading is more natural and more characteristic, and is closer to the indications of the Quarto punctuation.

3.182 *In the base court come downe: downe court, downe King,*

The line is mostly read *In the base court? Come down?* It seems more likely that Richard combined his two previous thoughts into one question here, which summarized his images. The Quarto punctuation also favours this reading. It might even be held that its colon suggests a dash rather than a question-mark, a reflection rather than a question. Perhaps a reflective question.

READ: *In the base court come down?*

ACT 4

1.52 *I taske the earth to the like*

Other Quartos read *take*. Folio omits a passage including this. Editors all read *task*, interpreted by the Clarendon editors 'I lay on the earth the task (of bearing the like gage)'. I suggest *tax*. The metathesis of *taske* for *takse*, and the spelling *takse* for *tax*, are not infrequent. The sense is much the same.

READ: *I tax the earth to the like,*

ACT 5

2.28 *Did scowle on gentle Ric. no man cried, God saue him,*

Folio omits *gentle*, and *New Cambridge* follows, to improve the metre. But are we to assume that the compositor of Quarto simply invented it? He may, of course, have neglected to observe the deletion of the word in Shakespeare's copy. But the line as it stands has an easy rhythm in the speaking as a six-footer. It should be retained, as by Kittredge and Alexander.

2.74 ff. Capell indicated that a stage-direction *Enter Servant* was necessary at l. 74, *Exit Servant* at l. 77, and *Re-enter Servant with boots* at l. 84. There can be no real doubt that this was so, as most editors read. *New Cambridge* would have York's call for his servant at l. 74, and his order to him at l. 77, to be impatient, and unobeyed until l. 84, mainly on the ground that the only stage-direction in Quarto is at l. 84:

His man enters with his bootes.

The first entry and exit, however, are clear in the dialogue. But the re-entry had to be marked in the prompt-copy, in order that the property, York's boots, should be ready when required. This is a common feature of existing prompt-copies. The real stage-business here is the Servant standing between York and his Duchess, obeying York against the anger of the Duchess. It is to the Servant that she addresses the line,

Hence villain, never more come in my sight.

3.10 *Which he yong wanton and effeminate boy,*

Pope read *While* for *Which*. Folio reads *Which*. Most editors retain *Which*, rightly, I think. *New Cambridge*, however, reads *While*, and supports it as a misprint 'of a common type'. It is certainly not plausible graphically, nor is it otherwise plausible as a misprint. *Which* gives excellent sense in Shakespeare's way of writing English, which was not Pope's, and is admittedly more difficult to analyse or parse. The later words, 'to support so dissolute a crew', are clearly in apposition to *Which*. 'Which, namely to support so dissolute a crew, he takes as a point of honour.' And so Kittredge and Alexander read.

READ: *Which*

5.42 *Ha ha keepe time,*

It is difficult to make clear that *Ha ha* is not laughter, as might well be suggested by the usual reading adopted, *Ha, ha!* Richard is listening, and his *ha*'s are inarticulate expressions of his critical attentiveness to the possibly false time kept by the music.

READ: *Ha—ha—keep time!*

5.106 *How now, what meanes Death in this rude assault?*

New Cambridge agrees with earlier commentators that the line is obscure and perhaps corrupt. Staunton suggested *How now? What? meanst death.* But there is no obscurity. Richard has a complex mind. And here he asks Death, 'what are your real intentions? To kill me? Yet you give me the weapons, in this very act of assault, to kill the murderers'.

READ: as in Q.

THE FIRST PART OF
KING HENRY THE FOURTH

ACT 1

Sc. 1 *Stage-direction*. **Enter the King, Lord Iohn of Lancaster, Earle of Westmerland, with others.**[1]

Capell's omission of Prince John has been followed by many editors, as by *New Cambridge*, but not by Kittredge or Alexander. But there is no justification for this departure from the text. The pretext presumably is that Prince John does not speak in the scene. Yet in Act 5, Sc. 1, he is permitted to enter (though again he does not speak) in most editions, including *New Cambridge*. His part is, nevertheless, a speaking part in the later scenes of Act 5, and there is every reason why he should appear at once upon the King's first entry in the play, apart from the question of 'dressing' the scene. He would, of course, be recognizable by his place beside the King, and probably by heraldry. It is significant that the King is accompanied here only by Prince John, and not by Prince Henry, the reason for which appears later in the scene, and in Sc. 2 immediately following.

Capell's addition of Blunt, on the other hand, is obviously right. He is present, 'new lighted from his horse', and is indirectly addressed by the King.

READ: Enter *King Henry, Prince John, Westmorland, Sir Walter Blunt*, and others.

2.27–8 *let not vs that are squiers of the nights bodie, bee called theeues of the daies beauty:*

There seems to be no need to consider this too curiously or to doubt whether it is corrupt. The meaning seems to be

[1] Citations are from the Quarto of 1598, which is basic for this play.

plain, and simple, with no more point than its euphuistic turn of phrase. 'It should not be said that we who are night-rakes are consequently a blot upon the world of daylight.'

3.83–5 *Against that great Magitian, damnd Glendower,*
Whose daughter as we heare, that Earle of March
Hath lately married:

Alexander retains the Quarto reading, *that...that.* *New Cambridge* reads *the...that* and argues that the second *that* is necessary for the audience to relate the Earl of March to a previous mention of Mortimer. This seems very laboured. The second *that* could only be justified as a distinction between one Earl of March and another. And the audience a few lines later again hears about 'revolted Mortimer', and is left in no doubt. (Folio reads *the...the.*)
    READ: *that great magician...the Earl of March*
So Kittredge also reads.

3.108 *Neuer did bare and rotten pollicy*

Folio reads *base* for *bare*, and many editors follow, including Kittredge and Alexander. *New Cambridge* rightly reads *bare*, but explains it as meaning 'patent'. The sense is rather 'bare-faced', as opposed to 'coloured' (by pretexts), as suggested in l. 109, 'Colour her working'.
    READ: *bare*

ACT 2

1.52–7   Enter Chamberlaine.
        Gad. *What ho: Chamberlaine.*

Most editors mark the entrance of the Chamberlain at l. 52, as indicated thus in Quarto. But it is surely apparent that it is not so. Gadshill's *What ho, Chamberlain* is of course a call, not a salutation. The Chamberlain answers ('within') 'At hand, quoth pickpurse'. And Gadshill's comment is obviously an aside for the audience, at the end of which the Chamberlain makes his appearance. And so *New Cambridge* also reads. The Quarto entrance is related to the Chamberlain's entry into the dialogue, not upon the stage.

READ: l. 57 *thou layest the plot how.*
            Enter *Chamberlain.*

1.84 *Burgomasters and great Oneyres,*

Folio reads *Oneyers*, and this spelling is generally adopted. But there is great debate upon the meaning of the word, and an infinity of comment. Malone's note upon the word comes near the truth, in his reference to *Coke on Littleton*, to the abbreviation *O.Ni* (for 'Oneratur nisi habet sufficientem exonerationem') in respect of officers in charge of Crown dues in money, who are therefore *Oni-ers*. Hence Dover Wilson's note interprets *oneyers* as 'Exchequer officials'.

Cowell's *Law Dictionary* or *The Interpreter* (1607), however, points the allusion much more precisely. The Exchequer entry *O.Ni* is related especially to a Sheriff entering upon his accounts with the King. The word *oneyer* therefore really means 'sheriff', and the whole phrase 'Burgomasters and sheriffs'. This is, of course, particularly apt in Gadshill's subversive mouth, as both should be pillars of the law.

READ: *oneyers,*

2.1–55: l. 1   Enter Prince, Poines, and Peto &c.
        l. 52 Enter Gadshill.
        l. 54 Po. *O tis our setter, I know his voice, Bardoll,*
                what newes.

There is much variety in editorial versions of stage-directions in this scene. Some make the first stage-direction, *Enter Prince and Poins. New Cambridge* makes

Prince, Peto, Bardolph and Poins all enter here, and rejects the generally accepted entrance of Bardolph with Gadshill at l. 52, on the ground that Gadshill is the 'setter' and not Bardolph, who was with the Prince's party. But I see no ground for departing from the Quarto direction at l. 1, or for resisting the addition of Bardolph after the Quarto direction, 'Enter Gadshill' at l. 52. Bardolph could well have been a look-out, he could have met Gadshill, heard the news from him on their way to the Prince, and be ready to answer Poins' question at l. 55, 'Bardolph, what news?' I do not see, moreover, why Bardolph, being of their party, should not be asked to report what he has been told. *New Cambridge*, to avoid this difficulty in its conduct of the scene, adopts Johnson's suggestion and makes Bardolph speak,

> Poins. *O, 'tis our setter. I know his voice.*
> Bardolph. *What news?*

in place of the original l. 55, as in the Quarto text. I see no ground for this radical rewriting of the text. It is to be noted that the universal speech-heading for Bardolph in this play is *Bar.*, and the spelling of his name in dialogue and direction is *Bardol* or *Bardoll*, without exception. The Quarto text and punctuation give no support to emendation.

READ: l. 1   Enter *Prince Henry, Poins,* and *Peto.*
    l. 52 Enter *Gadshill* and *Bardolph.*
    l. 54 Poins. *O 'tis our setter, I know his voice.*
      [Comes forward with *Peto.*] *Bardolph, what news?*

4.270 *you starueling, you elfskin,*

Hanmer's *eel-skin* for *elf-skin* is generally accepted. Kittredge retains *elf-skin*, but without gloss in interpretation. There is ample authority for *eel-skin* as relevant in meaning here, none for *elf-skin*, in Shakespeare's own vocabulary and elsewhere (e.g. 'my arms such eel-skins stuffed' in *King John* 1.1.141). I do not, I confess, see any plausible reason for the compositor's error. A spelling *eleskin* might have led him to improvise *elfskin*, but this is guessing. (The reading *elf-skin* in my recent edition was due to oversight in preparing copy, as is evident from my private notes.)

READ: *eel-skin*,

4.437 *Peace good pint-pot, peace good tickle-braine.*

4.528 *Stage-direction.* **Enter Bardoll running.**

I suggest that a stage-direction is required at l. 437, with an exit for Bardolph and Hostess. Quarto marks an entrance for Bardolph, 'Enter Bardoll running', at l. 528, and for Hostess at l. 532, 'Enter the hostesse'. The prevailing practice among editors is to mark the exit at l. 528 (exactly where Quarto directs Bardolph's re-entrance), along with Hostess and Francis:

Prince Henry. *I do, I will.* [Exeunt Hostess, Francis and Bardolph.]

And Bardolph re-enters immediately.

New Cambridge marks no exit, with the explanation that Bardolph and Hostess 'can exit any time unnoticed by the audience', which is certainly not the way of prompt-copies or of producers in any age.

There is a clear indication in the text and in the necessary action for an exit at l. 437, in Falstaff's words at ll. 433–4:

> For God's sake lords, convey my tristful queen,
> For tears do stop the flood-gates of her eyes.

It is probable that Francis as well as Bardolph should exit here, and I suggest this instead of my former limitation of the exit to Bardolph and Hostess. Falstaff's words now take on additional point and 'business'. As he has addressed the Hostess as 'Queen', so he addresses Bardolph and

Francis as 'Lords', bidding them take the Hostess-Queen away. Falstaff's words at l. 437 accompany the action of ushering her out. Poins is audience enough for the ensuing scene, a scene that is ticklish even in comedy and bears no audience save Prince Henry's confidant Poins. At l. 528 again, Bardolph's entrance and outcry becomes, as it should be, a genuine and unexpected interruption which annoys Falstaff: 'Out ye rogue, play out the play.' To mark a direction here, 'A knocking heard' (for which there is no authority), with Bardolph going to see what the trouble is, while all wait to hear, destroys this effect, and is indeed very awkward.

> READ: l. 437 Exeunt *Bardolph* and *Francis* with
> *Hostess.*
> l. 528 Prince Henry. *I do, I will.* [Entei
> *Bardolph.*]

4.541 *thou art essentially made without seeming so.*

Quarto and Folio alike read *made.* The Third Folio, followed by most editors, including *New Cambridge,* reads *mad.* A misreading of *madd* as *made* is of course quite plausible. But it may be doubted whether *mad* is relevant here, and whether *made* does not in fact give a better sense. (Indeed, *mad* seems to be the opposite of any possible trend of Falstaff's thought. For surely Prince Henry might *seem* mad, but *is* essentially not mad.) Falstaff's point is that the Prince is true gold and should recognize Falstaff's sterling worth too, when it is a question of defending him against the sheriff. And so he says, in effect, 'Do not, Hal, ever mistake true gold (including me) for counterfeit. You, for example, are made of the true, essential metal, though you may seem outwardly to be base metal for a Prince. (Remember this when the sheriff comes in after me.)'

> READ: *essentially made*

3

4.554 *Stage-direction.*

4.577–602 *Speakers' names.*

At l. 554 most editors read 'Exeunt all except Prince Henry and Peto'. At ll. 577 and 583 Quarto gives Peto as the speaker, as also at l. 602. At l. 601, moreover, Prince Henry concludes his speech with 'and so good morrow Peto'. The textual evidence is therefore strongly against Johnson's argument that *Peto* is an error for *Poins* throughout this part of the scene. Both Kittredge and Alexander retain the original readings here. *New Cambridge*, however, follows Johnson and Malone in reading *Poins*, justly I think on the balance of dramatic probability. There is, moreover, support for the emendation in the Dering MS. of part of the play, which appears to transmit the stage-practice of the time.

Poins, not Peto, is the Prince's confidant and attendant. The Carrier would have recognized Peto, who was one of the thieves, as Poins was not. The Prince's words, 'thy place shall be honourable' in the wars, are fitting in relation to Poins, but not to Peto, whose place in the wars was in fact 'lieutenant Peto' under Captain Falstaff with his lamentable company. The compositor, having misread *Po* (for *Poins*) as *Pe* (for *Peto*) and set the speaker's name as *Peto*, then *Pet* and again *Peto*, might well have changed *Poins* in his copy to *Peto* to suit, at the end of the Prince's speech. This seems on the whole more probable than that Shakespeare for some inscrutable reason suddenly made Peto play what was obviously the part of Poins, forgetting all distinctions between them elsewhere in the play.

READ: l. 554 [Exeunt all except *Prince Henry* and *Poins.*

ll. 577–602 For *Peto* read *Poins.*

ACT 3

1.1–20 The opening lines of this scene are printed as prose in Quarto, up to l. 12. And so *New Cambridge* prints them. Most editors on the contrary arrange all as verse, not without difficulty. It seems to me that there is a clear purpose in the writing which leads to a compromise between these extremes. The speeches of Mortimer and Glendower lend themselves readily to metrical arrangement, whereas those of Hotspur, up to l. 20, are certainly designed for prose. It can hardly be doubted that this was intentional, dramatically significant, and characteristic of the speakers. I would not, however, read ll. 6–10 as generally lineated by editors, but as follows:

> *No, here it is. Sit Cousin Percy,*
> *Sit good cousin Hotspur, for by that name,*
> *As oft as Lancaster doth speak of you,*
> *His cheek looks pale, and with a rising sigh*
> *He wisheth you in heaven.*

3.66 *the tight of a haire, was neuer lost in my house before.*

The Griggs facsimile of the Devonshire Quarto is misleading here, reading clearly *right*. Dr McManaway confirmed from the Folger copy the reading *tight* in the B.M. copy. Folio also reads *tight*. There can be no escape, I think, from the reading *tithe* suggested by Theobald and universally adopted. The word is entirely apt here. It is possible that *tithe* was spelled *tihte* in the copy—a kind of misspelling that is frequently met—and so gave birth to the compositor's *tight*.

READ: *tithe*

3.99 *the prince is a iacke, a sneakeup,*

Many editors, including Kittredge and Alexander, read *sneak-cup*, as read in Folio and later Quartos. The later reading is due to a worn *e* type in Quarto, which at first sight seems to read *sneakcup*. (Q2, however, also reads *sneakeup*.) The only ground for reading *sneak-cup* would be the unintelligibility of *sneak-up*. But the sense of the word is more obvious than that of *sneak-cup*. *New Cambridge* rightly reads *sneak-up*.

READ: *sneak-up*.

3.220–1 *Go Peto to horse, to horse, for thou and I*

See note on 2.4.554 ff. above. It is clear that Poins is in question here, as Kittredge reads (who stuck to Peto in Act 2, Sc. 4). Alexander, however, reads *Peto* still. Quarto marks no entrance for either.

READ: *Go Poins, to horse,*

ACT 4

1.20 Mes. *His letters beares his mind, not I my mind.*

Capell went so far as to emend this line to read, *not I, my lord*, and this reading is generally followed, e.g. by Kittredge, *New Cambridge*, and Alexander. Kittredge's textual notes make no reference to variant readings. Dover Wilson erroneously reports Quarto and Folio alike as reading *my mind*. Folio, in fact, reads *his minde*. The emendation proposed assumes therefore a fit of absent-mindedness in the compositor, repeating *mind* automatically, and a Folio editor seeking to make sense of an unintelligibility, leaving *carte blanche* for emendation.

But the original Quarto reading is perfectly intelligible, and recalls the dialogue of Viola as a messenger with Olivia in *Twelfth Night* 1.5.219–20. So the Messenger says here, 'Put your questions to his letters, which convey his mind: it is not my office to convey my own mind upon these matters.'

READ: *His letters bears his mind, not I my mind.*

1.98–9 *All plumde like Estridges that with the wind*
        Baited like Eagles hauing lately bathd,

The crux of the matter here is whether editors should, or should not, accept Rowe's conjecture of *wing* for *with* in l. 98, as did Johnson, Malone, *New Cambridge*, but not Kittredge or Alexander. Dover Wilson's note that *wing* could easily be misread in Secretary hand as *with* seems to me very difficult to sustain. The interpretation of *baited* as 'refreshed', necessary to this emendation, is also very questionable in this instance. (I find difficulty even in interpreting 'with the wind baited' as 'refreshed by the wind'.) There are alternative senses that the word can well bear. Of these, the most relevant here is surely the sense of 'beating the wings' (*battre les ailes*) as a term of falconry. The English knights are thus 'plumed like ostriches, when ostriches flutter and toss their wings in the wind, as eagles do after bathing'. The phrase *with the wind* conveys perhaps the suggestion of 'against the wind, into the wind'. To put it simply, the knights' plumes are displayed, extended, and fluttering in the wind. There is no need to improve on Shakespeare's writing here.

READ: *All plumed like estridges, that with the wind*
      Bated like eagles having lately bathed,

as do Kittredge and Alexander also.

2.34–5 *an olde fazd ancient,*

Folio reads *old-fac'd Ancient,* and most editors follow. But *old-faced* is a quite extraordinary phrase, none the less so for being applied to an *ancient* (in the sense of an officer in this reading). *New Cambridge* rightly keeps the Quarto reading, with *ancient* in the sense of a flag. *fazed* simply means 'frayed, tattered', and the sense of the whole phrase is quite clear and apt. The Folio reading is an over-facile editorial effort.

READ: *an old fazed ancient;*

ACT 5

3.11 *I was not borne a yeelder thou proud Scot,*

The Folio reading, *I was not borne to yeeld, thou haughty Scot* (misquoted by Dover Wilson in *New Cambridge* as *naughty*, doubtless a misprint), has attracted some editors, unreasonably, as it is clearly editorial in Folio. And so Malone proved. The Quarto text is, in any case, far superior, and more characteristic.

READ: as in Q.

3.22 *Ah foole, goe with thy soule whither it goes,*

Capell's emendation, *A fool go with thy soul,* is accepted by *New Cambridge*, Kittredge, and Alexander. But it seems extremely forced, and the sense given to the emended phrase difficult to justify. The Quarto original, on the other hand, gives a perfectly good sense, in harmony with Elizabethan ideas, which distinguished between a man and his soul as two entities (e.g. '*I* bequeath *my soul* to Almighty God'). 'You were foolish in your life. Go, you and your soul together, into the next world (to which your folly has brought you).' The Quarto punctuation must not simply be set aside, any more than the word *Ah*, without cogent reason.

READ: *Ah fool, go with thy soul*

5.36–7 *Towards York shal bend, you with your deerest speed*
To meet Northumberland

The Folio reading *shall bend you, with* is followed by most editors. *New Cambridge*, however, reads as in Quarto (misquoted in Dover Wilson's note as *bend, with you*) and with a comma after *bend*, indicating apparently that some particular *you* shall make especial speed, which seems difficult to justify. The normal form of the verb is reflexive, *bend you*, and the omission of the Quarto comma makes clear and good sense. And so Kittredge and Alexander read.

READ: *Towards York shall bend you with your dearest speed*
To meet Northumberland

THE SECOND PART OF
KING HENRY THE FOURTH

INDUCTION

L. 35 *And this worme-eaten hole of ragged stone,*[1]

Theobald's emendation, *hold* for *hole*, is universally accepted. The compositor's misreading of *hold* as *hole* is the commonest of possible errors. And *hole* gives no satisfactory sense. *worm-eaten hole* could only mean *worm-holed hole*.

READ: *hold*

ACT 1

Sc. 1 *Stage-direction.* The usual stage-direction 'Enter Porter at the Gate', or 'The Porter opens the Gate' (Alexander), is questionable. The Porter's words to Lord Bardolph, 'Please it your honour knock but at the gate', and Lord Bardolph's 'Here comes the Earl' (the Earl's coming evidently invisible to the Porter), require the Porter's entry 'above' the Gatehouse of the Castle. And so *New Cambridge* also reads.

READ: Enter *Porter* above.

1.101–3   *and his tongue*
            Sounds euer after as a sullen bell,
            Remembred tolling a departing friend.

The Quarto punctuation is not lightly to be overruled, and editors retain it. But the sense of these lines surely points to a comma after *Remembered*, not after *bell.* 'His

---

[1] Citations are from the Quarto, which is basic here, except in respect of passages cut in the Quarto copy and restored in the First Folio. Such passages are cited from the Folio and marked with an asterisk (*).

tongue *thereafter* sounds like a bell *remembered*'. 'tolling the death of a friend' explains *sullen,* not what was remembered. It is a fine point, but significant. The emendation is supported by Folio.

> READ: *as a sullen bell*
>   *Remembered,*

1.126 *So soone tane prisoner,*

Folio reads *Too* for *So,* and editors follow, including recent editors. But there is no difficulty in the Quarto reading to compel resort to Folio. (And there is no plausibility in the suggestion that *To* might be misread as *So.*) Indeed the preceding lines explain precisely why Worcester was *so soon* captured, because of the flight of the soldiers. Otherwise a doughty warrior like Worcester would not be an early capture.

> READ: *So soon*

1.161–2 Vmfr. *This strained passion doth you wrong my lord.*
>   Bard. *Sweet earle, diuorce not wisedom from your honor,*

Line 161 is given to Travers by Kittredge, to Lord Bardolph by Alexander and *New Cambridge,* and is omitted by Folio. It seems clear that at some stage in the preparation of the play Umfreville disappeared from the cast, and was replaced where necessary by Lord Bardolph. Line 162, again, attributed by Quarto and Folio to Lord Bardolph, is clearly the beginning of the speech of Morton, which in Quarto runs from l. 163 to l. 165, and in Folio is extended by a further fourteen lines, which are cut in Quarto. It can hardly be doubted that Folio here, as in some other places, is closer to the final form of the play as well as to the original copy from Shakespeare's hand.

> READ: Lord Bardolph. *This strained...lord.*
>   Morton. *Sweet earl, ...honour.*

1.183–4 *And yet we venturd for the gaine proposde,*
Choakt the respect of likely perill fear'd,

Capell's emendation, followed by most editors, as by Kittredge and Alexander, transfers the comma after *pro-posed* to after *ventured*, and I think rightly. *New Cambridge* supports and defends the Quarto punctuation. Both readings are in truth intelligible. But the natural structure of the thought is clearly 'And yet we ventured.... And... venture again', both with parentheses.

READ: *And yet we ventured, for the gain proposed Choked....*

2.8–9 *this foolish compoūded clay-man is*

Dover Wilson retains the Quarto *clay-man* as a compound word, but without any clear reason adduced. His note would serve equally for the usual reading *clay, man,*. *this clay-man* surely suggests an individual, *this clay, man,* the species, which is certainly Falstaff's thought, as indicated in the preceding 'Men of all sorts'

READ: *clay, man,*

2.24–6 *I will sooner haue a beard grow in the palme of my hand, then he shal get one off his cheek,*

Folio reads *on* for *off*. Editors read *off*. Dover Wilson suggests in a note that *off his cheek* denotes whiskers, but this seems to me to support the Folio *on*. I suggest *of*, a common use of the word, and a plausible emendation for the obscure *off*. It means 'in relation to, on'.

READ: *of his cheek,*

2.189–91 *and yet in some respects I grant I cannot go. I cannot tell, vertue is of so little regard*

Editors in their punctuation relate *I cannot tell* to the preceding sentence. *I cannot go—I cannot tell.*, or the equivalent. But surely the Quarto punctuation is precise,

SECOND PART OF KING HENRY IV—ACT I 43

and should be followed. *I cannot tell* is a frequent introduction to a paradox or a surprising statement in Elizabethan idiom, and it is so used here.

READ: *I cannot go. I cannot tell—virtue is of so little
regard*

3.28 *Eating the ayre, and promise of supplie,*

Folio reads *on promise*, and editors follow, except
Alexander. Dover Wilson, who reads *on*, quotes 'I eat the
air, promise-crammed' from *Hamlet*, which surely supports the Quarto *and*, 'eating the air, and eating promises'.
Having read *on* in my edition, I am now sure that we
should not emend Quarto.

READ: *air, and promise*

3.36–8* L. Bar. *Yes, if this present quality of warre,*
            Indeed the instant action: a cause on foot,
            Liues so in hope: As in an early Spring,

The difficulties felt by editors are best exemplified by
Mackail's suggestion, repeated by Cunningham, and widely
accepted, that *Indeed* is a verb meaning 'implement' or
'effect'. Dover Wilson very reasonably objects that this
would be unintelligible to the audience. It is in fact
incredible. *New Cambridge* reads as in Folio, with an
obelus, but suggests in a note that *warre* might be a misreading for *warrs*, i.e. *war is*.

The original Folio reading, however, offers no real
difficulty, if the punctuation is disregarded. 'Indeed the
instant action—a cause on foot' may be in apposition to
'this present quality of war' and a parenthesis in the clause,
'if this present quality of war lives so in hope.' The
argument is then plain. 'It never yet did any harm', says
Hastings, 'to be optimistic and reckon on probabilities'.
'Yes', says Lord Bardolph, 'if the present outlook or state
of affairs of our war—indeed the action we are now
engaged on, one actually in progress—rests upon hopes'.

Alexander's reading seems to support this interpretation. He reads:

> *Yes, if this present quality of war —*
> *Indeed the instant action, a cause on foot —*
> *Lives so in hope, as in an early spring,*

A better sense, however, and closer to the argument, can be drawn with less interference with the Folio punctuation. To Hastings' speech, Lord Bardolph replies, 'But it *does* do harm (*Yes*) if you are thinking of the conditions affecting our war now, in fact the action we are about to embark on. An enterprise already under way, if resting mainly on hope, is as deceptive as an early spring.' He then enlarges upon actions set on foot precipitately, as was Hotspur's, like an untimely early spring, which raises hopes destined to disaster. Such enterprises should be prepared and planned, and not rest on mere hope but on calculation. The crux of the passage is the word *Yes*, here used, as often, in an adversative sense, the French *Si*, or the German *Doch*. *Instant* means 'now facing us, but not yet in being.' *On foot* means 'already in progress, an action begun'.

READ: *Yes — if this present quality of war;*
   Indeed the instant action. A cause on foot
   Lives so in hope, as in an early spring

ACT 2

1.65–6 Boy. *Away you scullian, . . . catastrophe.*

Many editors, including Kittredge, have followed the Third Folio in attributing this speech to Falstaff. It is not at all characteristic of Falstaff. There is no ground for the emendation, and every reason against it.

READ: Page. *Away you scullion,*

2.80 **Poynes** *Come you vertuous asse,*

Theobald's attribution of this speech to Bardolph, followed in many editions, is quite unjustified. Poins makes fun of the Page's blushes, and the Page retorts the gibe upon Bardolph's red face. 'I have no tongue sir', says Bardolph later, and he certainly had no tongue for such a speech as Poins' here.

READ: Poins. *Come you virtuous ass,*

''A calls me e'en now' in l. 85, by the way, is the historic present. 'He called me a little while ago.'

2.115ff. **Prince** *I do allow this Wen...*

Some redistribution of the speeches of Prince Henry and Poins seems necessary here. Editors follow Quarto in making the Prince show Poins Falstaff's letter, taking his words *look you how he writes* literally, whereupon Poins reads *John Falstaff Knight,* and continues to speak. Hanmer, followed by many editors, including Kittredge, went so far as to transfer all the reading of the letter consequently to Poins, with a radical redistribution of the speeches after the Prince's *But the letter*— (l. 128). But Poins is surely replying to the Prince's reading of the words. And *look you* is merely 'listen to this', as usual. And presently the Prince reads the whole letter, interrupted again by Poins.

READ: Prince Henry. *I do allow this wen...for look you how he writes.* [Reads] John Falstaff Knight—

Poins. *Every man must know that...*

3.24* *And speaking thicke (which Nature made his blemish)*

The phrase *speaking thick* has been interpreted even of late on the stage as meaning either 'having a defect in speech' (Olivier's stutter) or 'having a guttural accent' (Redgrave's Northumbrian *r*). The phrase in fact means simply 'rapid, or hurried, speech', a frequent Elizabethan sense of *thick* (e.g. as in *All's Well* 2.2.47, 'O lord Sir—thick, thick, spare not me'). Hotspur was Hotspur in speech as in action. Lady Percy contrasts his speech with that of those who spoke 'low and *tardily*'. Over-haste in speaking, of course, might lead to want of clarity in enunciation, and words running into each other.

The origin of the stage-tradition of stuttering this part was Schlegel's translation of the word *thick* by *stottern*, after which German actors stuttered the part and set a fashion.

4.11 ff. (a) Fran. *Why then couer...musique.*
        (b) Dra. *Dispatch, the roome...straight.*
        (c) Francis *Sirra, here wil be...word.*
                Enter Will.
        (d) Dra. *By the mas...stratagem.*
        (e) Francis *Ile see if...Sneake.*

It is evident that in this passage the distribution among speakers is at fault. The Folio distribution is as follows: (a) First Drawer, (b) omitted, (c) Second Drawer, (d) First Drawer, but in variant reading, (e) Second Drawer. It would seem that the Quarto version allows for three Drawers, with its opening direction 'Enter a Drawer or two', i.e. Francis and another, and the later direction, 'Enter Will', a Third Drawer. One of these had been dispensed with before the time of the Folio text, which omits this direction.

Editors handle the problem variously. *New Cambridge* distributes as follows: (a) Francis, (b) Second Drawer, (c) Francis [Enter Falstaff, crosses the stage, and exit.], (d) Second Drawer, (e) Francis. Dover Wilson thus retains the Quarto distribution, and interprets *Enter Will* as 'Enter Will Kemp' who probably acted the part of Falstaff, and so inserts this apparently meaningless entrance and immediate exit of Falstaff, which seems improbable.

Alexander, whose edition I had not seen before deciding upon my own text, distributes: (a) Francis [Enter Third

Drawer], (*b*) Third Drawer, (*c*) Francis, (*d*) Third Drawer, (*e*) Second Drawer.

It seems most probable that *Enter Will* marks the entrance of a minor part and a minor actor, a Third Drawer, and that he enters at (*c*) to give the news which he has heard from Bardolph. Falstaff's true entrance is clearly marked at l. 35, *Enter Sir John*, and he speaks at once. A fleeting appearance at l. 21, possibly in time to hear the words 'Sir John must not know of it', and during discussion of the plot against him, is surely impossible. It is also reasonably sure that if Francis instructs the Second Drawer in (*a*) to find Sneak and his music, he is unlikely in (*e*) to go himself in search of Sneak. There is a hierarchy even among Drawers, and Francis is First Drawer. Francis is throughout imperative and the Second Drawer subservient. And he remains on stage until Falstaff sends him off at l. 36: 'Empty the jordan', a duty that in *New Cambridge* falls to Second Drawer. The following arrangement seems to me to represent the original intention of Shakespeare.

READ:

Francis. *Why then cover and set them down, and see if thou canst find out Sneak's noise; Mistress Tearsheet would fain hear some music. Dispatch, the room where they supped is too hot, they'll come in straight.*

Enter *Third Drawer.*

Third Drawer. *Sirrah, here will be the Prince and Master Poins anon, and they will put on two of our jerkins and aprons, and Sir John must not know of it. Bardolph hath brought word.*   [Exit.

Francis. *By the mass here will be old utis: it will be an excellent stratagem.*

Second Drawer. *I'll see if I can find out Sneak.*   [Exit.

.   .   .   .   .

l. 36 Falstaff. When Arthur first in court. *Empty the jordan.*   [Exit *Francis.*

4.232 *A rascall to braue me?*
4.239 *a villaine!*
4.240 *Ah rascally slaue!*

There is a difference between Doll's ejaculation and the contemptuous comments of Falstaff.

> READ: l. 232. *A rascal to brave me?*
> l. 239. *Ah villain!*
> l. 240. *A rascally slave!*

4.347–8 *that the wicked might not fall in loue with thee: in which doing,*

A stage-direction is required here to make the sense unmistakable. (Folio reads *him* for *thee*, and many editors follow.)

> READ: *that the wicked might not fall in love with thee* [turns to *Prince*], *in which doing,*

4.363–4 *for the boy there is a good angel about him, but the diuel blinds him too.*

Most editors follow the Folio reading here, *but the Deuill out-bids him too.* This seems to be an obviously editorial reading, for it cannot arise from mere corruption of Quarto copy. *New Cambridge* reads as in Quarto, with an obelus. Dover Wilson rightly finds the word *too* irrelevant in either reading. He suggests (*the devil's*) *behind* misread as *blynd*, giving *devils blind*, corrected to *devil blinds*.

I suggest the simple emendation of *to't* for this suspect word *too*, which is graphically plausible with a common form of *t* made with a loop after the downstroke before the cross-stroke. The sense then becomes clear. Falstaff is the Good Angel about the boy, but the devil prevents the boy from realizing it, *blinds him to't.*

> READ: *but the devil blinds him to't.*

4.420–21 Host. *O runne Doll, runne, runne good Doll, come,
         she comes blubberd, yea! will you come Doll?*

This speech has caused difficulty. *New Cambridge*
emends radically, with a redistribution among two speakers:

Hostess. *O run, Doll, run, run, good Doll.*
Bardolph [at the door]. *Come!*
Hostess. *She comes blubbered.* [dries Doll's face
Bardolph [enters]. *Yea, will you come, Doll?*

The difficulty is really due to the want of stage-directions,
and there is no need to break the speech up. We know that
Bardolph is *within.*

READ: Hostess. *O run Doll, run, run good Doll. Come.*
      [Leads her to the door. To *Bardolph* within.]
      She comes blubbered. [To *Doll.*] *Yea, will you
      come Doll?*

ACT 3

1.26–7 *Canst thou, ô partiall sleepe, giue them repose,
        To the wet season in an howre so rude,*

Folio reads *thy Repose* and *wet Sea-Boy,* and all editors
follow gratefully. Dover Wilson conjectures *season* as
emerging in the Quarto from a misspelling of *sea-boy,* the
compositor being attracted to *season* by *wet.* But there is
surely a simpler explanation which makes the Folio reading
decline into an editorial guess suggested by *ship-boy* in l. 19.
season is a slightly corrupted form of *sea's son,* and there is
no need for emendation here. 'Son of the sea' is a familiar
phrase even now. I think it certain, however, that we
should read *thy* for *them,* an easy misreading in Quarto.

READ: *Canst thou, o partial sleep, give thy repose
      To the wet sea's son in an hour so rude,*

2.61–2 *Good morrow honest gentlemen.*
        Bard. *I beseech you, which is Iustice Shallow?*

In Quarto l. 61 is a continuation of a speech by Silence,
but by some copies of Quarto it is given to Bardolph, as by

4   SSII

Kittredge. Folio gives it to Shallow. It is surely Shallow's place and manner to greet the newcomers, and certainly not for Bardolph to condescend to Shallow and Silence.

READ: Shallow. *Good morrow honest gentlemen.*
Bardolph. *I beseech you, which is Justice Shallow?*

2.336–7 *that his demensions to any thicke sight were inuincible,*

Kittredge retains *invincible,* and glosses 'invisible'. Most editors read *invisible,* and rightly. Dover Wilson's note on the spelling *invinsible—invuisible* is convincing, though there are other possibilities for the misreading.

READ: *invisible.*

2.350–2 *you might haue thrust him and all his aparell into an eele-skin,*

Folio reads *truss'd* for *thrust,* and *New Cambridge* follows. But it would be more natural for *trussed* to be followed by *in,* and for *thrust* to be followed by *into.* There is no difficulty in the Quarto reading to justify emendation.

READ: *thrust*

ACT 4

1.71* *And are enforc'd from our most quiet there,*

Vaughan's conjecture *shore* for *there* has been followed by *New Cambridge* as graphically plausible, and apt. Kittredge and Alexander retain the Folio reading, which seems to me difficult, though possibly *there* means 'in the stream of time' (l. 70), and *most* is an adjective. I suggest *flow,* which is also plausible. *quiet flow* is thus opposed to 'rough torrent' (l. 72), and is a favourite image of Shakespeare, the image of streams contained in their banks or overflowing them. In l. 176 below it recurs, 'We come within our awful banks again'.

READ: *our most quiet flow*

1.93 *And consecrate commotions bitter edge.*

1.95 *To brother borne an houshold cruelty.*

Later, corrected, copies of the Quarto omit these lines,
as does Folio. Line 95 is manifestly out of place, in the
absence of further reference to Lord Scroop, and l. 93
redundant. It is apparent that lines deleted by Shakespeare
in his copy have survived in the uncorrected Quarto, and
should be relegated from the text to a footnote.

1.139* *And bless'd, and grac'd, and did more then the King.*

The usual reading adopted by editors, e.g. Kittredge,
New Cambridge and Alexander, is *indeed* for *and did*, as
proposed by Thirlby. But it may well seem that there is
no need for emendation. Is it too simple to say that the
people blessed and graced Hereford, and *did more than the
King* to do due honour to him? I do not see *and did* as a
probable misreading of *indeed*.

READ: *and did*

1.197–8   *the King is weary
                    Of daintie and such picking greeuances,*

Johnson found this line corrupt. *New Cambridge* reads
as in Quarto, with an obelus, but conjectures in a note
search-picking. But surely there is no corruption. There is
no difficulty in the phrasing 'such dainty and picking', as
would be evident, or 'such dainty and such picking', or
'dainty and such picking'. No one would object to a
modern colloquial sentence, 'their grievances are dainty,
and *so* picking'.

READ: as in Q.

3.45–6 *that I may iustly say with the hooke-nosde fellow of
Rome, there cosin, I came, saw, and ouercame.*

Folio reads *of Rome, I came,* and most editors follow,
though *New Cambridge* prints with an obelus. Dover

Wilson records Johnson's *Rome there, Caesar*, and suggests
Rome, Ju. Caesar, misread as *Rome, thr Cosen*. The Folio
reading is surely editorial. Failing to make sense of *there
cosin*, the words were simply omitted.

I suggest *their Caesar*, Caesar being spelled *cesar* as often,
and easily misread as *cosin*. *There* for *their* is common
enough, and the catchword from the preceding page is
actually *their*. The sense is then clear, *that hook-nosed
fellow of Rome* (*their Caesar*), i.e. 'Rome's Caesar'.

READ: *the hook-nosed fellow of Rome, their Caesar,*

4.39–41   *giue him time and scope,*
           Till that his passions, like a whale on ground
           Confound themselues with working,

Folio reads *Line* for *time* and *New Cambridge* follows, as
do Kittredge and Alexander. But the image of line-fishing
is incongruous with the example given. The stranded whale
exhausts itself thrashing on the ground. The point of the
image of the whale is its size and uncontrollable power, in
which it resembles the 'greatness' (l. 26) of the Prince.
Like the Prince, it cannot be governed; it alone can
exhaust its own passions. Finally, it is not suggested that
Thomas of Clarence should 'play' his brother like a fish.
On the contrary, the King's advice is to let the Prince
alone 'when he is moody', to give him *time* in fact, and a
'wide berth', till he is no longer 'incensed'.

READ: *give him time and scope,*

4.104 *But wet her faire words stil in foulest termes?*
     Folio reads:

     But write her faire words still in foulest Letters?

I have no doubt that the Folio reading here restores
the original copy underlying the Quarto text, and that
there is no need for compromises such as *But write her*

fair words still in foulest terms? which offers the serious difficulty of having 'fair *words*' expressed in 'foul *terms*'. It is generally agreed that *write* could easily have been misread as *wette*, and printed *wet*, by the Quarto compositor. But it is no less plausible that *letters* should be misread as *terms*, given the almost universal spelling of *letters* as *lr̃es* or *lr̃s*, misread as *tr̃es* and interpreted as *termes*, a somewhat obvious guess in the context and supported by a frequent use of ∼. *New Cambridge* accepts the Folio reading with an obelus, and suspects it, in a note, as a makeshift, on the ground of its double variant from Quarto, which therefore probably conceals an undiscoverable original in Dover Wilson's view.

letters gives a clear sense, and offers no difficulty in the context. The word was familiar both in the sense of printed type-letters and of written alphabet-letters. It has no connection here with *letters* as epistles. 'Fortune conveys even her hopeful messages in crabbed writing.' (The image is suggested by the packet of writings just presented by Harcourt.) The King receives good news but it is accompanied by his own severe illness.

READ: *But write her fair words still in foulest letters?*

5.205 *And all thy friends which thou must make thy friends,*

Tyrwhitt's *my* for the first *thy* is universally accepted. Yet the trend of the King's advice is opposed to the change. The Prince has friends, stands surer than did the King once, yet is not firm enough in their friendship; they must be confirmed to him by his own care. The sense probably requires the use of italics in the text.

READ: *And all thy friends, which thou must make thy friends,*

ACT 5

3.77–9 Do me right, and dub me Knight, samingo:

This is certainly a snatch of a song, and should be so printed. Dover Wilson's suggestion that *samingo* is a 'corruption of "Sir Mingo" (identity unknown)' is surely right, except that the derivation from the Latin verb *mingo* is lamentably clear, and the mock-title could be applied to any toper, Sir John Falstaff for example, as indicated in this present play (2.4.36).

5.4–42 Stage-directions.

The Folio stage-directions, which differ from those of Quarto, have generally been adopted by editors, until Kittredge's edition of 1936. The Quarto directions, as followed by recent editors, provide for the entrance of the King's procession at l. 4 on its way to the Abbey for the coronation, and again at l. 42 on its way back from the Abbey. The Folio text provides only for the procession from the Abbey, at l. 42. But the dialogue of the Grooms opening the scene, with their reference to trumpets sounding, in Folio as in Quarto, leads naturally on to the third sounding at l. 4 which announces the entrance of the procession. It is clear that the Quarto directions form part of the original text and production.

It is important to attend to the phrasing of the Quarto direction at l. 4:

Trumpets sound, and the King, and his traine passe ouer the stage:

New Cambridge reads: 'the King and his train...pass into the Abbey;', and a note interprets this as entering at a side-door they move into the inner stage. It is very unlikely that this is a correct interpretation. To *pass over the stage* in Elizabethan directions means an entrance at one side-door, a passage over the whole stage, and an exit at the opposite door. In this instance the effect of the procession as a spectacle would be lost by curving it into a sharp bend, and it would be much more difficult to manage.

READ: l. 4   Trumpets. Enter the *King* and his train in procession and exeunt to the Abbey.

l. 41 [Shouts within, and trumpets sound.

l. 42 Enter the *King* and his train from the Abbey, with *Lord Chief Justice.*

5.16–20 (a) Pist. *It doth so.*
Falst. *It shewes my earnestnesse of affection.*

(b) Pist. *It doth so.*
Falst. *My deuotion.*

(c) Pist. *It doth, it doth, it doth.*

The attribution of these speeches to Pistol has given reasonable difficulty. Folio attributes (a) to Shallow, (b) and (c) to Pistol. Hanmer, followed by most editors, attributes all to Shallow. *New Cambridge*, while accepting Shallow for (a), follows Folio in giving (b) and (c) to Pistol. I have no doubt that Hanmer was right; (a) is certainly a reply by Shallow to Falstaff's preceding speech addressed to him. And it is clear that Falstaff's further speeches are equally addressed to him, with the borrowed 'thousand pound' in the minds of both. Pistol is an irrelevance here. The comic effect of the repeated 'It doth so' depends upon one speaker and his repetitions, *crescendo*. And they are not in Pistol's vein.

READ: Shal. *It doth so.*
Fal. *It shows my earnestness of affection—*
Shal. *It doth so.*
Fal. *My devotion—*
Shal. *It doth, it doth, it doth.*

KING HENRY THE FIFTH

ACT 1

2.94 *Then amply to imbarre their crooked Titles,*[1]

The Third Folio reads *imbar* for *imbarre*, followed by most editors, but yielding very doubtful sense. *New Cambridge* and Kittredge follow Warburton's conjecture *imbare*, with the general sense in which eighteenth-century editors read the passage, 'make bare' or 'unveil'. It may be questioned whether this nonce-word *imbare* could have the sense of the word *embare* cited from *N.E.D*. The double *rr* of *imbarre* cannot be ignored, and it is paralleled by *barre* two lines earlier. This suggests the possibility of a better antithesis in Shakespeare's mind than *bar, imbare*.

I suggest *unbar*, a minim variant of *imbarre*, and the direct antithesis of *bar* above, giving more point to the sentence. *unbar their crooked titles*, of course, by a frequent figure of speech, means 'unbar the crookedness of their titles'. The whole passage thus means, 'they would bar your claims, and conceal their own titles in verbiage, rather than unbar, disclose, reveal for examination, the crookedness of their titles'. Steevens suggested *unbar* in the sense of 'weaken'.

READ: *unbar*

2.166–73 Bish. Ely. *But there's a saying very old and true,...*

Capell and most editors make Westmorland the speaker here, on the ground that Holinshed does so. This is to deny to Shakespeare his necessary discretion in the use of his sources. There is some plausibility in attributing a reference to Border and Scottish affairs to a Northern Earl, but no implausibility either in attributing it to the Bishop. Henry

---

[1] Citations are from the basic Folio text.

himself opens the question, the Archbishop comments in reply, and the Bishop comments further. *New Cambridge* follows Folio, and rightly, for it cannot be claimed that emendation is necessary.

READ: Bishop of Ely.

2.173 *To tame and hauocke more then she can eate.*

Rowe read *tear* for *tame*, followed by most editors, including Alexander. Kittredge conjecturally reads *spoil*. Greg read *'tame* for *attame*, followed by *New Cambridge*, meaning to break into prey, which is surely irresistible. *tear* or *teare* offers little graphic plausibility and a less apt sense.

READ: *'tame*

2.197 *Who busied in his Maiesties surueyes*

Editors seem to be unanimous in reading Rowe's *majesty* for *majesties*. Yet *majesties* in the plural gives good sense, indeed better sense. To say that the King is 'busy in his majesty' suggests merely that he is absorbed in his lofty rank, whereas 'busy in his majesties' means occupied by all the diverse attributes and functions of a king. The word *royalties* is used in a similar sense.

READ: *his majesties*

2.208-9 *Come to one marke: as many wayes meet in one towne,*
        As many fresh streames meet in one salt sea;

Capell, followed by *New Cambridge*, proposed the insertion of *several* before *ways* in the Folio text, on the authority of the Quarto edition, thus making a complete line *As many several ways meet in one town*. The structure of the speech then falls into pattern, with *Come to one mark* as a broken line. This may well be an instance of the survival of a true reading in an untrustworthy early text. The omission of *several* by the Folio compositor is plausible, even its deliberate omission from an over-long line which fills the column without it, as Dover Wilson points out. The colon after *marke* suggests a broken line. And *several ways* seems more natural than *ways* after the *several ways* of l. 207, the words being now used in a different sense, and the sense requiring *several*. (Kittredge and Alexander follow the Folio reading.)

>   READ: *Come to one mark;*
>   *As many several ways meet in one town;*
>   *As many fresh streams meet in one salt sea;*

ACT 2

1.28–30 Bar. *Heere comes Ancient* Pistoll *and his wife: good Corporall be patient heere. How now mine Hoaste* Pistoll?

There can be little doubt that Bardolph's speech, as reported in the Folio text, ends with a sentence that is spoken by Nym, and not by Bardolph. And so it is read in the Quarto text, by *New Cambridge* and Alexander. Pistol's reply makes it certain, in the light of what has gone before. Nym is aggrieved by Pistol, as Bardolph makes plain, and instantly attacks Pistol, despite Bardolph's plea for patience. The attack in its form of words relates to his complaint, and is meant to be offensive. And so Pistol takes it and replies in kind, to Nym and not to Bardolph, with whom he has no quarrel.

>   READ: Bar. *Here comes . . . be patient here.*
>   Nym. *How now mine host Pistol?*

1.38–40 *O welliday Lady, if he be not hewne now, we shall see wilful adultery and murther committed.*

Hanmer's emendation, *drawn* for *hewn*, has established itself in the text, and is read by Kittredge and Alexander

among recent editions. *New Cambridge* retains the Folio
reading, and surely rightly. The emendation requires for
plausibility a compositor who deliberately altered a word
familiar in the context to a less familiar word, the *durior
lectio* in fact. There is no possibility of a mere misreading of
his copy. The emendation requires further a radical
revision of the punctuation to arrive at *if he be not drawn
now! We shall see.* The original Folio reading gives good
sense, and is a better reflection of Mrs Quickly's complex
mind. She can be ruthless with 'swaggerers'. (Bardolph's
words are enough to show that Nym has drawn his sword.)
Her immediate feeling is that he must be cut down, even
if presently she bids him put his sword up.

READ: *O well-a-day lady, if he be not hewn now,*

1.110–11 **Nym.** *I shall have my eight shillings I won of you
at betting?*

This speech, contained in most editions, as in *New
Cambridge* and Alexander, is not to be found in Folio, but
is derived from Quarto. There is no necessity for its
insertion here, and it reads like an actor's improvisation.
The question at issue has already been made plain by Nym
a few lines previously, in almost identical words, and there
is no need whatever to recapitulate it here.

READ: as in F.

3.17–18 *for his Nose was as sharpe as a Pen, and a Table of
greene fields.*

It is almost blasphemous to question closely the most
brilliant of emendations, which we owe to Theobald,
babbled for *Table.* It is highly plausible that a compositor
should misread *babld* as *table.* Yet in fact Shakespeare, if
we accept Hand D in *Sir Thomas More* as his normal hand,
and as sole criterion of plausibility (though I think this an
error), does not post-link *b*, and does not write a *t* that is

to be confused with a *b*. The compositor, moreover, printed *Table* with a capital *T*, still less to be confused with a *b*, capital or minuscule. Finally, was Falstaff truly represented in this scene of his death as *babbling* in delirium? Apart from this, Mrs Quickly tells us that he 'cried out God, God, God', which is not babbling, and that "a bade me lay more clothes on his feet'. Indeed, she represents him as entirely in his right mind, mindful of God and his soul's welfare, and of his bodily comfort. It would perhaps be in harmony with the 'finer end' he was making that the twenty-third psalm should be in his mind, with its reference to 'green pastures'. Or, more simply, his 'green fields' were a return to memories of childhood. But I am offended, to put it frankly, at the notion of the unconquerable Falstaff disintegrating in mind even on his death-bed. It is Mrs Quickly and his Page who report that even *in extremis* his irrepressible spirit played freely as of old upon various themes.

It is no less possible, or probable, that Shakespeare wrote *talkd* than that he wrote *babld*, with the compositor's error more plausible. And it so happens that the Quarto reads 'and talk of floures', as I found after arriving at this possibility. It is painful to decide. We may not, however, ignore Mrs Quickly's tendency towards the dramatic. Her word might then naturally be *babbled*, rather than *talked*, as it was traditional for a dying man's mind to wander. In the end, tempted as one may be to read *'a talked of green fields*, Theobald's emendation has now the authority of tradition and of proverbial use. Only a certainty could hope to oust it.

As for the Folio compositor's processes of mind, it may be supposed that he was satisfied with some vague notion of a *table* (a framed picture) of green fields being relevant here.

READ: *'a babbled of green fields.*

4.107 *The dead-mens Blood, the priuy Maidens Groanes,*

For *privy* Quarto reads *pining*, and most editors follow. Alexander, however, retains *privy*, in the sense of 'secret', no doubt, as suggested by Schmidt. I cannot see why maidens should groan *privily* for separation from their declared, betrothed lovers. It is easy to understand, on the contrary, why they should *pine* during their absence at the wars. And *priuy* is no difficult misreading of *pining* in a current hand. *Pining* is relevant, *privy* irrelevant, and *pining* plausible in every way.

READ: *pining*

ACT 3

1.7 *commune vp the blood,*

Rowe's *summon* for *commune*, universally accepted though inexplicable, may now be superseded by J. H. Walter's reading *conjure* in the *New Arden* edition. *commune* for *coniure* is an easy misprint, and *conjure up* carries conviction.

READ: *conjure*

1.17 *On, on, you Noblish English,*

Noblish is variously emended to *noble* or *noblest*. There can be no reasonable doubt that *noblest* was in the original copy misread as *Noblish*, as *noble* could not be so misread. Miss Husbands suggests attraction from '*English.*' The King's address is to his army in two groups, first the 'noblest English' (though all were noble after their fashion, as the King presently says), the nobility and gentry, and then the 'good Yeomen'.

READ: *you noblest English,*

5.11 Mort du ma vie, *if they march along*

Greg suggested *Mort Dieu! Ma vie!* followed by *New Cambridge* and Alexander, doubtless because of the Folio *du* and the Quarto *Mordeu*. But the Folio expression is entirely natural and idiomatic French as it stands with *de* for *du*, whereas *Mort Dieu! Ma vie!* is a very odd phrase. The Quarto reading is what we might expect as an improvisation, and should not dictate the abandonment of a better Folio text.

READ: *Mort de ma vie,*

5.54–5 *And in a Captiue Chariot, into Roan*
        Bring him our Prisoner.

To read *And in a chariot, captive into Rouen*, as did Daniel, followed by *New Cambridge*, is rewriting Shakespeare, not restoring his true text. The sense is plain, and the expression forcible and effective as it stands, much more so than, in effect, 'captive into Rouen bring him our captive'.

READ: as in F.

ACT 4

1.65 *'So, in the Name of Iesu Christ, speake fewer:*

fewer here seems very suspect, though *New Cambridge* and Alexander concur in accepting it. Dover Wilson dismisses the Quarto *lewer* as a misprint for *fewer*, whereas it is a much more probable misprint of *lower*, the reading of Q3, accepted by Malone and most editors. But one hardly needed authority for suggesting *lower*. The whole point of this little discussion is the need to avoid loud speech, audible to the enemy. Gower's share in the talk is decisive. First, he objects that 'the enemy is *loud*, you hear him all night', and presently he agrees, 'I will speak *lower*,' and Fluellen is appeased. Henry, listening, applauds Fluellen's prudence. Fluellen of all men is not correcting volubility (he is voluble himself even here, and Henry, immediately afterwards, is extremely voluble); he is recommending voice-control for reasons of security. Graphically there is little difficulty in the misreading of *lower* as *fewer*.

READ: *speak lower.*

1.307–9   *Take from them now*
The sence of reckning of th'opposed numbers:
Pluck their hearts from them.

New Cambridge reads *or* for the second *of*, Theobald *lest*, which can hardly be justified as plausible. Quarto gives an obviously rewritten version of the whole passage, and cannot help. Tyrwhitt's suggestion, *if* for *of*, followed by most editors, is surely the most probable graphically, and gives the best sense. It is not only that Henry's prayer, read thus, is at least as sound an argument to present to God as that of the *New Cambridge* reading. *if* here means 'since', as often. There are clear hints in the preceding dialogue that their hearts *are* plucked from them by the weight of opposing numbers. Henry has heard, for instance, the opening exchange between Bates and Williams, and has himself spoken of the need for the King to show no fear, 'lest he by showing it should dishearten his army'. The battle is a forlorn hope, and so the whole scene shows. The compositor's *of* is obviously attracted by false sense, as is his colon.

READ: *if th' opposed numbers*

2.5 Rien puis le air & feu.

The general quality of the French suggests that *Rien puis* is a corruption. The sense is plain. 'Only water and earth? Nothing more? Surely air and fire.' And *puis* does not bear this sense. These passages were almost certainly written in an italic hand. And with the frequent very short *l*, *plu* could easily be read as *pui*.

READ: *Rien plus?*

3.44 *He that shall see this day, and liue old age,*

Pope's transposition of *see* and *live* in this line has found general acceptance, as with Kittredge and Alexander among recent editors, but not with *New Cambridge*. It is, however, a desperate measure to defeat an unreal difficulty, and it damages the sense. To 'live this day' is almost meaningless, or at best is a repetition of l. 41 above, 'He that outlives this day, and comes safe home', a thought that is perhaps more typical of Pistol than of Henry, and certainly not one to stress by repetition. But to 'see this day' is a second thought, and refers clearly to those who take part in its great events. To *live old age* cannot be said to offer difficulty, and but for Pope there would probably be no comment upon the line.

READ: *He that shall see this day, and live old age,*

4.4 *Qualtitie calmie custure me.*

It is perhaps vain to debate the exact form of Pistol's gibberish, though editors may well accept Malone's emendation of *calen o* for *calmie*, on the authority of a known ballad with an Irish refrain. But I suggest that the gibberish was continuous here and is more effective so, and not a corrected exclamation *Qyality!* followed by his bit of Irish. I see no reason for correcting Pistol's version of the Frenchman's 'qualité' to *quality* or *cality*. The compositor set *qualitee* up without difficulty in l. 3.

READ: *Qyaltitie calen o custure me!*

4.15 *for I will fetch thy rymme out at thy Throat,*

Theobald corrected Pistol's threat, reading *or* for *for*, followed by all editors, and I cannot imagine why. Threats, even if conditional, need not be expressed conditionally according to any law of human nature, and generally are not, being more effective so, as effective here as later on, 'for I will cut his throat'. Theobald no doubt would have been more logical. But this was Pistol.

READ: *for*

4.38 ce soldat icy est disposee tout asture de couppes vostre gorge.

Editors all translate *asture* into modern French, *à cette heure*, after Theobald. But this Folio spelling clearly represents the sixteenth-century abbreviation in common use then, as in de Baïf, La Boétie, Montaigne, or Brantôme, in various forms, e.g. *asteure, asture, astheure,* or *ast'heure*. We should certainly follow Folio, which here is exact. Cotgrave (1611) glosses *asteure*.

READ: *tout asteure*

4.58 Ie me estime heurex que Ie intombe, entre les main. d'vn Cheualier

Theobald's French lessons for Shakespeare again corrected this sentence, reading *je suis tombé* for *ie intombe*, which is manifestly taking it out of the hands of Shakespeare no less than of the compositor, for no process of textual criticism avails to support this reading. All editors follow. There can be no reasonable doubt that *j'ai tombé* is the underlying copy here, or rather *je ai tombé*, with every plausibility for the misreading. It need hardly be added that even today in France this solecism may frequently be heard.

READ: *j'ai tombé*

5.3 Mor Dieu ma vie,

See note on 3.5.11 above.

5.11 *Let vs dye in once more backe againe,*

It is evident that a word has been omitted here after *in*. It seems natural to supply the word that has some authority in the Quarto text as probably remembered from the

5   SSII

acting of the play, 'Lets dye with honour.' There is no difficulty in the antithesis of *honour* here with *shame* in l. 10. 'We have won shame so far. Let us at least die in honour.' No other word, either on authority, or in sense, can rival *honour* here.

READ: *Let us die in honour*.

7.57 **Gow.** *Heere comes his Maiesty*.

Surely there must be an *exit* for Gower at some point in this scene before l. 158, when the King sends Williams to call him to his tent, and a little later sends Fluellen on the same errand. It is plain for other reasons also that Gower has left the stage. Miss Husbands drew my attention to this question. Editors seem to ignore the problem, and no *exit* is marked for Gower in Folio (though exits are marked for Williams and Fluellen to go to seek him). Fluellen, at least, would be aware of Gower's presence. And there is no doubt that the scene is continuous. The most plausible suggestion is that Gower slips away as Henry makes his entrance.

READ: Gow. *Here comes his Majesty*.   [Exit.

7.76 *To booke our dead, and then to bury them,*

The reading *look* for *book* has been popular with editors, presumably because *book* is 'low', but fortunately not of late. The dead have to be listed. And presently the King reads the 'Note' of the dead French.

READ: *To book our dead,*

ACT 5

1.86 *my* Doll *is dead i'th Spittle*

Capell read *my Nell* for *my Doll*, and it seems irresistible, except to Dover Wilson who finds here support for his theories concerning the revision of the play. It seems more probable that it is mere inadvertence on the part of Shakespeare, or of the compositor. Pistol is speaking. And in 2.1.33 we have 'Nor shall *my Nell* keep lodgers'.

READ: *my Nell*

2.77 *I haue but with a curselarie eye*

Most editors read *cursorary* after Q 3, which as Dover Wilson rightly remarks is an editorial attempt to make sense of Folio and Quarto corruptions. There is no other authority for the existence of this word. *New Cambridge* reads *cursitory*, for which there is example. And *curselarie* is a perfectly credible misreading of *cursitorie* in the compositor's copy, but not of *cursorarie*.

READ: *cursitory*

THE FIRST PART OF
KING HENRY THE SIXTH

DRAMATIS PERSONAE

The indications are clear that Joan of Arc's name was thought of as *Joan Pucelle* or *Joan de Pucelle*, not *Joan la Pucelle*, i.e. as if *Pucelle* were a surname, not a title. She should therefore be entered in *Dramatis Personae* as *Joan Pucelle*. (A twelfth-century seal of a Bishop of Coventry bears the inscription *Magister Gerardus Pucella*. Francis Godwin, in *A Catalogue of the Bishops of England*, 1601, p. 256, refers to him under the heading 'GIRARDUS PUELLA' as 'Magister Girardus cognomento Puella, &c. Master Gerard surnamed Puella.')[1]

ACT 1

1.50 *Our Ile be made a Nourish of salt Teares,*[2]

Pope's emendation, *marish* for *nourish*, is surely right. *Nourish* cannot be forced into good sense, even with Dover Wilson's gloss as a variant of *nurse*. It can hardly be argued, despite the preceding words 'babes shall suck', that the sense is, 'our isle will be like a nurse yielding salt tears in place of milk', a repetition in worse taste of the preceding line. *marish* is easily misread as *nourish*, and the compositor might well have been suggestible to 'babes shall suck' in this misreading. The word was in very common use, and in this form. *New Cambridge* and Alexander

---

[1] I owe knowledge of this seal, and the reference to Godwin, to Mr Ellis of the Shakespeare Birthplace Library.

[2] Citations are from the First Folio, which is basic for this play.

retain *nourish*, though Dover Wilson's note leans heavily towards *marish*.

READ: *marish*

1.56 *Then* Iulius Cæsar, *or bright—*

I have little doubt that this is a genuine interruption, and not due to illegible copy to be supplied by editorial guesses. The Messenger's news is dreadful enough to justify his manners. The dash is a kind of stage-direction. He enters tumultuously and speaks so. Bedford indeed chides him for shouting: 'Speak softly'.

READ: *or bright—*

4.33 *Rather then I would be so pil'd esteem'd:*

Pope, followed by most editors including Kittredge and Alexander, read *vile* for *pil'd*, an easy way out of a difficulty, for it is quite implausible graphically. There is no need for emendation. *Pilled* or *peeled* meaning 'stripped' in various associations, as in 'peeled priest' (1.3.30), expresses a clear and relevant thought here. Talbot would not be judged to be so stripped of his rank and honour by defeat as to be exchanged for an inferior. Dover Wilson accepts *pilled*, but interprets the word as an adverb, meaning 'beggarly'.

READ: *pilled*

ACT 3

1.51–5 Winch. *Rome shall remedie this.*   [Winch.]
    Warw. *Roame thither then.*   [Warw.]
    My Lord, it were your dutie to forbeare.   [Som.]
    Som. *I, see the Bishop be not ouer-borne:*   [Warw.]
    Me thinkes my Lord should be Religious,   [Som.]
    And know the Office that belongs to such.

From Theobald and Malone onwards down to the most recent editions these exchanges have been radically altered by a redistribution of speakers, as indicated in square brackets, for which I see no necessity, or even desirability. Warwick intervenes for the first time in the debate between Gloucester and the Bishop of Winchester when the Bishop threatens an appeal to Rome. After something of a jeer, *Roam thither then*, he answers more seriously to the threat, 'My Lord, you should forbear such a threat, if you knew your true duty'. Somerset, like Warwick a second string, but on the other side, now joins in, and replies aptly.

To justify this, I propose a minor emendation, to read *so* for *see*. *See the Bishop be not overborne* is surely odd, and irrelevant. (It is only explicable in Warwick's mouth as a weak taunt.) The misreading *see* for *soe* is one of the commonest types of error, with obvious graphic plausibility. Somerset then replies to Warwick, 'You say it is his duty to forbear, but the danger is that he will be overborne, and so driven to the appeal to Rome.' And he continues, with a logical sequence of thought, 'it is for a Bishop to safeguard religion. You speak of his *duty*, but the Bishop knows his *office*, his duty as a Bishop.' And the exchange continues on these lines.

READ: as in F., with the F. distribution of speakers. But at l. 53 for *see* read *so*:

Ay, so the Bishop be not overborne.

2.22 *Here is the best and safest passage in.*

Rowe, followed by Kittredge and *New Cambridge*, and most editors except Alexander, read *Where* for *Here*. But there is no need to make an emendation, especially where the original text gives the same sense, and without graphic plausibility.

READ: *Here*

3.45-9 *And see the Cities and the Townes defac't,*
By wasting Ruine of the cruell Foe,
As lookes the Mother on her lowly Babe,
When Death doth close his tender-dying Eyes.
See, see the pining Maladie of France:

Most editors divide this into two, with a full stop after *Foe* (*foe!*) and a comma after *Eyes*. Kittredge and *New Cambridge* rightly follow the Folio punctuation, which is obviously deliberate and precise, and gives a much more effective reading.

3.84-5 *So farwell* Talbot, *Ile no longer trust thee.*
　　　 Pucell. *Done like a Frenchman: turne and turne againe.*

Much of the dramatic effect of this later part of Sc. 3 is lost without due attention to the distinction between asides and open speech. Burgundy's speech at ll. 58-9, for example, is spoken aside. And in this second speech ll. 78-80 are spoken aside. He then speaks ll. 81-4 openly, and the Pucelle replies. The whole of the line is generally marked as an aside, e.g. in *New Cambridge* which marks no other aside. But surely it is plain that the Pucelle applauds Burgundy's decision openly, and then secretly comments upon it. The Folio colon is plainly significant, and is there to good purpose. Kittredge and Alexander concur in this reading, though they vary in the extent of asides elsewhere in this scene.

READ: *Done like a Frenchman*—[aside] *turn and turn again!*

ACT 4

1.180 York. *And if I wish he did. But let it rest,*

Capell's reading *wist* for *wish* has been generally followed, I think rightly. *New Cambridge* reads *iwis* after Theobald. The sense, though close, is not the same. And the trend of thought favours *I wist*. 'The King meant no harm in wearing Somerset's badge', says Warwick. And Richard very naturally replies, 'If I only knew that to be true', much more naturally than 'If that was certainly true'. The confusion of *wist* with *wish* offers no graphic difficulty. Elsewhere *iwis* is only used absolutely by Shakespeare. (The decision that Shakepeare wrote this scene may have affected the textual reading here in *New Cambridge*.)

READ: *An if I wist he did.*

7.58–60 **Char.** *For prisoners askst thou? Hell our prison is.*
But tell me whom thou seek'st?
Luc. *But where's the great Alcides of the field,*

Alexander retains the second *But*. *New Cambridge* also retains it, but argues that the two successive *Buts* indicate the arrival of a new author at l. 60, thus at any rate accepting them as very awkward and needing explanation. It can hardly be doubted that the second *But* is a corruption, and that the compositor picked it up from the preceding line. Lucy was a Herald, and this *But* would have been most incorrect, a kind of mocking or defiant echo of the Dauphin. He has his message to deliver in due form and style, and learned by heart, as all this speech shows clearly.

READ: *Where is the great Alcides of the field,*

ACT 5

3.10–11 *Now ye Familiar Spirits, that are cull'd*
Out of the powerfull Regions vnder earth,

The emendation of *legions* for *regions* has been generally accepted, indeed much too readily, as formerly by me. Tempting as it is, there is no necessity for emendation, and *regions* gives a perfectly good sense, with ample authority. And so Alexander and *New Cambridge* read.

READ: *regions*

3.47–9 *For I will touch thee but with reuerend hands,*
I kisse these fingers for eternall peace,
And lay them gently on thy tender side.

This passage was for long read in a changed order of lines:

For I will touch thee but with reverent hands,
And lay them gently on thy tender side.
I kiss these fingers for eternal peace.

There is, of course, no need for emendation, and a suitable stage-direction suffices to make this clear.

READ: *I kiss these fingers for eternal peace* [kisses her hands and releases them.

3.68 *Hast not a Tongue? Is she not heere?*

It can hardly be denied that there is a lacuna here, whether on grounds of sense or of a marked stumbling jolt in the metrical pattern. The Second Folio supplies the words *thy prisoner* which are necessary to the sense and can hardly be merely editorial. And so most editors agree, though *New Cambridge* reads as in Folio without comment.

READ: *Hast not a tongue? Is she not here thy prisoner?*

3.192 *Mad naturall Graces that extinguish Art,*

Collier's '*Mid* for *Mad*, adopted by *New Cambridge*, seems to be the obvious emendation here, but to me it sounds artificial, forced, and modern. I arrived at *And* as the probable and natural reading on graphic grounds as in respect of the sense, and find it to be read by Capell and by most editors, as by Kittredge and Alexander. The misreading is graphically plausible, assuming with every reason that the word was written in minuscules in the copy, and with an initial open *a*. The difference is one minim, as with Collier's emendation.

READ: *And natural graces*

4.36–8 *First let me tell you whom you haue condemn'd;*
        Not me, begotten of a Shepheard Swaine,
        But issued from the Progeny of Kings.

There is every reason for accepting Malone's suggestion
of *one* for *me*, though Alexander and *New Cambridge*
retain the Folio reading. *Not one* seems necessary to the
sense of the passage, and is clearly the sequel to the previous
line, ' I am descended of a gentler blood'. To read *Not me
begotten . . . but issued* is surely corrupt. There is no difficulty
in the compositor's error, with an open *o* in the *one* of his
copy. And taking l. 37 alone he could well have found it
good sense and obvious.

  READ: *Not one begotten*

5.59–61 *And therefore Lords, since he affects her most,*
         Most of all these reasons bindeth vs,
         In our opinions she should be preferr'd.

Line 60 has been variously emended. Rowe's *It most*
has been generally followed, as by Kittredge and Alexander.
New Cambridge adopts C. B. Young's *Which most*. These
emendations may improve the metre, but are not otherwise
justified or plausible. They merely change the original
syntax of the passage to a more modern syntax. The
original is in fact plain enough and gives perfect sense,
better sense than the emended versions. The subject to
bindeth us is *since he affects her most*, and this is a turn of
sentence familiar in Elizabethan English. The word *since*
has a double function in this frequent type of construction.
' And therefore since among all these reasons his particular
affection for her must be our guide, in our opinions she
should be preferred.' The metrical argument alone can
hardly be said to be cogent for emendation.

  READ: *And therefore lords, since he affects her most*
        Most of all these reasons bindeth us,
        In our opinions she should be preferred.

THE SECOND PART OF KING HENRY THE SIXTH

ACT 1

3.13–15 1. *Pet. I pray my Lord pardon me, I tooke ye for my Lord Protector.*
  Queene. *To my Lord Protector?*[1]

Rowe, followed by *New Cambridge* and other editors, got over the difficulty by a stage-direction making Margaret's words a reading from one of the petitions. But this is improbable, for a moment later she says 'Let me see them' (the petitions). There can be no reasonable doubt that the original text was *For my Lord Protector?*, an echo of the First Petitioner's words. The compositor possibly edited his copy on the simple logic of Margaret's second sentence being 'Are your supplications *to* his Lordship', or more probably 'carried' his line incorrectly because of that second *to*.

READ: Margaret. *For my Lord Protector?*

3.93 *That she will light to listen to the Layes,*

Most recent editors, with Malone, follow the Folio. But Kittredge reads *their* for *the*, correctly as I think. *their* follows inevitably upon the preceding line, 'a choir of such enticing birds'. It is surely a clear instance of the mis-reading of copy in which the word *their* was written *y^r*, mistaken by the compositor for *y^e*, a familiar instance indeed.

READ: *to their lays,*

---

[1] Citations are from the Folio text, which is basic for this play.

3.153 *Shee's tickled now, her Fume needs no spurres,*

Editors seem to be content with the Folio reading *Fume*, although it makes the line halt metrically, and this use of the word *fume* is odd here. I suggest that Shakespeare wrote *furie*, which is easily misread as *fume*.

READ: *her fury*

3.214–15 *This is the Law, and this Duke* Humfreyes *doome.*
  Som. *I humbly thanke your Royall Maiestie.*

Some editors, Kittredge among them, supply lines from the Quarto to fill a presumed gap between l. 214 and l. 215. I see no need for emendation of the Folio text. Gloucester (Humphrey) is speaking as the King's mouthpiece, and there is no difficulty in Somerset replying to the King directly.

4.19 *Deepe Night, darke Night, the silent of the Night,*

Most editors retain the Folio *silent*. Quarto reads *silence*. There is every graphic plausibility for a misreading of *silenc* as *silent* by the compositor, as Dover Wilson points out in *New Cambridge*, and evidence enough for the spelling *silenc*.

READ: *the silence*

ACT 3

1.140 *That you will cleare your selfe from all suspence,*

The emendation *suspects* for *suspense* has been current since Capell. Alexander, however, reads *suspence*, and Hart and *New Cambridge suspense*, and surely rightly. There is no sort of difficulty in reading *suspense*, meaning 'a state of suspense or of suspended judgment', a meaning for which there is ample authority.

READ: *from all suspense.*

1.260 *As* Humfrey *prou'd by Reasons to my Liege.*

The established reading, now taken for granted, *As Humphrey, proved by reasons, to my liege.* ignores the Folio punctuation. The line is thus treated as in apposition to l. 258, 'By nature proved an enemy to the flock'. 'The fox is proved by nature to be an enemy to the flock, as Humphrey (proved by reasons) to the King.' This seems very forced, elliptical, and unnatural. The Folio reading as it stands gives a better sense, with *Humphrey* as subject to the verb *proved*, and refers back to ll. 165 ff. in this scene and to Gloucester's words explaining to the King that ways would be found to justify his own death, that 'A staff is quickly found to beat a dog'. This was what 'he proved by reasons to the King', as Suffolk sardonically recalls the conversation. 'Do not stand on quillets how to slay him', he continues.

READ: *As Humphrey proved by reasons to my liege.*

2.120 *Dye* Elinor,

The confusions in the text between Elinor and Margaret (who is here plainly speaking of herself), as also in *Nell* for *Meg* at l. 26 in this scene and elsewhere, cannot be laid at the compositor's door. *New Cambridge* adduces this as evidence for divided authorship and revision, and reads as in the Folio, though marked with an obelus. The errors must, however, have been corrected in the course of preparation for the stage-presentation. The Folio text therefore cannot in this respect transmit the final text, and there is every justification for emending to *Die Margaret* in a modern edition.

2.146 *Stage-direction.* Bed put forth.

The Folio stage-direction is given at l. 146, two lines before Warwick's speech to which it is related, 'Come hither gracious Sovereign, view this body'. To cite in a modern text this direction as it stands, as is usual, is misleading. It suggests that a bed was 'put forth' on to the main stage. But the direction is given from the point of view of the back-stage hands, of the prompter. It is given in good time to be ready for l. 149. And it merely means that the prompter gives warning, if necessary, that the bed must be 'put forth' into the inner stage, so that when Warwick speaks at l. 149 and draws the curtains, the bed will be revealed there. And this is, in effect, the Quarto form of the stage-direction. It is pedantic to cite the *ipsissima verba* of the Folio text here, especially as they were probably not inserted by Shakespeare. (And so *New Cambridge* rightly reads.) Warwick's entrance, it should be noted, after his exit at l. 135, is from the inner stage. He draws the curtains as he enters.

READ at l. 148: [*Warwick* draws the curtains and shows *Gloucester* in his bed.

2.121–287 *Stage-directions.*

The problems offered by the conduct of this scene have been variously met by editors. It is clear that we cannot proceed as if there were two groups of *Commons*. It seems reasonable that at l. 135 Salisbury 'retires' with the Commons, who have seen the corpse of Gloucester and heard Warwick's attack upon Suffolk and Beaufort. At l. 202 Salisbury and the Commons exeunt along with Beaufort and Somerset. At l. 241 Salisbury re-enters, with the Commons at the door (*within*), following upon *Noise within* at l. 235. Salisbury addresses the Commons at the door, and they shout in reply within. There has to be time for the Commons to instruct Salisbury upon 'their mind', and the interval between l. 202 and l. 235 provides this.

The arrangement in *New Cambridge*, whereby the Commons never 'enter' but remain throughout 'at the door' offers much difficulty. In some other recent editions the Commons 'enter', evidently upon the stage, but make no exit, yet are found later on indicated as *within*.

READ: l. 121 Noise within. Enter *Warwick*, *Salisbury* and *Commons*.

l. 135 [Exit *Warwick*. *Salisbury* and *Commons* retire.

l. 202 [Exeunt *Beaufort*, *Somerset*, *Salisbury*, and *Commons*.

l. 235 [Noise within.

l. 241 Enter *Salisbury*, and *Commons* at the door.

l. 288 [Exeunt *Salisbury* and *Commons*.

ACT 4

1.35 *And told me that by Water I should dye:*

The pun is clear in reference to '*Walter* Whitmore' in l. 31. The *l* was not pronounced in *Walter* (as indeed often even today). It is best to read *Water* here with a capital *W* as in Folio. An amazing instance of this pronunciation occurred in Chancery records of the time. A witness's name was entered as *Walter Tonpayn*. His name was in fact, as he signed it, *Waterton Payne*.

1.70. Poole, *Sir* Poole? *Lord*,

Here there can be little doubt that the Folio text is corrupt, and that the Quarto, with *Yes Poull...I Poull*, assists us to arrive at the true text. Editors vary in the form given to the exchange. New Cambridge reads:

> Lieut. *Yes, poll!*
> Suff.   *Pole!*
> Lieut.   *Sir Pool! Lord Pool!*

Kittredge reads:

> Lieut. *Yes, Pole.*
> Suff.   *Pole?*
> Lieut.   *Pool? Sir Pool? Lord!*

I concur in this latter reading, except that I would read the final line as

>   Lieut.   *Pool? Sir Pool? Lord*,

with a final comma instead of an exclamation-mark, as in Folio, thus marking the Lieutenant's contempt in the succeeding words, 'Lord, ay kennel, puddle, sink'.

Dover Wilson's reading *poll* introduces a suggested pun related to the previous words, 'Strike off his head'. But the name *Pole* was pronounced *Pool*, and the pun would be unperceived. The reading, surely, misses the point. The point of *Pole* in this line is quite different. The Lieutenant addresses Suffolk with deliberate discourtesy, without title or honour due, merely as *Pole*. 'You dare not behead me', says Suffolk, 'lest you lose your own.' The Lieutenant replies, 'I dare, Pole', his defiance underlined by contempt. Suffolk asks, 'Do *you* call *me* Pole?' And the Lieutenant then puns on his name, with a withering reply to Suffolk's protest, imitating his voice, 'I omit your titles, do I? Well, then, Pole, *Sir* Pole, *Lord*, you are only a ᴘool, a kennel, puddle, sink.'

Alexander, upon consideration of the Quarto sources, deletes the Folio *Sir* and *Lord*, thus arriving at,

>   Lieut. *Poole!*
>   Suff. *Poole?*
>   Lieut. *Ay, kennel. . . .*

But this is to reject the authoritative text along with the evidence of a less authoritative text which supplements it.

READ: Lieut. *Yes, Pole.*

>   Suff.   *Pole?*
>   Lieut.   *Pool? Sir Pool? Lord*,

1.117 **Pine gelidus timor occupat artus,** *it is thee I feare.*

Editors mostly omit *Pine* and leave it at that. So Kittredge and Alexander. *New Cambridge* reads *Perii!*

gelidus, after a suggestion of J. A. K. Thomson, which is at any rate an attempt to face the textual facts, though difficult to educe from the possible copy. My own suggestion is *Sive*. It is perhaps less difficult to misread an initial *S* as *P* in italic script, and *u* as *n*, and *Sive* seems to fit reasonably into the sense of the line, perhaps by confusion with *sicut*, as in *Love's Labour's Lost* 5.1.22.

READ: *Sive gelidus timor*

3.8–9 *And thou shalt haue a License to kill for a hundred lacking one.*

There is no need to append the words *a week* to this sentence, as did Malone on Quarto authority, followed by many editors. No Elizabethan would need these explanatory words concerning a familiar condition for licences to kill during Lent.

7.75 *Kent to maintaine, the King, the Realme and you,*

Johnson, followed by most editors, including recent editors, read *But* for *Kent*, and Dover Wilson suggests that it is graphically plausible, *k* resembling *b*, as indeed it can. I think the misreading of the whole word implausible. But, more important, I see no need whatever for emendation. Say is addressing the men of Kent, and is asserting his especial care for Kent, as any politician would in his place. The Folio comma after *maintaine* is not to be ignored. And 'to maintain Kent' is not synonymous with 'to maintain the men of Kent' (*you*).

READ: *Kent to maintain,*

ACT 5

3.1-2 Yorke. *Of Salsbury, who can report of him,*
          That Winter Lyon,

Alexander and *New Cambridge* retain the first *Of*. It seems likely that they fall into the error of the compositor, who was influenced by the phrase *of him* later in the line, and interpret accordingly. The opening words *Of Salisbury* would surely be most awkward and artificial. The speech goes on to lay the utmost stress upon the point of Salisbury's age: 'winter lion', 'aged contusions', 'brush of time', and presently Richard joins in with 'his old feeble body', supported by Salisbury himself, 'God knows how long it is I have to live'. It is surely irresistible to read *Old*. And so Kittredge reads.

READ: *Old Salisbury,*

THE THIRD PART OF
KING HENRY THE SIXTH

ACT 1

1.19–20 **Nor.** *Such hope haue all the line of* **Iohn of Gaunt.**
Rich. *Thus do I hope to shake King* **Henries** *head.*[1]

Alexander and *New Cambridge* (without comment)
retain the Folio *hope* in l. 19. All editors agree that *have* is
optative, 'may all the line of John of Gaunt have', and
those that read *hope* doubtless treat it as ironical, and as an
exclamation, which seems very weak. I have little doubt
that *hap* is the true reading, and that the compositor was led
to *hope* partly by the pattern, and partly by *hope* in l. 20.
There is clearly some play of words with *hap* and *hope* in
close succession, here as in 2.3.8–9:

> *Warw.* How now my lord, what hap? What hope of good?
> *George.* Our hap is loss, our hope but sad despair.

READ: *Such hap have all the line of John of Gaunt.*

ACT 2

5.119 *Men for the losse of thee, hauing no more,*

Capell's emendation, *Even* for *Men*, has been generally
accepted, but it appears to be barely relevant here, and a
mere makeshift or expletive. I suggest *Meet*, as apt and
significant in the context. 'Thy father will take full care
for thy obsequies, as is meet for the loss of thee, his only
son'. The misreading of *mete* or *meet* as *men*, with a short
t, is at least as plausible as misreading *even* as *men*.

READ: *Meet for the loss of thee,*

[1] Citations are from the basic Folio text.

6.42–5 Rich. *Whose soule is that which takes hir heauy leaue?*
A deadly grone, like life and deaths departing.
See who it is.
  Ed. *And now the Battailes ended,*
  If Friend or Foe, let him be gently vsed.

Most editors, including *New Cambridge*, follow Capell in adopting changed speakers' names as set out in the 1595 Octavo. (Alexander, however, retains the Folio reading.) It seems entirely probable that the changes are necessary. Edward is the senior of the brothers, takes the lead throughout, and gives instructions. It is quite clear that Richard obeys the instruction, *See who it is*, and announces "'tis Clifford'.

READ:
  Edw. *Whose soul is that which takes her heavy leave?*
  Rich. *A deadly groan, like life and death's departing.*
  Edw. *See who it is, and now the battle's ended,*
  If friend or foe, let him be gently used.

Life and death's departing, of course, means the dividing point between life and death.

ACT 3

1.24 *Let me embrace the sower Aduersaries,*

Recent editors are agreed upon following Dyce's *embrace thee, sour adversity.* I would, however, read *adversities* on graphic grounds, taking into account the pattern of the Folio reading more precisely. *aduersaries* and *aduersities* could readily be confused, as *aduersaries* and *aduersitie* could not.

READ: *Let me embrace thee, sour adversities,*

ACT 4

8.6 King. *Let's leuie men, and beat him backe againe,*

It has been argued that the speaker here must be
Oxford, not the King. And so Kittredge reads. There is
some support for this in the 1595 Octavo. The scene,
again, opens with Warwick addressing the lords (not the
King), 'What counsel, lords?' Finally, Henry is anything
but warlike throughout. The sum of these arguments
seems inadequate. Henry is King, after all, and later in the
scene speaks to Exeter of his 'power'. Stronger reasons
are required to desert the authoritative text here.

READ: as in F.

8.32 *New Cambridge*, after an *Exeunt omnes* ('they go')
at l. 32, begins a new scene at l. 33, at 'The Bishop of
London's palace adjoining St Paul's'. The reasons adduced
are P. A. Daniel's, and are unconvincing. The King speaks
of his levies as already in existence. Warwick is spoken of
as at Coventry. But these are normal in dramatic fore-
shortening. The lords have set off at l. 32 to raise levies,
and the King considers it done. Warwick leaves for
Coventry at l. 32, and Edward at l. 58 assures himself that
he will find Warwick at Coventry. The only valid point is
that Exeter is not included in the entry at the beginning of
Sc. 8, and this is slight ground for such conclusions, which
involve an exit by the King and an immediate re-entry in
a new scene. There is no real ground for this radical
emendation, which really rests upon a desire to reconcile
the play with the chroniclers who place Henry's capture by
Edward in the palace of the Bishop of London.

ACT 5

2.44 *Which sounded like a Cannon in a Vault,*

The 1595 Octavo reads *clamour* for *cannon*, with almost universal acceptance, e.g. by Kittredge and Alexander, but not by Hart or *New Cambridge*. There is no justification for this emendation, unless one accepts the Octavo as of equal authority with Folio. The sound of a cannon discharged in a vault is surely entirely appropriate here, reverberating with a deep hollow noise, confused, echoing.

READ: as in F.

KING RICHARD THE THIRD

ACT 1

1.64–5   Clarence '*tis shee*,
That tempts him to this harsh Extremity.[1]

For *tempts* Quarto reads *tempers*, and omits *harsh*. There
can be no reasonable doubt that this is the true original
text. The point of Richard's speech is the effect of the rule
of men by women, not their temptation, as is evident in the
words, 'when men are *ruled* by women', and 'Was it not
she . . . That *made* him send Lord Hastings to the Tower'.
Temper has the sense of 'mould', 'prepare' by pressure.

READ: *That tempers him to this extremity.*

1.138 Rich. *Now by S. Iohn, that Newes is bad indeed.*

Quarto reads *Now by Saint Paul*. There is contemporary
authority for Richard's use of St Paul as his usual oath, and
elsewhere Folio so uses it (e.g. 1.2.36, 41). It was, with
other personal characteristics referred to in the play,
common knowledge. Alexander retains *St John*.

READ: *Now by Saint Paul*

1.142 *Where is he, in his bed?*

Quarto reads *What is he in his bed?* a much more natural
and intelligible question in this form. Richard's question is
not of the King's whereabouts, but whether he is ill enough
to be in bed. The Folio reading is surely makeshift, though
Alexander retains it.

READ: *What, is he in his bed?*

---

[1] Citations are from the Folio text, which is basic for most of the play:
where the Folio text appears to be derivative or incomplete, citations are
from the First Quarto, and are marked with an asterisk (*).

2.14–16 *O cursed be the hand that made these holes:*
Cursed the Heart, that had the heart to do it:
Cursed the Blood, that let this blood from hence:

Quarto omits l. 16, and for ll. 14–15 reads:

> *Curst be the hand that made these fatall holes,*
> *Curst be the heart that had the heart to doe it.*

It is to be observed that a little later in this speech, l. 25 is also omitted in Quarto, though it is significant in Anne's argument. It seems unreasonable therefore to depart from Folio in ll. 14–15, on slight stylistic preference, and yet to depart from Quarto in favour of Folio in l. 11 above, where Quarto reads,

> *Stabd by the selfesame hands that made these holes,*

and Folio, surely rightly, reads *wounds* for *holes*. But it is indeed difficult to avoid a stylistic eclecticism in this play, whose textual history is obscure and uncertain. And so the next note, and many others, show.

READ: as in Folio.

2.38–9 Gen. *My Lord stand backe, and let the Coffin passe.*
Rich. *Vnmanner'd Dogge,*
Stand'st thou when I commaund:

Quarto reads *stand thou when I command*, and it can hardly be doubted that this is the true reading, for the Folio reading is almost nonsense. Richard's reply to the Gentleman's order to him to *stand back* is 'stand *thou*'.

READ: *stand thou when I command.*

2.94 *Thy murd'rous Faulchion smoaking in his blood:*

Quarto reads *bloudy faulchion*, and this repetition of *blood* surely vindicates Folio here, and justifies a general acceptance of the Folio text in this region of the play.

READ: *murderous*

3.68 *Makes him to send, that he may learne the ground.*

Quarto reads here:

> *Makes him to send that thereby he may gather*
> *The ground of your ill will and to remoue it.*

Editors, fearing the loss of a drop of Shakespeare's blood, have mostly adopted the Quarto reading, with its two lines to the Folio's one, and with the emendation *and so remove it* for *and to remove it.* The Folio text appears to be adequate, and the additional idea introduced in the Quarto text, *and to remove it,* is out of character for Elizabeth.

READ: as in F.

3.109 *To be so baited, scorn'd, and stormed at,*

Quarto reads: *To be thus taunted, scorned, and baited at:*

It might seem to be apparent in the Folio reading that the compositor, if working from manuscript copy, would have difficulty in distinguishing between *scorned* and *stormed.* It looks like duplication of one word in the copy, *scorned* read for something else, and *stormed* read for *scorned.* And this use of *stormed at* seems curiously unnatural, where *baited, scorned,* and *taunted* seem natural in Elizabethan English. It is probable that there was confused copy from the beginning, with some truth in both Quarto and Folio. The Quarto *baited at* is certainly odd too. There seems to be nothing for it but a guess, on the material supplied by both texts.

READ: *To be so baited, taunted, and scorned at.*

4.46 *that sowre Ferry-man*

Quarto reads *grim* for *sour,* and most editors have preferred *grim,* though not Kittredge or Alexander. *sour* is indeed a superior epithet for Charon, and in tune with 'the *melancholy* flood' in l. 45.

READ: *that sour ferryman*

4.101–8 *2 *What shall I stab him as he sleepes?*
       1 *No then he will say twas done cowardly*
          When he wakes.
       2 *When he wakes,*
          Why foole he shall neuer wake till the iudgement
          day.
       1 *Why then he will say, we stabd him sleeping.*

Folio reads:

2 *What, shall we stab him as he sleepes.*
1 *No: hee'l say 'twas done cowardly, when he wakes*
2 *Why he shall neuer wake, vntill the great Iudgement*
  day.
1 *Why then hee'l say, we stab'd him sleeping.*

Making the best of both worlds, I suggest that Folio and
Quarto each contain part of the original text. So often in
this play each supplements the other beyond reasonable
doubt. Editors vary in their versions here.

READ:

Sec. Murderer. *What, shall I stab him as he sleeps?*

First Murderer. *No. He'll say 'twas done cowardly, when
he wakes.*

Sec. Murderer. *When he wakes? Why fool, he shall never
wake till the judgment day.*

First Murderer. *Why then he'll say we stabbed him
sleeping.*

This reading seems to me to agree with the indications
elsewhere of differences in the characters and ways of the
two murderers, the First more of a dangerous clown, the
Second more complicated in thought and soul.

4.121 *my holy humor*

Folio reads: *this passionate humor of mine,*

Kittredge and Alexander both read as in Folio. But the
Second Murderer has religious qualms (not emotional),
connected with the *Judgment Day,* being *damned,* and

conscience. There is a grim humour in being limited to a short duration of such moods (l. 122).

READ: *this holy humour of mine*

4.263–77 The Folio text is here manifestly a more faithful transmission of the original copy than the Quarto, unless we are dealing with the revision by Shakespeare of an unsatisfactory first draft, a theory to which all analysis of the text is in opposition. Yet it is no less manifestly gravely disordered in its arrangement of lines, and Quarto also furnishes material for a probable reconstruction of the true original.

READ:

Sec. Murderer. *What shall we do?*
Clar.   *Relent, and save your souls.*
First Murderer. *Relent? 'Tis cowardly and womanish.*
Clar. *Not to relent is beastly, savage, devilish.*
Which of you, if you were a Prince's son,
Being pent from liberty, as I am now,
If two such murderers as yourselves came to you,
Would not entreat for life?
[To *Second Murderer*]. *My friend, I spy some pity in thy looks.*
O if thine eye be not a flatterer,
Come thou on my side, and entreat for me,
As you would beg, were you in my distress.
A begging prince what beggar pities not?
Sec. Murderer. *Look behind you my lord.*
First Murderer. *Take that, and that* [stabs him]. *If all this will not do,*
I'll drown you in the malmsey-butt within.
                                        [Exit, with the body.

And so most recent editors agree.

ACT 2

1.5–6 *And more to peace my soule shall part to heauen,*
       Since I haue made my Friends at peace on earth.

Various readings have been adopted by compromise with
a variant Quarto text, which is manifestly corrupt here. It
seems clear that in the Folio the first *to* in l. 5 is an error
for *at*, by attraction from the second *to* and the apparent
sense, 'my soul shall go to heaven and to peace'.

READ: *And more at peace*

1.56 *vnwillingly,*

Quarto reads *vnwittingly*, the true reading beyond doubt,
as recent editors agree, and easily misread in copy.

READ: *unwittingly,*

4.65 *Or let me dye, to looke on earth no more.*

Quarto reads *death* for *earth*. The Folio reading is
evidently an improvisation. The Duchess is complaining of
the long series of wars and violent *deaths* which 'her eyes
have beheld'.

READ: *death*

ACT 3

4.57 *By any liuelyhood he shew'd to day?*

Quarto reads *likelihood*, followed by Kittredge. Derby's
argument, however, is in direct reference to Hastings'
preceding 'His Grace looks cheerfully and smooth this
morning'. *livelihood* is used here, as often in Elizabethan
English, in the sense of 'liveliness'. *live* could easily be
misread as *like*.

READ: *livelihood*

5.33-5 *Well, well, he was the couertst sheltred Traytor*
       That euer liu'd.
       Would you imagine, or almost beleeue,

There is an apparent lacuna in l. 34. In Quarto, there
is in the preceding speech an excrescent phrase, 'Looke ye
my Lo: Maior', which is lined separately, and is clearly out
of place there. But it fits precisely into the gap in the Folio
text, and is required there to indicate to whom Buckingham
is speaking. It is to be noted that Buckingham, throughout
the scene, does not address the Mayor without referring to
his office or his 'lordship' as Lord Mayor. Alexander,
however, reads as in Folio.

READ: *That ever lived. Look ye my Lord Mayor,*

5.50-1 **Buck.** *I neuer look'd for better at his hands,*
       After he once fell in with Mistresse **Shore**:

Folio gives these lines to Buckingham, as the beginning
of his speech; Quarto to the Lord Mayor at the end of his
preceding speech. There can be no doubt that Quarto is
right. The Mayor picks up Richard's hint at l. 31.

READ: as in Q.

ACT 4

2.45-8 *How now, Lord* **Stanley**, *what's the newes?*
       Stanley. *Know my louing Lord, the Marquesse*
      Dorset
      As I heare, is fled to **Richmond**,
      In the parts where he abides.

Quarto reads:

    How now, what neewes with you?
    Darby. *My Lord, I heare the Marques Dorset*
    Is fled to Richmond, in those partes beyond the seas
     where he abides.

It is clear that both are printed from imperfect copy, in which the original text and lineation are lost. Various editors attempt various reconstructions and restorations, all eclectic. I suggest the following:

> READ: *How now Lord Stanley, what's the news?*
> Derby.   *My lord,*
> *I hear the Marquess Dorset's fled to Richmond,*
> *In the parts beyond the seas where he abides.*

2.101–20: l. 101 **A king perhaps, perhaps.*
          l. 120 **Whie then resolue me whether you wil or
                  no?*

Folio, followed by recent editors, reads:

> *May it please you to resolue me in my suit.*

It is clear that Quarto throughout this passage transmits the original text, whereas in Folio some sixteen lines are wanting. It has been suggested that these lines were cut because of censorship, but there is no clear ground for this explanation. The indications point rather to imperfect copy in Folio. In l. 101, at the beginning of the cut in Folio, where Quarto reads *A king perhaps, perhaps.*, Folio reads *A King perhaps.* Few will question that Quarto here represents Richard's brooding meditation in this repeated *perhaps*, and that the text should follow Quarto here. The omitted lines are, if not dramatically indispensable, dramatically most effective and crucial. The Quarto version of l. 120 represents surely the growing tension and anger of Buckingham, and explains more fully the sudden brusqueness of Richard's reply to this line.

> READ: l. 101 *A King—perhaps—perhaps—*
>   l. 120 *Why then resolve me whether you will or
>   no.*

4.323 *Aduantaging their Loue, with interest*
       Of ten-times double gaine of happinesse.

Editors, including recent editors, have emended *love* to
loan, presumably plausible as a misreading of *love* for *loan*
spelled *lone*. Dover Wilson (privately) cites *lone* in Sonnet 6.
But there it is an eye-rhyme. The metaphor, difficult as it
is, is made more difficult by insisting thus upon *loan, interest*.
It may seem unnecessary to emend. *love* may well be closely
related to *happiness* in the poet's mind. 'The love that you
have shown in your tears for those you have lost (*their
love*) will be rewarded by increased gain of happiness.'
    READ: *Advantaging their love*

4.348 *To vaile the Title,*
    Quarto reads *waile* for *vaile*. The Folio reading is clearly
a misreading of manuscript copy, of *v* for *w*.
    READ: *To wail*

ACT 5

3.204–13 **Me thought the soules of all that I had murtherd,*
          Came to my tent, and euery one did threat,
          Tomorrows vengeance on the head of Richard.
                    Enter Ratcliffe.
          Rat. *My Lord.*
          King. *Zoundes, who is there?*
          Rat. *Ratcliffe, my Lord, tis I, the earlie village
          cocke,*
          Hath twise done salutation to the morne,
          Your friendes are vp, and buckle on their armor.
          King. *O Ratcliffe, I haue dreamd a fearefull
          dreame,*
          What thinkst thou, will our friendes proue all true?

The passage as it stands in Quarto, as in Folio with
some omissions, offers difficulty. Lines 204–6 form a very
odd epilogue to Richard's long soliloquy after the procession

of ghosts, and seem quite out of place there. He hardly
needs to tell himself what he has seen. And this epilogue
ruins the unity of his magnificent soliloquy. On the other
hand, there is a curious disjointedness in his speech to
Ratcliffe after his initial alarm, in ll. 212–13, and he is
oddly uncommunicative to him about his 'fearful dream'.
Ratcliffe, moreover, has little to go upon to lead him to bid
Richard 'be not afraid of shadows'.

There is clearly serious dislocation in the text, in both
Quarto and Folio, and I suggest that ll. 204–6 are out of
place and should form part of Richard's explanation of his
fears to Ratcliffe, his closest confidant. They also help to
explain his desire to be reassured about the loyalty of his
friends. Johnson suggested inserting them after l. 192.

READ: Enter *Ratcliffe*.

Ratcliffe. *My lord.*

Richard. *Zounds, who is there?*

Ratcliffe. *Ratcliffe, my lord. 'Tis I. The early
village cock
Hath twice done salutation to the morn.
Your friends are up, and buckle on their armour.*

Richard. *O Ratcliffe, I have dreamed a fearful
dream.
Methought the souls of all that I had murdered
Came to my tent, and every one did threat
Tomorrow's vengeance on the head of Richard.
What thinkest thou, will our friends prove all true?*

3.302–4 *Nor. *A good direction warlike soueraigne,*
                    he sheweth him a paper.
            This found I on my tent this morning.
            Iocky of Norfolke be not so bould,

Folio omits any stage-direction, but otherwise reads as
in Quarto. Editors have taken the Quarto direction to
mean that Norfolk shows Richard the paper and Richard
reads it. I have no doubt that Norfolk shows Richard the

paper, but reads it himself, as the Folio text would suggest. And this is indeed the natural course of events. 'Gives him a paper' would be a different direction and is no unusual form of words for a direction.

READ: *This found I on my tent this morning.*
[Shows a paper, and reads.
Jockey of Norfolk be not so bold,

KING HENRY THE EIGHTH

ACT 1

1.78–80
> *and his owne Letter*
> *The Honourable Boord of Councell, out*
> *Must fetch him in, he Papers.*[1]

This passage has given difficulty, and has been variously emended, unnecessarily except in regard to punctuation. The Folio punctuation in l. 80 in fact points to the construction, with *him* as object of the verb *papers* (or rather *whom* understood).

'His own mere letter is sufficient to call in anyone to whom he sends a paper, without reference to the Council.'

READ:
> *and his own letter,*
> *The honourable Board of Council out,*
> *Must fetch him in he papers.*

1.221 Buck: *O Michaell Hopkins?*

Hopkins' name was Nicholas, in fact. And in 1.2.147 he is referred to as '*Nicholas* Henton'. An abbreviated form *nich* might well be misread *mich*.

READ: *O Nicholas Hopkins?*

2.67 *There is no primer basenesse.*

Editors, including recent editors, have accepted the emendation *business* for *baseness*, as more consonant with Katharine's request for 'quick consideration', and with the adjective *primer*. It is plausible in every way, though an *e* is not always easily to be confused with an *i*. But emendation is not obligatory, and may indeed seem to weaken the sense and to be out of harmony with Katharine's argument and Henry's indignant comment. The exactions

---

[1] Citations are from the Folio text.

are 'pestilent to the hearing'; they reflect on the King and affect the loyalty of his subjects, giving rise to disloyal comment and even disobedience. The Folio reading should be retained.

READ: *baseness.*

2.139 *This dangerous conception in this point,*

Editors seem satisfied with the Folio reading. But the insistence in Wolsey's speech, as in the Surveyor's preceding speech, is throughout on *him, he, his*; and *this* weakens the line. It was probably attracted from *his* by the second *this* in the line. *This conception* and *this point* have the effect of tautology.

READ: *His dangerous conception in this point.*

2.147–8 Nicholas Henton.
          Kin. *What was that* Henton?

This is obviously a reference to the Nicholas Hopkins of 1.1.221. Editors (not Alexander) therefore emend, reading *Hopkins* for *Henton.* But this is no compositor's misreading or error. It is at worst a slip of Shakespeare's. The Surveyor is speaking this time, whereas Buckingham made the earlier reference, and the monk was in fact known by name in this form also, *Henton* being the name of his convent. The audience is left in no doubt that it is the same man ('Sir, a Chartreux friar'). It is surely deliberate.

READ: *Nicholas Henton.*

2.164 *vnder the Commissions Seale,*

It is not possible to justify the Folio reading on grounds of sense. The sense demands *confession's*, and there is no question of the issue of a commission to take evidence here. The Folio reading could not be a mere misreading of the copy, but may well have been an editorial change. The 'seal of the confession' was by now less familiar than 'a commission under seal'. It was hardly likely to be a censorial change.

READ: *under the confession's seal*

2.169–70   *bid him striue*
              To the loue o' th' Commonalty, the Duke

Sense and metre alike indicate a defective line here. *gain the*, or *win the*, must be supplied.

READ: *To win the love*

ACT 2

4.182–4 *The bosome of my Conscience, enter'd me;*
        Yea, with a spitting power, and made to tremble
        The region of my Breast,

Many editors have emended *bosom* to *bottom*. Dover Wilson (privately) cites Holinshed's 'bottom of my conscience.' But the whole of the image refers to *bosom* and *breast*, and *conscience* is not unreasonably associated with the inward *heart*. *spitting*, again, has been emended, as by Kittredge and Alexander, to *splitting*, which gives an entirely different, and false, sense. The sense of *spitting*, which is not unfamiliar even today, is 'piercing, pricking through', as by a spit, or a rapier.

READ: *The bosom of my conscience, entered me,*
        Yea, with a spitting power,

ACT 3

1.21–3 *I doe not like their comming; now I thinke on't,*
        They should bee good men, their affaires as righteous;
        But all Hoods, make not Monkes.

Editors, including Kittredge and Alexander, read as directed by the Folio punctuation, with a full stop after

coming, and a new sentence beginning *Now I think on't.*
But the sense would then be, 'I do not like their coming.
But now I remind myself that they should be good men,
though you cannot trust all men in canonicals. (Therefore
I should like their coming.)' Surely the trend of Katharine's
thought is much plainer, and much less woolly. 'What can
two Cardinals want from me when I am so out of favour
with the King? And now I think about it, I do not like
this visit. Cardinals *should* be good men, on a good errand,
but you cannot trust all men in canonicals (and I do not
trust these).'

READ: *I do not like their coming, now I think on't.*
　　　　They should be good men,

2.171 *Yet fill'd with my Abilities:*

Editors read *fil'd* (*filed*) for *filled*, which seems to me to
increase the difficulty of the line. Indeed, I am not clear
upon the sense of *filed* here. But the phrase as in the Folio
text has a clear and relevant sense, 'yet fulfilled to the best
of my abilities'. These interpretations of *filled* and *with my
abilities* are familiar in Elizabethan English.

READ: *Yet filled with my abilities.*

2.342–3　　　*Goods, Lands, Tenements,*
　　　　　　　　Castles, and whatsoeuer,

The Folio reading is an excellent example of a plausible
false text. But for knowledge of the sources used, an
editor could hardly question the word *castles*. This passage,
however, follows Holinshed closely, and Theobald naturally
suggested *Chattels* for *Castles*, on this evidence. Holinshed's
text, moreover, gives a clue to the origin of the false reading
of Shakespeare's copy, in his spelling of the word, *Cattels*,
which is indeed the usual Elizabethan spelling, and is closer
graphically to *Castles* than is *Chattels*.

READ: *Chattels,*

2.350–1 *So farewell, to the little good you beare me.*
          Farewell? A long farewell to all my Greatnesse.

These two lines are universally read with insufficient
respect for the Folio punctuation:

> *So farewell to the little good you bear me.*
> *Farewell, a long farewell to all my greatness.*

A great deal is thus lost of the dramatic effect of the
opening of this great soliloquy, to which the Folio text
clearly points. Wolsey is replying to the parting words of
Norfolk as he goes:

> *So fare you well, my little good* Lord Cardinal.

His first words are an echo of Norfolk's mockery, and are
spoken to the nobles as they leave. He then turns to his
own thoughts which play upon these *farewells* and emerge
in fragments, until they flow into the full stream of
imagery.

READ: *So farewell—to the little good you bear me.*
        Farewell? A long farewell to all my greatness.

ACT 4

2.97–8   *How pale she lookes,*
         And of an earthy cold? Marke her eyes?

Editors have swayed between retaining the Folio *cold*
and the emendation *colour*. I have no doubt that the
emendation gives the true text. Patience throughout this
speech is referring to appearances. The Queen is *altered,*
drawn, pale, and her eyes look ominous of death. Nor is
of an earthy colour synonymous with *pale*. She is pale, and
her paleness is of an earthy texture and shade. The sentence
means in effect, 'she looks pale and corpse-like'. The
emendation is plausible graphically, for with *colour* written
color, as frequently, the *or* could easily be misread as *d*.

READ: *And of an earthy colour?*

ACT 5

Scs. 2 and 3 *Stage-directions.*

There is some obscurity in most editions concerning the conduct of these scenes on the stage. I suggest the following arrangements. Sc. 2 opens *Before the Council Chamber.* Cranmer approaches the curtained inner stage (the Council Chamber) from which the Doorkeeper enters. At l. 19 Henry and Butts enter *above*, in the gallery, and begin to watch the proceedings. In Sc. 3, the curtains of the inner stage are drawn and the stage becomes the Council Chamber, with table and chairs brought in and set in front of the State (which is in the inner stage), after which the procession of nobles enters from the inner stage and is set at the Council Table. At the end of Sc. 2 the King and Butts do not 'exit', though they close the gallery-curtains, and they continue watching the proceedings through the part-closed curtains, as they must to make the scene intelligible. At l. 109 in Sc. 3, the King exits *above* and at l. 113 enters *below*. Scenes 2 and 3 are, in fact, continuous.

The Folio direction at l. 19, in Sc. 2,

> Enter the King, and Buts, at a Windowe aboue.

need not necessarily be taken as indicating literally a window, and I do not take it so, though there is of course room for debate on this point. Certain additional stage-directions are required to make this course of business clear. And their precise timing is of importance.

3.109 READ: *Would I were fairly out on't.*
                                        [Exit *Henry* above.
The preceding speeches approach a climax which reaches its height at these words, and is the cue for the King's action.

3.113 *Ye blew the fire that burnes ye: now haue at ye.*
          Enter King frowning on them, takes his Seate.

In the text and directions as given in editions, as in Folio, it is difficult to see why Cromwell suddenly turns to the menace of *now have at ye!* The explanation, of course, is that he sees that the King is now in presence, and will take charge.

READ: *Ye blew the fire that burns ye—*
          Enter *Henry* below.
                    now have at ye!
                         [*Henry* takes his seat.

It is a question whether Cromwell's final words here should not be spoken aside. But the whole speech is aside in a way, a soliloquy.

3.133 *Then but once thinke his place becomes thee not.*

this place is generally read for *his place*, an emendation for which I find no justification. The King is speaking of the Council and of Councillors. 'That Councillor (*he*) had better starve than think that you are not fit to be a Councillor like himself.' *his place*, then, means the office of a member of the Council. Foxe, one of Shakespeare's sources here, uses the phrase, 'He is a counsailour as well as you'.

READ: *his place*

THE TRAGEDIES

TROILUS AND CRESSIDA

ACT 1

1.30–1 *And when faire* Cressid *comes into my thoughts,*
        So traitor then she comes when she is thence.[1]

Editors have of late (e.g. Alexander and *Variorum*)
returned from Rowe's emendation to the original text, but
with dubious interpretation, conveying a halting and flat
thought. It might seem likely, however, that the compositor has followed the most obvious logic in a perversion
of his copy. Cressida could not well *come* into Troilus'
thoughts *except* when she was *thence*. And the interpretation hardly accounts for *So, traitor!* The whole trend of
the passage points to insistence upon Cressida's constant
presence in Troilus' mind, and upon his suffering from
absence from her. Graphic plausibility is not to be claimed,
but all else points to the emendation. And there are
various indications of damaged copy for the Quarto text, as
also indications of its origin in a transcript.

READ: *And when fair Cressid comes into my thoughts—*
      So, traitor! When she comes? When is she thence?

2.92 Hector *shall not haue his will this yeare.*

The Yale editor alone rejects Rowe's emendation, *wit*
for *will*, which is fully justified by the context and is
plausible graphically, with the spellings *wit, witt; wil, will*
frequent.

READ: *his wit*

---

[1] Citations are from the First Quarto of 1609. But the Folio text is agreed
to have authority also, as resting upon a copy of the Quarto corrected from
manuscript sources. Occasional citations from Folio are marked with an
asterisk (*).

2.282 *You are such a woman*

Folio reads *such another woman*, a far more idiomatic expression in Elizabethan English, and Pandarus is nothing if not colloquial. Alexander and Dr Walker prefer *such a.*

READ: *such another woman!*

3.36 *Vpon her ancient brest,*

Folio reads *patient,* and editors are agreed in following it. There is no possibility of one being misread for the other, and we may conclude upon damaged copy ( )*tient*) and a guess by the Quarto compositor (*auntient* and *pacient* are both frequent spellings.)

3.53–4 *And with an accent tun'd in selfe same key,*
        Retires to chiding fortune.

Pope read *Returns* for *Retires.* Dyce's *Retorts* is by far the most popular emendation, and is now universal, though graphically impossible. *Returns,* on the other hand, could well be misread as *Retires,* gives an admirable sense, and is used elsewhere by Shakespeare in that sense, a stronger sense than commentators seem to realize in Elizabethan English.

READ: *Returns*

3.70–4 *Aga. Speak Prince of Ithaca, and be't of lesse expect:*

        .   .   .   .   .

We shall heare Musicke, Wit, and Oracle.

These lines are wanting in Quarto. They are not indispensable, for Ulysses could well continue his speech without Agamemnon's intervention. But it can hardly be doubted that they are Shakespeare's. They may have been omitted by a transcriber, if we accept Dr Walker's theory. Or they may have been added after 1609, possibly marginally. There was need to break up the series of long speeches.

And a response by the King to Ulysses' direct appeal gave good opportunity.

READ: as in F.

3.92 *Corrects the ill Aspects of Planets euill,*

Quarto reads, *Corrects the influence of euill Planets,* and editors agree generally in preferring the Folio reading. It may well be thought probable that we have here evidence of revision by Shakespeare.

READ: as in F.

3.238–9 *Good armes, strong ioints, true swords, & great*
          Ioues accord
          Nothing so full of heart:

Folio reads *& Ioues accord,.* The passage has given difficulty. Theobald read as in Folio, and made sense of a kind out of *accord.* Alexander reads:

> *and, Jove's accord,*
> *Nothing so full of heart.*

This leaves the essential difficulty of *accord,* and treats *great* as a mysterious intrusion. If the metre is to be tolerable in the Quarto reading, a word of two syllables is required with the accent on the first syllable. I suggest *accent* as meeting all requirements, including that of graphic possibility, fortified by l. 53 above:

> And with an accent tuned in selfsame key...

The Trojans, in fact, 'have arms, joints, swords, and speak to their enemies in godlike voices: full of heart in all things beyond other men.'

READ: *Good arms, strong joints, true swords, and great*
          Jove's accent;
          Nothing so full of heart.

3.359–62   *let vs like Marchants*
First shew foule wares, and thinke perchance theile
*   sell;*
If not; the luster of the better shall exceed,
By shewing the worse first: do not consent,

Editors have preferred the ampler Folio version of this passage, which offers metrical difficulties. *Variorum* feels certain that it is a late revision and authoritative, as also an improvement. I am impressed by the lameness of the verse in Folio, as in Quarto, and I am not convinced that either is free from corruption. It is probable that both rest here upon 'foul papers', and each is a partial reflection of a true original, and I resort to an eclectic reading which derives in part from Quarto and in part from Folio.

READ: *Let us, like merchants, show our foulest wares,*
And think perchance they'll sell; if not,
The lustre of the better shall exceed,
By showing the worse first. Do not consent

ACT 2

1.15 *Speake then thou vnsalted leauen,*

Folio reads *whinid'st* for *unsalted*. The change cannot be other than deliberate. But the word should be represented in its more normal form, *vinewdst*, in its accepted sense of 'mouldiest'.

1.30 *I would thou didst itch from head to foote, and I had the scratching of the, I would make thee the lothsomest scab in Greece,*

Editors ignore the comma of Quarto and Folio after *foot*, and read *I would...head to foot and I had...thee. I would....* I see no difficulty in preserving the indications of the original texts, with much better sense. *And* here is *an* ('if').

READ: *I would thou didst itch from head to foot; an I had the scratching of thee, I would make thee the loathsomest scab in Greece.*

1.63 *You see him there? do you?*

Editors read, *You see him there, do you?* It may appear to be a small and fine matter, but the retention of the original precision of the text is significant, and is supported by Thersites' next speech, 'Nay, look upon him.'

READ: *You see him there. Do you?*

2.51–2 *Brother, shee is not worth, what shee doth cost the keeping.*

Editors, except Alexander, prefer the Folio *holding* for *keeping*. But *keep* is the idea in Shakespeare's mind, as appears presently: 'Why keep we her?'; 'Is she worth keeping?', in Troilus' speech.

READ: *cost The keeping.*

3.86 *He sate our messengers*

Folio reads *sent* for *sate*, which gives no sense, and is obviously an editorial counsel of despair. Among a mass of conjectures, Theobald's *shent* has been generally adopted, as also in recent editions, but with no plausibility of derivation from either the Quarto *sate* or the Folio conjecture *sent*. *Variorum* considers it unchallengeable, none the less.

I suggest *fobbed*, which gives good sense and is graphically plausible in the spelling *fobd*, easily misread as *sate*. *fobbed* is used thus absolutely in Elizabethan English, with the sense of the modern *fobbed off*. 'He put our messengers off with excuses'.

READ: *He fobbed our messengers,*

3.139 *His course, and time, his ebbs and flowes,*

Folio reads, *His pettish lines, his ebs, his flowes,* and Hanmer's emendation, *lunes* for *lines*, is generally accepted,

despite attempts to justify *lines* with support from *N.E.D.*
Graphically, this minim error is easy. And the collocation
of *ebbs and flows*, with *predominance* in l. 138, and *tide*
in l. 141, supports the image of *lunes* irresistibly. The
Quarto text in this area is exceptionally poor and shows
other guesses from difficult copy. The sense of the word
lunes, if accepted, must surely be 'variations like those of
the moon, but capricious'. If *lunes* be not accepted, I think
times preferable to *lines*, and indeed we might return to the
quite intelligible Quarto reading. But *pettish* carries conviction of a revised, or more authentic, text.

READ: *His pettish lunes,*

3.253–4 *Fam'd be thy tutor, and thy parts of nature,*
          Thrice fam'd beyond all thy erudition:

Folio reads for l. 254, *Thrice fam'd beyond, beyond all*
erudition; and its reading must certainly be followed, as
preferable in sense as in metre, and repairing a clearly
corrupt Quarto line which has been vamped to fit in with
the single *beyond*. The sense is, 'and may thy parts of nature
be thrice famed beyond the fame of thy tutor, beyond all
mere erudition (nature being superior to nurture)'. And
so recent editors rightly read.

READ: *and thy parts of nature*
          Thrice famed beyond, beyond all erudition.

3.267–8 Aiax. *Shall I call you father?*
          Nest. *I my good Sonne.*

Folio makes Ulysses reply to Ajax. Johnson set the
example for future editors in vindicating the Quarto reading.
A few recent editors, however, seek to justify Folio, very
improbably. Ulysses has just called Nestor 'father Nestor',
and has drawn Ajax' attention to him. Ajax naturally
responds by deferring to Nestor as Ulysses does, to the fount
of wisdom and experience.

READ: Nest. *Ay my good son.*

ACT 3

1.92-4 Pan *What saies my sweet Queene? my cozen will fall out with you.*

　　Hel. *You must not know where he sups.*

So both Quarto and Folio. Most editors transfer Helen's words to Pandarus' preceding speech, following Capell, and most unreasonably. The change is a grave injury to the text. Why should not Helen, like Paris, guess where Troilus is supping, and like Paris tease Pandarus, interrupting him with her 'Nay but my lord—'? And so Alexander rightly reads.

READ: as in Q. and F.

1.116 *I, I, prethee, now by my troth*

Folio reads *I, I, prethee now: by my troth,* followed by editors, including Alexander. But surely Quarto is preferable. Helen contemptuously and carelessly accepts Pandarus' offer to sing, then at once breaks in with an irrelevance. (The Folio reading is affected by Pandarus' preceding 'I'll sing you a song now'.) There is much of Millamant in Helen here, and there is a long provocation in her reception of Pandarus as a singer, since early in this scene.

READ: *Ay, ay, prithee. Now by my troth,*

2.210 *let all constant men be Troylusses*

The arguments for *inconstant* as an emendation for *constant* are dismissed generally of late, though the arguments for the Quarto *constant* are equally odd sometimes, e.g. Empson's suggestion that the lines were spoken from 'well on the front of the apron-stage' and are, in fact, out of the action, an interjection to the audience. But the plain fact is that Pandarus' words are, in effect, dictated by Troilus, 'As true as Troilus' (l. 189), and by Cressida, 'As false as Cressid' (l. 203). He is carrying out their

8   SSII

instructions in his prophecy, and the three speeches are
closely linked together. The speech of Pandarus is far from
being an aside to the audience.

READ: *constant men*

2.215–18 *Wherevpon I will shew you a Chamber, which bed*
because it shall not speake of your prety encounters presse it to
death;

So Quarto and Folio alike, with obvious difficulty.
Editors meet this by inserting *and a bed* or *with a bed* after
Chamber, and sometimes omitting *bed* in *which bed*.
Kittredge reads after Hanmer, *a chamber with a bed, which,*
because; Alexander, after Capell, *a chamber and a bed*;
which bed; neither plausible in reference to any possible
misreading of copy. I suggest that what the compositor
saw was *a Chamber wth bed, wch bed because*, and that he
thought *wch bed* a repetition, *w^{th}* and *w^{ch}* being indistin-
guishable. This leads to a reading satisfactory at all points.

READ: *a chamber with bed, which bed because*

3.4 *That through the sight I beare in things to loue,*

So Quarto and Folio alike. Editors generally follow F 4
and Rowe in reading *come* for *love*, or Johnson's *Joue*,
though Kittredge for one follows the original text. Steevens
suggested, *That through the sight I bear in things, to loue I*
have abandoned Troy,. The original reading could be
forced into a meaning, 'through my insight into the things
that are worth loving, that it would pay to love, i.e.
Greece'. *leave*, easily misread, if spelled *leue*, as *loue*, gives
a similar sense more readily. But I am now convinced that
come, the obvious reading, is also the authentic reading.
This is Calchas' first appearance, and his especial gift as a
seer is referred to at once. Chaucer does the same, at the
beginning referring to Calchas as 'a gret devyn', a diviner
or seer. And Shakespeare used Chaucer. I do not follow
Tannenbaum's suggestion of plausibility, resting on an

italic lower-case *c* as a common feature of writing Secretary hand, which I do not recall meeting, though I have met a capital italic *C* often enough, and this might be the clue to the misreading. *things above* would be more easy graphically, as misread *to loue*. Quarto shows every sign of rough papers in its copy hereabouts, as in l. 197, and elsewhere.

One is a little shaken by the possibility of the absolute use of *things* in *the sight I bear in things*, as in *Antony and Cleopatra* 1.2.8, where Charmian asks the Soothsayer, 'Is't you sir that know things?', and presently he says, 'I make not, but foresee'. But *come* is irresistible.

READ: *in things to come,*

3.225 *Be shooke to ayre.*
      Ach. *Shall* Aiax *fight with* Hector.

Alexander resists the general following of the Quarto reading, and reads *airy air* with Folio. The Quarto reading is more satisfactory, and metrically superior, and there is every reason for suspecting a repetition of *ayre* in the copy for Folio (possibly by a transcriber), which could readily be rationalized as *ayrie ayre*. Or the copy might have read *ayrie* (deleted) *ayre*. Both are arguable.

READ: *Be shook to air.*

ACT 4

2.74 Æn. *Good, good my lord, the secrets of neighbor* Pandar
       Haue not more guift in taciturnitie.

Folio reads *the secrets of nature Haue,* followed by most editors, though Pope, Johnson, and Alexander retain the Quarto reading, and other conjectures are offered to reconcile the two. I have no doubt that Folio gives the true reading, which we may compare with 'nature's infinite book of secrecy' in *Antony and Cleopatra. neighbor*

Pandar, moreover, is quite alien to the character and the mode of speech of Æneas, especially in his attitude towards Pandarus. Æneas is not given to such comic irony as would be involved in attributing taciturnity to the loquacious Pandar. He is reassuring Troilus in earnest, 'I will be as silent and inscrutable as you could wish'. The *Pandar* of Quarto is apparently an anticipation of a speech-heading for the following speech of Pandarus, repeated two lines below in the catchword for the next page.

READ: *the secrets of nature*

4.78–80   *The Grecian youths are full of qualitie,*
             Their louing well compos'd, with guift of nature,
             Flawing and swelling ore with Arts and exercise:

Quarto omits l. 79 and *Flawing* in l. 80. Commentators vary between the views that the words added in Folio are the result of revision, or were omitted in Quarto, but editors rightly agree in including them in their texts. Kittredge and Alexander read as in Folio, with a variation adopted from early editors, and followed by many others:

    They're loving, well compos'd with gifts of nature,

I see no difficulty in the original *Their loving*. 'Their love-making, or art of love, has all the perfection of the combination of natural gifts with arts and exercise, well composed of nature with nurture.' *They're loving* has a faintly ludicrous effect. The construction of *Their loving well composed* is absolute, 'their loving (being) well composed'.

READ: *Their loving well composed, with gift of nature*
        flowing,
        And swelling o'er with arts and exercise.

5.59 *That giue a coasting welcome ere it comes.*

Theobald's *accosting* for *a coasting*, followed by some editors, is an unnecessary modernization of Shakespeare.

'To coast' means to move, or approach, with circum-
spection. *a coasting* could therefore be 'a circumspect
approach', and the word *coasting* a noun. The whole line
thus means, 'That give a welcome to a circumspect
approach, to an accosting, before it begins.' The words
coasting and *accosting* are, of course, etymologically closely
allied. To consider *coasting* as an adjective offers more
difficulty.

   R E A D : as in Q.

5.163 **Agam.** *Worthy all armes as welcome as to one,*

   The Folio reading *of Armes* suggests incomprehension.
A stage-direction should perhaps be added. All the Greek
heroes are to embrace Hector, e.g. Nestor at l. 199.

   R E A D : *Worthy all arms*—[embraces him] *as welcome as
to one*

5.176 **Hect.** *Who must we answer?*
        Æne. *The noble* Menelaus.

   The words attributed by Quarto, as by Folio, to Æeneas
were for a time given by editors to Menelaus, presumably
because Hector thereupon addresses Menelaus. Later
editors, including recent editors, have returned them to
Æneas. I am convinced that they should be attributed to
Ajax. Hector and Ajax have been fighting, and are now
brothers in arms. Hector has embraced Ajax and called
him 'cousin', as Ajax calls him in return. At l. 157 they
are hand in hand. And at l. 160 Hector asks Ajax to name
the Greek lords to him. At l. 176 he asks who the speaker
is, when Menelaus addresses him. Surely it is Ajax who
answers him, giving Menelaus' name. As for the name
Æneas in the original text, the abbreviated forms *Ai* and *Ae*
for *Ajax* and *Aeneas* could readily be confused by the
compositor.

   R E A D : Ajax. *The noble Menelaus.*

5.193 *When that a ring of Greekes haue shrupd thee in,*

Folio reads *hem'd* for *shrupd*, and is followed by recent editors. But the Quarto *shrupd* is not to be ignored, as in *Variorum*, in favour of the easier Folio reading. The *English Dialect Dictionary* records a word *shrape*, meaning to catch or trap, and the reading *shraped* is feasible, as giving good sense, and is graphically plausible, with the easy misreading of an *a* as a *u*. The Folio reading then becomes patently editorial, with the obvious word *hemmed* replacing the unfamiliar *shraped*. Dr Walker agrees (*M.L.R.* XLV, 460 n. 2).

READ: *have shraped thee in,*

5.201 Æne. *Tis the old* Nestor.

This line should also be attributed to Ajax, for the same reasons as l. 176. Hector thinks better of Ajax than do most commentators. And in this scene he is a hero of stature and of courtesy.

READ: Ajax. *'Tis the old Nestor.*

ACT 5

1.4 *How now thou curre of enuy.*

Folio reads *core* for *curre*, and is rightly followed. The metaphor is of an apple, followed by an image of bread, 'thou crusty batch'. The Folio text is greatly superior to that of Quarto in Act 5, Scenes 1 and 2, with full evidence of MS. sources.

READ: *core*

2.160 *are giuen to* Diomed.

Folio reads *bound* for *given*. All the imagery of the passage rests upon *bonds*.

READ: *bound to Diomed.*

3.19 ff. **And.** *O be perswaded, do not count it holy,*
            It is the purpose that makes strong the vow,
            But vowes to euery purpose must not hold:
            Vnarme sweet Hector.

   *And. *O be perswaded, doe not count it holy,*
            To hurt by being iust; it is as lawfull:
            For we would count giue much to as violent thefts,
            And rob in the behalfe of charitie.
    Cass. *It is the purpose that makes strong the vowe;*
            But vowes to euery purpose must not hold:
            Vnarme sweete Hector.

There is no doubt of the superiority of the Folio text
here. Rival explanations have been offered of the apparent
corruption and incompleteness of the Quarto text. It
seems difficult to conceive that the Folio text was the out-
come of revision and addition, and it seems more probable
that the copy for Quarto was here seriously damaged. The
speeches of Andromache and Cassandra in Folio are
notably characteristic of the speakers. And surely the
words *Unarm sweet Hector* must have been from the
beginning Cassandra's, adding her urgency to that of
Andromache in l. 3.

The obvious intrusion of *count* in l. 21, from l. 19 above,
suggests a transcriber's error rather than a compositor's.
Line 21 offers further difficulty, which is removed by
reading *use* for *as*, as suggested by Tyrwhitt, an error of
reading which could easily be made as between *vse* and *ase*,
and is now generally accepted. *For* is used in the sense of
'because, in order that', and the sense is, 'it would be as
lawful to resort to violent thefts because we want to give
generously, and so rob for the sake of charity.'

   READ: *it is as lawful,*
            For we would give much, to use violent thefts,

[3.113ff.] *Pand. *Why, but heare you?*
          Troy. *Hence brother lackie; ignomie and shame*
          Pursue thy life, and liue aye with thy name.

Quarto omits, as do editors. See note on 5.10.32ff. below.

7.11 *now my double hen'd spartan,*

Folio reads *sparrow* for *spartan,* an apparent editorial emendation to fit the preceding *double-henned.* The image of the Spartan Menelaus as a cock-bird with two hens is inexplicable, and is absurdly out of place in this bull-fighting picture by Thersites, though weak attempts have been made to justify the Folio reading. The solution *double-horned,* conjectured by Kellner, carries conviction and is graphically very plausible. Menelaus is doubly horned, not only in the sense of having two horns, but of wearing horns like a bull, and also as a cuckold. And so Alexander reads.

READ: *Now my double-horned Spartan.*

10.6–7 *Frowne on you heauens, effect your rage with speed,*
        Sit gods vpon your thrones, and smile at Troy.

Hanmer's emendation, *smite all* for *smile at* (or Warburton's *smite at*), has been widely followed, as also recently by Kittredge, on the ground that it is absurd to adjure the gods to *frown* in l. 6, and to *smile* in l. 7. But the heavens are not the gods. 'Let the heavens frown (carrying out the orders of the gods), and let the gods sit on their thrones mocking Troy.' There are, of course, Biblical parallels.

READ: *and smile at Troy.*

10.32–4 Pan. *But here you, here you.*
         Troy. *Hence broker, lacky, ignomyny, shame,*
         Pursue thy life, and liue aye with thy name.

See note on 5.3 [113ff.] above, where a variation of these lines occurs in Folio as well as here, though not in Quarto. It is evident enough that these facts bear witness to a revision in the course of writing the play. Shakespeare, having decided at the end of the play to make Pandarus the Epilogue, gave him an entrance into the play proper, with the great advantage that Troilus could now give him his contemptuous dismissal at the right moment, and with greater effect. Troilus, on his way to heroic death, has found himself, and Pandarus is as remote from him as Falstaff from the new King Henry. Shakespeare therefore transferred this rejection from Act 5, Sc. 3, and deleted the lines already written there. We may be less sure of the facts concerning the copy for Quarto and Folio respectively. But it may seem most probable that Folio in Act 5 was using Shakespeare's 'foul papers', and that the compositor ignored the deletion in Act 5, Sc. 3. The constancy of the Folio reading of l. 33 in both scenes (apart from *brother* for *broker* in Act 5, Sc. 3), as well as its superiority, vindicates the Folio form of the line. There is ample authority for the form of the word *ignomy* in Folio.

READ: Pand. *But hear you, hear you!*

Troilus *Hence, broker, lackey; ignomy and shame*
Pursue thy life, and live aye with thy name.

CORIOLANUS

DRAMATIS PERSONAE

It is right to return to forms of names which are clearly
those used by Shakespeare himself and his actors in this
play, e.g. *Martius* or *Caius Martius* for Coriolanus himself, *Volce* for *Volscian*, and *Corioles* for *Corioli*. We cannot
assume universal distortion in this respect by the compositor who set up his autograph copy here, while accepting
'Imogen' in *Cymbeline* without question.

ACT 1

1.28–9 All. *Against him first: He's a very dog to the
Commonalty.*[1]

This speech is clearly to be given to *First Citizen*, not to
All. *First Citizen* is differentiated as the irreconcilable
throughout as contrasted with *Second Citizen* and the body
of *Citizens*. And so Alexander reads.

1.58 ff. 2 Cit. *Our busines...strong arms too.*

1.81 ff. 2 Cit. *Care for vs?...they beare vs.*

Editors vary in the attribution of these speeches. Both
surely are spoken by *First Citizen*, as Alexander rightly
reads. *Second Citizen* has so far put the case fairly for
reconciliation. There is no easier misprint than that due to
the confusion between Arabic *1* and *2* in Secretary hand.

READ: ll. 58 ff. First Cit. *Our business...strong arms
too.*

ll. 81 ff. First Cit. *Care for us?...they bear us.*

---

[1] Citations are from the text of F 1, the basic text here.

1.262-3 *The present Warres deuoure him, he is growne*
          Too proud to be so valiant.

Editors read after Hanmer, (may) *The present wars*
devour him! But the sense is surely 'the present wars eat
him up with increased pride in being so valiant'. To emend
the punctuation thus is to change the meaning radically.

READ: as in F.

4.41-2 *If you'l stand fast, wee'l beate them to their Wiues,*
          As they vs to our Trenches followes.

There is no need to accept, as Kittredge and Alexander
do, the usual emendation:

          As they us to our trenches. Follow me.

Follow us is a common enough colloquialism, and here
continues 'Look to't. Come on', in l. 40.

READ: *As they us to our trenches. Follow's.*

4.54 *Thou art left* Martius,

Alexander retains *left*. But the sense seems to demand
lost, and the emendation is plausible graphically. *left* can
only suggest 'deserted'. But all Lartius says indicates loss
and not desertion, not least his use of the past tense—'Thou
wast a soldier', and the answer of the soldiers to his inquiry,
'Slain, sir, doubtless.'

READ: *Thou art lost, Martius.*

4.57 *Euen to* Calues *wish,*

Theobald's emendation, *Cato's* for *Calues*, is certain,
and plausible graphically.

READ: *Even to Cato's wish,*

6.76 *Oh me alone, make you a sword of me:*

Editors read *Oh, me alone?* or *Oh, me alone!* This
suggests misunderstanding of the sense. The soldiers are
treating Coriolanus as sole warrior, where he is asking for

volunteers. 'Are you making your sword out of me, and only me? (Where are your own swords?)' And he adds that any of them, willing to follow him and not only shout, is worth four Volscians.

READ: *O' me alone? Make you a sword of me?*

9.45–6 *When Steele growes soft, as the Parasites Silke,*
      Let him be made an Ouerture for th'Warres:

The whole of this passage has evoked vast discussion, and various emendations have been proposed, e.g. *coverture* for *overture*, as read by Kittredge, to suit *silk*. There is no real difficulty. *him* refers to the *parasite*, not his *silk*, nor to *steel*. 'When steel grows as soft as the court-parasite's silken clothes, let the parasite be made the herald of war (instead of a soldier).'

9.65, 67 Marcus Caius Coriolanus.

Editors all emend to *Caius Marcius Coriolanus*, apparently to ensure higher marks in classics and consistency for Shakespeare, for this order of names cannot well be attributed to the compositor. The form *Marcus* is exceptional here. The hero is known as 'Martius' elsewhere, and in speech headings, and this name naturally enough is placed first. The same order is repeated elsewhere, e.g. in 2.1.181, and in that scene Volumnia's words point the moral:

> My gentle Martius, worthy Caius, and
> By deed-achieving honour newly named—
> What is it? Coriolanus must I call thee?

So again in 2.2.50, even if in 4.6.29 we find *Caius Martius*.

READ: *Martius Caius Coriolanus.*

ACT 2

1.270–1   *when his soaring Insolence*
                 Shall teach the People,

Hanmer's emendation, *touch* for *teach*, is generally followed, as in recent editions. But the original *teach* offers no difficulty and gives a far more potent and apt sense. The whole trend of the conversation supports *teach*, in close relation to the education of the people by the Tribunes. The sentence is involved. The words *which time...dogs on sheep* are a parenthesis. The sense is, 'Coriolanus will teach the people their *time* for revolt: then this suggestion will be fire to their stubble'.

READ: *Shall teach the people—which time...on sheep— will be his fire*

2.8 *'Faith, there hath beene many great men*

Editors, including Alexander, obey the eighteenth century and 'correct' *hath* to *have* unconscionably.

READ: *hath been*

2.30–2 *Bonnetted, without any further deed, to haue them at all into their estimation,*

Pope's *heave* for *have*, and Johnson's *unbonnetted* for *bonnetted*, are fortunately losing currency in modern editions. The sense of the Folio text is clear, and superior.

READ: *bonneted, without any further deed to have them at all into their estimation*

2.109–10   *as Weeds before*
                  A Vessell vnder sayle,

The Second Folio read *waves* for *weeds*, widely followed, as by Kittredge even recently, with no plausibility and with considerable damage to the sense and the aptness of the image.

READ: *weeds*

3.122 *in this Wooluish tongue*

Editors are agreed upon *toge* for *tongue*. The misreading of the compositor is plausible if he read *tōge* for *toge*, and so arrived at a more familiar word.

3.251 *And Nobly nam'd, so twice being Censor,*
        Was his great Ancestor.

There is no doubt that this passage is corrupt in the Folio, and that the name *Censorinus*, certified by Plutarch, Shakespeare's source, was omitted.

READ: *And [Censorinus] nobly named so,*
        Twice being censor, was his great ancestor.

ACT 3

1.48 **Com.** *You are like to doe such businesse.*

Editors have transferred to Coriolanus this speech given in Folio to Cominius, as with other speeches in this scene. Here Cominius has been silent on the stage for a long time, and presently speaks again to much the same effect. It is not in Coriolanus' vein.

READ: as in F.

1.231–2 **Com.** *Stand fast, we haue as many friends as enemies.*

This speech is again rightly given by Folio to Cominius. It is difficult to see why this should be editorially interfered with, as even Alexander does, in obedience to Warburton, who attributed it to Coriolanus. Cominius is more of a soldier than a politician, and is close to Coriolanus. He stands in this scene half-way between Coriolanus and the Senators who counsel discretion. The finer lineaments of character are blurred by this unnecessary emendation.

Coriolanus would die fighting one against the world, not considering (as Cominius does here) the balance of forces.
READ: as in F.

1.237 ff. Corio. *Come Sir, along with vs.*
          Mene. *I would they were Barbarians, as they are,*

                    .   .   .   .

There can be no real doubt that l. 237 is in fact spoken by Cominius, and that ll. 238–40, here opening a speech of Menenius, are spoken by Coriolanus. And so all editors agree. One might suggest that the practice of inserting speakers' names after the dialogue has been written has led here to confusions in the Folio copy. But it seems to me probable that we have here a marginal addition in the copy, prefixed by the compositor in error to the existing speech of Menenius, whose words, *Be gone*, seem to follow directly upon Cominius' *Come Sir*.
READ: Com. *Come Sir, along with us.*
          Cor. *I would they were barbarians, as they are,...*
          Though calved i' th' porch o' th' Capitol.
          Men. *Be gone;*

1.287–8   *to eiect him hence*
                 Were but one danger,

The emendation *our* for *one* seems to me certain in the light of the succeeding words, which point the contrast between *our danger* and *our death. one danger* seems to lack meaning or association.
READ: *Were but our danger,*

2.20–1   *Lesser had bin*
                 The things of your dispositions,

Theobald's *thwartings* for *things* (from Rowe's *things that thwart*) has found great acceptance and, though graphically implausible in the extreme, has been adopted in recent editions also. The sense, moreover, is forced and irrelevant. I suggest *taxings*, as relevant and graphically plausible, on a hint from Mrs Nowottny. *h* and *x* are readily confused in Secretary hand, and so *th* and *tax*, the rest of the word being identical. The sense required is satisfied, the thought in Volumnia's mind being public criticism and response to her son's attitude to the people. 'You would have been less criticized publicly if you had concealed your disposition until you were in a more secure position', a very politic observation. There are ample instances of this common use of the words *tax, taxing, taxation*, elsewhere in Shakespeare, e.g. in *As You Like It* 1.2.91, 2.7.71, 86. (In *Titus Andronicus* 3.1.282 we have a similar reading of *things* by a desperate Folio compositor.)

READ: *Lesser had been*
            The taxings of your dispositions,

2.32 *Before he should thus stoope to' th' heart,*

It might seem clear that Menenius is here picking up Volumnia's preceding words, 'I have a *heart* as little apt as yours'. But this is misleading, for the thought will not bear the reading of *heart* here without forcing. It is likely, indeed, that the compositor was misled into reading *heart* for *herd* (spelled *heard*). There is general, and reasonable, agreement upon *herd* as an emendation.

READ: *stoop to the herd,*

3.54–5   *do not take*
            His rougher Actions for malicious sounds:

Theobald's *accents* for *actions* is certain, and is plausible graphically, *actions* being normally written *accõns*, which the compositor thought he saw here.

3.130 *Making but reseruation of your selues,*

Capell's emendation, *not* for *but*, still has its supporters. It destroys the powerful sense of the original, 'banishing all

defenders but yourselves', and so finding yourselves
defenceless. Alexander agrees.

READ: *Making but reservation*

ACT 4

4.23–4 *My Birth-place haue I, and my loues vpon*
        This Enemie Towne:

Capell's *hate* for *have* is certain, and is plausible graphically. The compositor mistook *hate* for *have*, the *t* resembling
a *v* with its preliminary ascender, and set up the normal
haue.

5.201 *hee might haue boyld and eaten him too.*

Pope's *broiled* for *boiled* is strangely popular, and
Kittredge and Alexander adopt it. The reason given
derives from culinary science; a *carbonado* is not *boiled*. But
two servants are speaking, and it is a comic conversation,
not a lesson in cookery. The Second Servant is not bound
to the First Servant's metaphor, and offers his own suggestion of a boiled Aufidius as edible. Graphically, there is no
likelihood of the misreading suggested. Finally, pork is in
fact often 'scotched' before boiling, in the Midlands at
least.

READ: *he might have boiled and eaten him too.*

5.237 *It's sprightly walking, audible, and full of Vent.*

Kittredge and Alexander read *it's spritely, waking*,
following Pope. There is no need for this emendation, or
for Collier's *vaunt* for *vent*. The image is clearly that of
war as a hunting dog, and there is need to bring this
metaphor into precise opposition to the succeeding description of peace as an apoplexy. *vent* is 'scent', and *audible*
refers to the hound's cry upon scent.

READ: as in F.

6.2–5 *His remedies are tame, the present peace,*
    And quietnesse of the people, which before
    Were in wilde hurry. Heere do we make his Friends
    Blush, that the world goes well:

This passage has been largely re-set and emended, as by recent editors also, with a period after *tame* and a comma after hurry, and deleting *we*. So Alexander reads:

> *His remedies are tame. The present peace...*
> *Were in wild hurry, here do make his friends...*

Other emendations have been proposed, e.g. *ta'en* for *tame*. But such emendation is corruption. It has been assumed that *his remedies* means 'remedies prescribed by Coriolanus'. But the words mean 'remedies *against* Coriolanus, antidotes to Coriolanus', and the original text offers no difficulty, *remedies* being in apposition to *peace* and *quietness*. 'The remedies for Coriolanus are the peace *etc.*, and are tame kinds of remedy.'

READ: *His remedies are tame—the present peace*
    And quietness of the people, which before
    Were in wild hurry. Here do we make his friends
    Blush that the world goes well;

6.58 *some newes is comming*

Editors all read *come* or *come in* for *coming*, after Rowe or Malone, very unnecessarily. A modern equivalent would be 'coming in'. Some has arrived, and more is to come.

READ: *coming*

7.14–15   *but either haue borne*
        The action of your selfe,

All editors read *had* for *have*, in line with the previous 'had not joined', without excuse unless we wish to rewrite Shakespeare. 'I wish you had', 'I wish you could have', are both idiomatic, and the constructions are readily mixed in ordinary speech. Shifting of construction is a characteristic of Shakespeare's later style and is a stumbling-block to early, and even later, commentators and editors.

READ: as in F.

7.54–5 *One fire driues out one fire; one Naile, one Naile;*
Rights by rights fouler, strengths by strengths do faile.

Line 55 'has no manner of sense', wrote Warburton. After vast comment, Malone's *founder* and Dyce's *falter* for *fouler* are most popular as emendations. Tucker Brooke, Kittredge and Alexander read *falter*, Chambers and Case *founder*, all taking both *rights* as plural nouns. Neither reading is in the least plausible as a misreading of copy. But emendation is unnecessary. If we read *Right's by rights fouler* we have a plain sense in full parallel with the other instances in the passage. 'A right which seems fair in itself may appear foul in the light of other rights.' *falter* or *founder*, again, is the same image as *do fail*, whereas *fouler* gives a different image, 'right losing its clear perfection', and is more varied in expression. The phrase is intentionally compressed and gnomic.

READ: *Right's by rights fouler,*

ACT 5

1.69 *Bound with an Oath to yeeld to his conditions:*

Editors have found great difficulty because of taking *Bound* to refer to Coriolanus, and so resorted to emendation. Alexander seems to make *bound* a verb with subject *he* understood, and rewrites ll. 67–9 as follows:

> *What he would do,*
> *He sent in writing after me; what he would not,*
> *Bound with an oath to yield to his conditions;*

But this makes an artificial division of the *conditions* sworn to, though there is authority for it in the Folio colon after *me*, and it is indeed possible. I think that *bound with* is an adjectival phrase referring equally to both sets of conditions, *what he would do*, and *what he would not*, and that the Folio colon has the effect of a parenthesis '*what he would do (and what he would not)*'. The word *bound* suggests not only 'coupled with' but also 'binding together' the two sets.

READ: *What he would do*
          He sent in writing after me, what he would not,
          Bound with an oath to yield to his conditions.

1.70–3 *So that all hope is vaine, vnlesse his Noble Mother,*
          And his Wife, who (as I heare) meane to solicite him
          For mercy to his Countrey: therefore let's hence,

Various emendations have been proposed to overcome the obvious incompleteness of the syntax here. Kittredge reads *in his* for *his* in the first line. Alexander reads as in Folio, with a full stop after *country*, presumably taking *hope* as in apposition to *mother* and *wife*. I suggest that we have here a broken construction, significant of Cominius' perturbation. Relining seems necessary.

READ: *So that all hope is vain,*
          Unless his noble mother and his wife,
          Who, as I hear, mean to solicit him
          For mercy to his country—therefore let's hence,

2.68 ff. *guesse but my entertainment with him:*

Hanmer read *by* for *but*, Malone (followed by Alexander) *but by* for *but*, evidently in order to make a continuous sentence with what follows, 'if thou stand'st not i' th' state of hanging'. But there is no difficulty if l. 68 is an independent sentence, as indicated by the Folio punctuation, and much more in Menenius' vein so.

READ: *Guess but my entertainment with him. If thou stand'st not . . . suffering, behold now presently . . . upon thee.*

3.11–17   *Their latest refuge*
                Was to send him: for whose old Loue I haue
                (Though I shew'd sowrely to him) once more offer'd
                The first Conditions which they did refuse,
                And cannot now accept, to grace him onely,
                That thought he could do more: A very little
                I haue yeelded too.

The passage has been reconstructed by editors. Kittredge
and Alexander read:

                And cannot now accept. To grace him only
                That thought he could do more, a very little
                I have yielded to.

This is, of course, a radical change in the meaning, which
seems unjustified, since the Folio punctuation gives
excellent and superior sense. 'Because I loved Menenius
of old, and to grace a man who hoped he could do more, I
have offered again the conditions which they had refused
(and cannot well accept now). I did not yield much!'
    READ: as in F.

TITUS ANDRONICUS

ACT 1

Sc. 1. *Stage-direction.*

I think it likely that the inner stage was the monument, and that the Senate was in the upper stage.

READ: Before the Capitol; a tomb below.

Enter *Marcus, Tribune,* and *Senate* above. Enter below, *Saturninus* with *Soldiers* at one door, *Bassianus* with *Soldiers* at the other, and *Romans.*

1.35 ff.   *and at this day,*
           To the Monument of that Andronicy
           Done sacrifice of expiation,
           And slaine the Noblest prisoner of the Gothes,

Editors since 1904, when the unique copy of Q1 was discovered, in which alone these lines appear, have rightly agreed that they belong to a first draft, and either were, or should have been, deleted in the copy for the final version. The *sacrifice* in question here is actually performed later in this scene. It is clear, as Greg showed, that this passage in the draft agreed with the entry for Tamora with two sons only, omitting Alarbus the eldest, at l. 69, and that the inclusion in the action of the execution of Alarbus was an afterthought, which would have involved a change in the 'plot' of the play. Greg, however, suggests reading *as this day* for *at this day,* i.e. 'as (he proposes to do) this day' (*M.L.R.* XLVIII, 439–40). This would permit the passage to stand, on conditions. The entry for Tamora with two sons only must be interpreted as including only speakers. And no conclusions may be drawn from the fact that Alarbus

---

[1] Citations are from the First Quarto of 1594, basic for this play. The readings of editions before 1904 suffered from ignorance of this edition.

does not open his mouth, when his younger brothers both
do. I find this too difficult to accept. The entry is specific,
'Tamora the Queene of Gothes, & *her two Sonnes Chiron
and Demetrius*, with Aaron the Moore'; Aaron, be it
noted, is also silent, yet is included in the entry. Greg is
himself unconvinced. These lines should be relegated to a
footnote.

As for 'Andronicy', I suggest that the compositor simply
mistook the sign 9 (=*us*) in italic writing for *y*. (This
might perhaps be thought to be more characteristic of a
University man's writing than of Shakespeare's.)

READ: *that Andronicus*

1.138 *Vpon the Thracian Tyrant in his Tent,*

Theobald was more learned than Shakespeare, and read
her (Hecuba's) tent, followed by *New Cambridge*, which
assumes a classical scholar, Peele, as author here.

READ: *his tent,*

1.341–2 Marcus. *O Titus see: O see what thou hast done*
In a bad quarrell slaine a vertuous sonne.

New Cambridge here, as also at ll. 355 and 362, makes
Martius the speaker instead of the Quarto Marcus. It
appears to be a mere slip. The Quarto reading is certified
by the dialogue in several places.

1.358–60 Titus two sonnes speakes.
And shall or him wee will accompanie.
Titus. *And shall. what villaine was it spake that
word?*
Titus sonne speakes.
He that would vouch it in any place but here.

There is no difficulty in accepting these speakers' names
as Quintus and Martius, and Quintus, respectively. So
New Cambridge reads. Quintus is the elder. Quintus replies

alone to Titus' question, which could well be addressed to both: 'he is a villain that says "and shall"'. Bolton's suggestion to read *Titus' 2 son* ('Titus' second son') is ingenious. But the compositor distinguishes well enough elsewhere in a number of instances. Only Maxwell of recent editors accepts it.

1.372 Titus. *Speake thou no more, if all the rest will speede.*

New Cambridge in a note finds this obscure. But Titus is angry with the previous speaker, Quintus, as appears plainly in ll. 359–60. 'The less you say, Quintus, the better for the others.'

1.397 *That brought her for this high good turne so farre.*

In the Folio text, and in *New Cambridge*, the following line is added to conclude this speech of Titus:

    Yes, and will Nobly him remunerate.

I have no doubt that this line belongs to the true text, and that (as Malone suggested) it was spoken by Marcus and not by Titus. It is, like the previous speech of Marcus, ironical, and is a comment by Marcus upon the words of Titus. And so Alexander reads also.

READ: *That brought her for this high good turn so far?*
    Marc. *Yes, and will nobly him remunerate.*

1.474–6 *Wee doo,...*
    Tendring our sisters honour and our owne.

These lines, in Quarto, conclude a speech of Tamora, but in Folio are given to 'Son' as speaker, correctly. In Folio 'Two sons' signifies Quintus and Martius, and 'Son' Lucius.

READ: Luc. *We do....*

ACT 2

1.71–2 *I care not I, knew shee and all the world,*
      I loue Lauinia *more than all the world.*

So Quarto and Folio alike punctuate. Recent editors, however, make l. 72 a new sentence, which is unjustified and less effective.

READ: *I care not I, knew she and all the world*
           I love Lavinia more than all the world.

1.122 *Will we acquaint withall what we intend,*

Editors follow the late Quarto and Folio in reading *with all that.* But *acquaint withal* is an idiomatic expression, naturally followed by *what we intend.* There is no corruption in Quarto, as Maxwell also saw.

READ: *withal what*

1.135 Per Stigia, per manes Vehor.

Editors correct *Stigia* to *Styga,* though they leave *manes* (for *amnes*) in the line misremembered here from Seneca (*Hipp.* 1180). The English adjective is 'Stigian', which doubtless explains the reading, not a compositor's error.

READ: *Per Stygia,*

3.85 *The King my brother shall haue notice of this.*

So Quarto and Folio read. Pope, followed by Kittredge and *New Cambridge,* emended *notice* to *note,* on metrical grounds. But the metre is satisfactory, except to Pope, and *notice* more Elizabethan than *note* here. There is no possibility of a compositor's error.

READ: *notice*

3.88 *Why I haue patience to indure all this.*

F 2, followed by editors except Alexander and Maxwell, reads *Why have I* in the form of a question. But Tamora is speaking ironically, and in character, and is plotting revenge. The original text is far superior.

READ: *Why I have patience to endure all this.*

3.131 *But when yee haue the honie we desire,*

New Cambridge follows F 2, which reads *ye* for *we*. Certainly it hardly seems possible for Tamora to desire Lavinia's *honey*, i.e. to enjoy her. But Tamora may vengefully desire Lavinia to be robbed of her *honey*, i.e. her treasured chastity, and so share in her sons' desires (cf. ll. 124–6). I now think the F 2 reading to be editorial and erroneous, and so Alexander thinks.

READ: *we desire,*

3.147 *Doe thou intreat her shew a womans pittie.*

The whole trend of Lavinia's speech points to *show a woman's pity*, the pity natural to a woman, as in Quarto, not *show a woman pity*, pity shown to a woman, as in Folio.

READ: *a woman's pity.*

3.222 *Lord* Bassianus *lies bereaud in blood,*

The Second Quarto and Folio read *embrewed heere* for *bereaud in blood,* and many editors follow. The unique Folger copy of Q 1 has a marginal correction in a contemporary hand: *heere reav'd of lyfe.* Its significance, however, is diminished by its apparent derivation from l.282 below: 'Haue here bereft my brother of his life'. *New Cambridge* reads *berayed in blood,* and the reading seems at all points acceptable, to me as to Alexander, as arising from a misreading by the compositor of *bereied* as *bereaud.*

READ: *lies berayed in blood,*

ACT 3

Sc. 1 *Scene-heading.*

The entry of Judges and Senators seems to include the Tribunes among the senators, as the dialogue indicates, though it is clear that Marcus enters at l. 58 with Lavinia.

1.17 *That shall distill from these two auntient ruines,*

For *ruines* Hanmer read *urns*, and all recent editors follow. It may be argued that the misreading of *urns* as *ruins* is plausible, and that *ruins* is caught up from *rain* in l. 16. But the emendation is unnecessary, and indeed may seem to be injurious to the sense. The word *distil* is hardly relevant to the suggested image, for you do not *distil* liquid, you *pour* it, from an urn. Tears, on the other hand, are *distilled* from eyes. There is no difficulty in interpreting *these two ancient ruins* as referring to the two eyes of Titus, eyes *ruined* by age and grief. (Urns, incidentally, are generally used for ashes, not for liquids, in Elizabethan imagery.)

READ: *these two ancient ruins,*

1.33–6 *Why tis no matter man,...*
         And bootlesse vnto them.

The Folio version seems plainly to be corrupt and incomplete, and therefore negligible here. Alexander and *New Cambridge* follow the Quarto text, though Dover Wilson marks l. 36 with an obelus and suggests in a note that its deletion removes all difficulty. (It is wanting in Folio.) The only 'difficulty' is a broken line. The sense seems clear and logical in the Quarto text.

READ: as in Q.

1.226 *I am the sea. Harke how her sighs doth flow:*

The Second Folio emends *flow* to *blow*, and all editors follow. I see no need for an emendation which is editorial and substitutes a common cliché of poetic diction. In this wild speech the imagery is wild too, but there is clear insistence upon the image of the movement of water as the expression of grief and anger, with *overflow* occurring in ll. 222 and 230, as well as here.

READ: *I am the sea—hark how her sighs doth flow!*

1.282 *And* Lauinia *thou shalt be imployde in these Armes,*

Folio reads *things* for *Armes*, an obviously despairing improvisation, though Kittredge follows it. *New Cambridge* and Alexander omit *Armes*, following Lettsom, with Greg's approval, and Alexander reads *this* for *these*. Maxwell (in *New Arden*) finds no solution possible.

I suggest *charms* for *Armes*. The compositor's misreading is plausible, if he guessed at a capital *A* of a well-known shape in a *ch* with the descender of the *h* missing or illegible in a torn or damaged manuscript. (It is an error which I have actually made in reading such a manuscript.) The context gives strong support for this conjecture in its associations of ritual and incantation: 'circle me about', 'swear', 'vow'. And it gives perfect sense.

READ: *And Lavinia thou shalt be employed in these charms.*

1.291–2 *Farewell proud Rome till* Lucius *come againe,*
　　　He loues his pledges dearer than his life:

Rowe emended *loues* to *leaues*, with a stop after *Rome*, thus making radical changes in the meaning. The emendation is adopted by recent editors, except Ridley who reads *loans*. But emendation is unnecessary and harmful. The lines as they stand simply mean, 'Farewell Rome till I return; I will carry out my vow and return even at the risk of life', a meaning that is supported by later lines of the speech.

READ: *Farewell proud Rome till Lucius come again;*
　　　He loves his pledges dearer than his life.

ACT 4

1.15 *Canst thou not gesse wherefore she plies thee thus.*

This line is printed in Quarto and Folio as the concluding line of a speech of Titus. But the Boy's reply is plainly addressed to Marcus, referring to his 'grandsire' Titus in his reply, and quoting his words. And this line is a sensible inquiry, in the vein of the previous inquiry by Marcus at l. 8, in contrast with the more sentimental observations of Titus. And so Alexander reads. *New Cambridge* reads as in Quarto. Maxwell in *New Arden* gives l. 9 to Titus, and ll. 10–15 to Marcus, on the ground that *Lucius* occurs in both ll. 9 and 10. But the repetition is exactly in the manner of the old grandsire.

> READ: Marc. *Canst thou not guess wherefore she plies thee thus?*

2.152–3 *Not farre, one* Muliteus *my Countriman*
          His wife but yesternight was brought to bed,

Steevens, followed by *New Cambridge* and *New Arden*, emended *Muliteus* to *Muly lives,*. Dover Wilson, ignoring the italics, suggests a very difficult graphic error of Secretary hand in explanation of such a misreading. Alexander reads as in Quarto, but with a dash after *countryman* indicating a break in thought. The construction, in fact, follows the common Elizabethan idiom which uses *his* as a genitive—*my countryman his wife* means 'my countryman's wife'. There were many variations of Moorish names of which *Muly* formed part. No emendation is necessary.

> READ: *Not far one Muliteus my countryman*
>   *His wife but yesternight was brought to bed,*

3.106 ff. *Giue me pen and inke....*

Much unnecessary difficulty has been felt about this scene. At l. 106 Titus only adds the superscription to his

'oration'. The insertion of the knife into the folded
'oration' changes its appearance from that of an ordinary
petition. There is no need to emend *For* in l. 117. The
thing to be presented to the Emperor is now a knife
wrapped in the paper of the 'oration', not a petition as
folded in the ordinary way by Marcus.

4.23–6 *But he and his shall know that iustice liues*
          In Saturninus *health, whome if he sleepe,*
          Hele so a wake as he in furie shall,
          Cut off the proud'st conspiratour that liues.

In ll. 24 and 25 Rowe read *she* for *he*, as referring to
Justice and not to Saturninus. Recent editors except
Kittredge follow in l. 24, but vary between *he* and *she* in
l. 25. (Capell read *who* for *whom* and retained *he*.) There
is no need to read *she*, which it is impossible to justify
graphically. Justice and Saturninus are one, sleeping and
waking together. (Cf. 'Justice shall neuer hear ye, *I am
Justice*,' in Fletcher's *Valentinian* 3.1.) The want of
immediate clarity is not sufficient evidence of textual
corruption. The thought and its expression are clear
enough. There are two entities, Saturninus-Justice and
Saturninus, in this complex thought.

READ: As in Q.

4.53 *May this be borne as if his traitorous sonnes,*

New Cambridge, following Folio, reads *borne? As if*,
and Alexander *borne—as if*. But the Quarto reading gives
better sense as it stands, continuous sense, as I now see.
And so Maxwell reads.

READ: as in Q.

4.62 *Arme my Lords, Rome neuer had more cause,*

Capell, followed by *New Cambridge*, regulates the
metre, reading *Arm, arm, my lords*, against the text of
Quarto as of Folio, and unjustifiably. If we read as

follows, with a broken line 63, even metrical purists would submit:

    Sat. *What news with thee Æmilius?*
    Æm.   *Arm my lords,*
    Rome never had more cause.
    READ: *Arm my lords,*

4.100 *Goe thou before to be our Ambassador,*

    New Cambridge and Maxwell read *before, be,* again in deference to Capell's metrical purism and with no support from text, sense, or even metre. (Folio reads *before to our.*)
    READ: as in Q.

ACT 5

2.18 *Wanting a hand to giue that accord,*

    Folio reads: *Wanting a hand to give it action,* The metre of the line in Quarto is truly deficient. Pope's emendation, *to give it that accord,* is plausible, given a copy which read *to give yt yᵗ accord,* with the compositor omitting one *yt.* Maxwell is attracted by the Folio reading, which gives scope for an elaborate note upon Elizabethan acting, with a suggestion for an implausible confusion between *accõne* and *accord* in the MS. copy. The Folio reading seems to me an improvisation.
    READ: *to give it that accord?*

2.52 *And finde out murder in their guiltie cares.*

    There can be no doubt that *cares* is a misprint for *caves.* But it is otherwise with Capell's emendation of *murderers* for *murder,* though followed by all editors. *murder* is used as personified and plural in sense, and refers plainly back to preceding lines, 'a hollow cave...Where bloody murder... can couch' (ll. 35–8).
    READ: *murder in their guilty caves.*

3.73–95 **Romane Lord.** *Let Rome her selfe bee bane vnto her selfe.*

· · · · ·

While I stand by and weepe to heare him speake.

Folio reads *Goth.* for *Romane Lord* as speaker here. Capell, however, appended this speech to the foregoing speech of Marcus (ll. 67–72), and read *Lest* for *Let*, a very high-handed proceeding, though followed by all editors. I do not understand the necessity for it, nor the explanation offered by *New Cambridge* of the possible features of the copy underlying the text thus emended.

The difficulty that is felt seems to arise from the speaker in Quarto. The error in Folio seems to be an editorial fancy. I suggest that the *Roman Lord* of Quarto is Æmilius, and that this speech is entirely apt from him, indeed far more relevant and comprehensible than from Marcus. Æmilius *is* a 'noble Roman' who in some measure stands for Rome, aged and venerable, and he intervenes here to reinforce the previous words of Marcus. His speech has clearly been misunderstood, and has been distorted by punctuation, e.g. a stop after *herself* in l. 76, and a dash indicating a break in sense at the end of l. 79, as well as the emendation *Lest* for *Let* in l. 73.

Marcus has spoken of the benefits of regained unity in Rome. Æmilius continues, 'Let Rome be an evil to Rome, and Rome destroy Rome, *unless (But if)* my age and experience can induce you to follow my advice', i.e. 'Rome will be an evil to Rome and destroy herself, unless...'. There is an apparent change of construction in the *cannot*, in this involved sentence, when it is analysed. But this passes unperceived in the speaking, and it is in fact merely another 'double negative' construction. There is much insistence on the speaker's great age. Marcus is an active Tribune. But Senators were almost by definition 'reverend' and 'aged men'. And at l. 119 the words of Marcus, 'Now is my turn to speak', hardly suggest a previous uninterrupted speech of twenty-nine lines. In l. 80 the words, 'as erst our ancestor', merely refer to Æneas as ancestor of all Romans. Æmilius is not an ordinary 'messenger', even on his first appearance. For there he seems to be a spokesman for the Senate, and Saturninus addresses him by name.

READ: *Æmilius. Let Rome herself be bane unto herself,*
And she whom mighty kingdoms curtsy to,
Like a forlorn and desperate castaway,
Do shameful execution on herself,
But if my frosty signs and chaps of age,
Grave witnesses of true experience,
Cannot induce you to attend my words.
[To Lucius] Speak Rome's dear friend, as erst our ancestor,

.   .   .   .   .

While I stand by and weep to hear him speak.
It follows that a stage-direction is required at l. 16:
Enter *Saturninus* and *Tamora*, with *Æmilius, Tribune, Senators* and others.
Also that Æmilius speaks ll. 176–8 as well as ll. 137–40 in this scene, in which he is, indeed, a prominent figure. There is no need to introduce a new character in the 'Roman Lord' of Q1.

3.124 *And as he is to witnes this is true,*

Theobald, followed by *New Cambridge* and Alexander, read *Damned as he is,* with no plausibility and unnecessarily. Read as it is in Quarto the line gives good sense in the context. Maxwell reads *And as he is to witness, this is true.* But there is no need even to re-punctuate.

READ: as in Q.

3.165 ff. Folio reads as follows:

Meete, and agreeing with thine Infancie:
In that respect then, like a louing Childe,
Shed yet some small drops from thy tender Spring,
Because kinde Nature doth require it so:
Friends, should associate Friends, in Greefe and Wo.

The Folio text, derived from Q3 of 1611, in turn derived from Q2 of 1600, perpetuated here a passage improvised for Q2 to fill a gap in the damaged copy of Q1 used for Q2, as demonstrated independently by Bolton and McKerrow. The Q1 text is naturally to be read here.

3.170–1 *Bid him farewell commit him to the graue,*
        Doe them that kindnes and take leaue of them.

Folio reads *him—him* for *them—them*, followed by *New Cambridge* and Maxwell. But the Quarto text is referring back to 'these poore *lips*' in the first line of this speech. Alexander retains *them—them* rightly. There is no difficulty in the return to this thought after l. 170. 'Bid him farewell and bury him; and kiss his lips for the last time.'
   READ: as in Q.

3.176–8 **Romane.** *You sad Andronicie haue done with woes,*
   READ: Æmilius. *You sad Andronici, have done with woes.*

3.198 *But throw her forth to beasts and birds to pray,*

Folio reads *of prey:* followed by *New Cambridge*, but not by Alexander or Maxwell, rightly as I now think. *To prey*, meaning 'to prey upon, to devour', is much more effective in any case, and the Folio reading is surely editorial.
   READ: *to prey.*

3.200 *And being dead let birds on her take pittie.*   Exeunt.
Folio reads as follows, adding four lines:

> *And being so, shall haue like want of pitty.*
> *See Iustice done on* Aaron *that damn'd Moore,*
> *From whom, our heauy happes had their beginning:*
> *Then afterwards, to Order well the State,*
> *That like Euents, may ne're it Ruinate.* Exeunt omnes.

See note on ll. 165 ff. above. This passage had a similar
origin in Q 2. Recent editors rightly follow the Q 1 text
here also.

ROMEO AND JULIET

ACT 1

1.27 *I will be ciuil with the maides, I will cut off their heads.*[1]

The agreement of Q2 and Folio upon *civil* is of no consequence, Folio being derivative. The logic and wit of Sampson's speech is all in favour of the emendation *cruel*, as a sequel to *a tyrant*. If *civil* is retained, as by Alexander, it introduces an incongruous and ineffective irony, in place of the parallel 'fought with the men...cruel with the maids'. The misreading of *cruel* as *ciuil* is entirely plausible.

READ: *cruel*

1.159 *Or dedicate his bewtie to the same.*

Theobald's *sun* for *same* is acceptable on graphic grounds, as on grounds of sense. To 'dedicate beauty to the air' (*the same*) is feeble. And Montague's previous speech shows that it is the sun that Romeo shuns.

READ: *sun.*

1.217 *From loues weak childish bow she liues vncharmd.*

Editors, including Alexander, have agreed on *unharmed* for *uncharmed*, taken from Q1, unnecessarily as I think. The misreading, it is true, would be graphically plausible. But the sense is greatly weakened by the change. *uncharmed* means 'free from the charm or enchantment' of Cupid's bow.

READ: *uncharmed.*

[1] Citations are from the Second Quarto of 1599, which is basic for this play.

2.76–8 Ser. *Vp.*
     Ro. *Whither to supper?*
     Ser. *To our house.*

Editors, following Theobald, all read:
     Rom. *Whither?*
     Serv. *To supper. To our house.*

There is every argument, however, for the Quarto reading, as punctuated in Folio, without emendation. The dialogue reflects the Servant's inconsequent evasiveness and Romeo's naturally insistent questions. Only thus does the dialogue read with its intended effect.

READ: Rom. *Whither? To supper?*

4.58 *ouer mens noses*

Editors have preferred *athwart* for *over*, from Q1. But Q1 is peculiarly untrustworthy in Mercutio's famous speech. And in l. 77 we have 'she gallops *o'er* a courtier's nose', and in l. 82 'driveth *o'er* a soldier's neck'.

Q1 cannot be treated as equal in authority to Q2, and no graphic confusion could account for the Q2 and Folio *over* for *athwart*, or *side* for *face* in l. 103.

READ: *over*

4.103 *Turning his side to the dewe dropping South.*

Q1 reads *face* for *side*, and most editors follow, with no necessity, for *side* gives good sense. So Alexander reads.

READ: *side*

5.1–17 *Stage-directions.*

The conduct of this scene offers some problems. The stage-direction in Q2 at the end of Sc. 4 reads:

They march about the Stage, and Seruingmen come forth with Napkins.   Enter *Romeo.*

And at l. 17 in Sc. 5, after an *Exeunt.* for the servants:

Enter all the guests and gentlewomen to the Maskers.

Folio agrees, except in reading *Enter Seruant* for *Enter* Romeo. It might seem clear, from these directions, that Sc. 5 is continuous with Sc. 4, that the Maskers remain on the stage at the end of Sc. 4 (no exit is given for them), that they are joined there first by the servants and, upon their departure, by the 'guests and gentlewomen'. Editors have nevertheless cleared the stage at the end of Sc. 4 for the entry of the servants at Sc. 5, and have made the Maskers re-enter with the 'guests and gentlewomen' at l. 17. Alexander, however, compromises, making the Maskers enter with the servants at the beginning of Sc. 5, in order to meet the direction 'Enter...*to the Maskers*'.

There is manifest difficulty in obedience to the Quarto directions, even to this minor extent. The dialogue of the servants in Sc. 5 could hardly be conducted in the presence of the Maskers. 'Enter Romeo' adds to suspicion of the directions. 'They march about the Stage' is usually indicative of an exit after the march, and there is every reason for considering the entry of the servants as following upon this exit. There is no difficulty in interpreting the meaning of 'Enter...to the Maskers' as a dual entrance from two doors, the Maskers at one door, and the Capulets and guests at the other, meeting. The relevant direction here should read:

Enter the *Maskers* at one door, and at the other *Capulet, Lady Capulet, Juliet, Nurse, Tybalt,* and others of the house, and *Guests,* meeting.

The servants also need attention. Quarto requires four servants, two entering first, with Anthony and Potpan entering when called at l. 11. The first speaker (*Ser.*) is clearly giving orders, and it is he who calls for Anthony and Potpan. The Quarto directions thus indicate a senior servant (*Ser.*) a subordinate servant (*1*), Anthony (*2*), and Potpan(*3*), who speak in that order. These are Shakespeare's

intentions. Folio eliminates *3* and gives what is clearly
Potpan's speech to *1*.

A further need is for an entry for the musicians, who are
addressed by Capulet at l. 27.

> READ: Enter *Musicians*, and two *Servants* with napkins.
>   1. Serv. *Where's Potpan, . . . trencher?*
>   2. Serv. *When good manners . . . foul thing.*
>   1. Serv. *Away with . . . and Nell.* [Exit *2. Serv.*
>   *Anthony and Potpan!*
>   Enter *Anthony* and *Potpan.*
> Anth. *Ay boy, ready.*
>   1. Serv. *You are looked for . . . chamber.*
> Potpan. *We cannot be . . . take all.*   [They retire.

5.19 *will walke about with you:*

Editors have followed the Q 1 reading, *have a bout with
you*, in preference to the natural word *walk* in reference to
dancing of the time. *walk about*, on the other hand,
ignores the reference to dancing. *walk a bout* means 'dance
a turn'.

> READ: *walk a bout*

5.47 *It seemes she hangs vpon the cheeke of night:*

So all early editions read, until F 2, whose reading *Her
beauty hangs* is followed by editors until Kittredge and
Alexander recently returned to the original text, with
every justification.

5.95-6 *If I prophane with my vnworthiest hand,*
This holy shrine, the gentle sin is this,

Q 1 reads *finne* for the *sin* of Q 2 and Folio, and editors,
including Kittredge and Alexander, read *fine* as suggested
by Theobald. *finne*, however, is improbable as a variation
of *fine* (which is never spelled *finne* or *fin*), but is the easiest
of errors for *sinne*. *fine*, moreover, runs contrary to the

whole trend of the passage. There is a contrast between the profaning of Juliet's hand by the rough touch of Romeo's and the gentle sin of kissing it by tender lips. The thought of his *sin* runs through the exchange, and is caught up again, by both speakers: *my sin is purged; Then have my lips the sin; Sin from my lips.*

READ: *the gentle sin*

ACT 2

1.13 *Young* Abraham: Cupid *he that shot so true,*

All original texts read *Abraham.* Upton's emendation *Adam* has been universally adopted. Yet *Abraham* or even *Abram* is impossible as a misreading of *Adam* or *Addam.* It is pure conjecture, and unnecessary. An 'Abraham-man' is well known as a type of Elizabethan beggar, crippled and purblind, a suitable 'nickname' for Mercutio to give to Cupid. It may be doubted whether *Adam* Bell the archer of balladry was as well known. He was certainly not 'purblind'. Editors, including Kittredge and Alexander, have preferred the Q 1 reading, *trim* for *true,* for which I see no necessity or graphic plausibility. *true* is very apt in opposition to *purblind.*

READ: *Young Abraham Cupid, he that shot so true,*

1.38 *An open, or thou a Poprin Peare.*

Q 1 reads *et cætera, thou,* and is rightly followed by editors. The copy clearly read *etc* (not *&c*) which was easily mistakable for *or* by the compositor.

READ: *An open et cetera, thou*

2.44 *By any other word would smell as sweete,*

Editors follow the Q 1 reading *name* for *word.* There is little plausibility for a graphic error here. The reading *name* seems weaker by its repetition, and was surely a memorial error in Q 1. The Q 2 reading is preferable on all grounds.

READ: *By any other word*

2.59 *Of thy tongus vttering,*

Here again the Q 1 reading, *that tongue's utterance,* for so long accepted, should be rejected in favour of the original *thy tongue's uttering,* as in Alexander.

2.61 *Neither faire maide, if either thee dislike.*

The Q 1 *fair saint* has obvious attractions, too obvious in view of the 'dear saint' preceding it in l. 55, which clearly affected the copy for Q 1. At l. 61, moreover, the dialogue has come nearer to ordinary speech between man and maid. And *saint* is not a word to be repeated.

READ: *fair maid,*

2.101 *Then those that haue coying to be strange,*

Q 1 reads *more cunning* for *coying,* and should be followed. *coying* is a not impossible reading, but its difficulty, along with the metrical flaw, suggests corruption in the copy for Q 2. The misreading of *coñing* as *coiing* (*coying*) is entirely plausible.

READ: *that have more cunning*

2.107 *Lady, by yonder blessed Moone I vow,*

I vow should be retained, in place of the accepted *I swear* from Q 1. There are *swears* enough to follow, to explain the Q 1 reading. Alexander concurs.

2.153 *To cease thy strife, and leaue me to my griefe,*

Editors, including Alexander, follow Q 4 in reading *suit* for *strife.* This is only justifiable if Q 4 is accepted as a prime authority, or if Q 2 is a possible corruption of *suit,* even if *suit* is supported, as it is, by the parallel passage in Brooke's poem used by Shakespeare as a source. But *strife* is not a possible misreading of *suit*, and gives good sense as it stands. Romeo is striving against the circumstances of their love.

READ: *To cease thy strife,*

2.168 Ro. *My Neece.*

Q1 reads *Madame*, Q4 *My dear*, followed by editors including Alexander, F2 *My sweet.* The *My Neece* of Q2 and Folio is manifestly a corruption. The capital *N* of *Neece* gives the clue. Once we realize that *sw* can easily be misread as *Ne, t* asc and so *swete* as *Neece*, the reading of F2 becomes imperative as a restoration of Shakespeare's copy.

READ: *My sweet.*

3.1–4 *The grey-eyed morne*...Titans *burning wheeles:*

These four lines have already appeared, in a slightly variant form, in Romeo's concluding speech in Sc. 2. They are, indeed, more in his idiom than in that of the Friar, and the night has passed as he and Juliet talk. The Friar's opening speech in Sc. 3 could perfectly well begin at l. 5: 'Now ere the sun advance his burning eye.' It is a temptation to consider these lines as out of place in the Friar's speech, and to leave them in Romeo's. Q1, however, includes them in the Friar's speech only. It seems more likely on the evidence that Shakespeare originally wrote those lines into Romeo's speech, then deleted them there, and rewrote them into the Friar's speech as he moved on to Sc. 3. The improvement of l. 4 is marked in this second version. The reverse process seems to be difficult to conceive as possible. There are other instances in this play of lines deleted in the copy surviving in the print.

4.107 ff. Ro. *Heeres goodly geare.* Enter Nurse and her man.
    A sayle, a sayle.
    Mer. *Two two, a shert and a smocke.*

Editors follow Q 1, reading:
    Mer. *A sail, a sail!*
    Ben. *Two, two; a shirt and a smock.*

I see no ground for departing thus from Q 2 and Folio.
Romeo is not to be limited to a love-sick mood. He does
not yet know the Nurse. And in the whole scene he is as
much the young spark as the others, so long as Mercutio
and Benvolio are with him. *Here's goodly gear*, moreover,
is linked closely with *A sail, a sail!* as comment upon the
entrance of Nurse and Peter (not upon the preceding
dialogue).
    READ: Enter *Nurse* and *Peter.*
        Rom. *Here's goodly gear! A sail, a sail!*
        Mer. *Two, two; a shirt and a smock.*

ACT 3

1.94 *A plague a both houses, I am sped,*

Q 1 reads *on your houses*; Q 2 at l. 103 reads *a both your
houses;* and the metre also of l. 94 requires this effective
repetition.

    READ: *A plague a both your houses,*

1.117–18   Tybalt *that an houre*
            Hath bene my Cozen,

Most editors have preferred *my kinsman* from Q 1, for
no reason. Both Juliet and Nurse refer to Tybalt as Juliet's
cousin (3.2.66, 96, 100).

    READ: *my cousin.*

1.127 *He gan in triumph and* Mercutio *slaine,*

Editors, including Alexander, adopt the Q 1 reading,
Alive in triumph, which has no possibility of derivation

from the copy for Q2. I suggest that this copy read *agen*, which the compositor read as *a gan* (*He gan*). Romeo is repeating Benvolio's words in the preceding line, 'the furious Tybalt back again,' pointing them with *in triumph*.

READ: *Again? In triumph! And Mercutio slain.*

1.129 *And fier end furie,*

Q1 reads *fier eyed*, easily derivable from the same copy if it read *fier eied*, misread in Q2 as *fier end*.

READ: *fire-eyed*

2.6 *That runnawayes eyes may wincke,*

The sense of this phrase has given great difficulty, and the *runaway* has been taken to refer to the night, the stars being its eyes, to Juliet herself, or to chance prowlers of the night. The reference is surely, in fact, to Romeo, the obvious *runaway*, a secret night-wanderer to Juliet. 'When night comes, Romeo may relax his vigilance (he dare not be caught coming to Juliet, or he dies), and come to my arms.' It is the more acceptable because of the audience's, and Shakespeare's (though not Juliet's), knowledge that Romeo has been banished. 'Untalked of and unseen', in l. 7, is a second thought, not an explanation of l. 6. There is no need for wild conjectures like Collier's *enemies*'.

2.9 *And by their owne bewties,*

Editors omit *And*, apparently to reduce syllables to ten. The line is metrical as it stands. The word *And* is not insignificant, but is emphatic in this parenthesis between the opposition of 'Lovers can see' to 'or if love be blind.'

READ: *And by*

2.34–5 *Now Nurse, what newes? what hast thou there,*
     The cords that Romeo *bid thee fetch?*

It seems more likely that Juliet is not making a simply curious inquiry as to what the Nurse was carrying, as in

PLATE I

Romeo and Juliet (act 3, sc. 3, ll. 38ff.)

(*a*) Alternative reconstructions of Shakespeare's MS.

Who euen in pure and veſtall modeſtie
Still bluſh, as thinking their owne kiſſes ſin.
This may flyes do, when I from this muſt flie,
And ſayeſt thou yet, that exile is not death?
But *Romeo* may not, he is baniſhed.
Flies may do this, but I from this muſt flie:
They are freemen, but I am baniſhed.

(*b*) The Quarto version of 1599, sig. G 4

the accepted reading, *What hast thou there?*, but is asking her whether she has carried out her orders, a matter of importance to Juliet.

READ: *What, hast thou there*
                    The cords

3.40 ff. (a) *This may flyes do, when I from this must flie,*
            (b) *And sayest thou yet, that exile is not death?*
            (c) *But Romeo may not, he is banished.*
            (d) *Flies may do this, but I from this must flie:*
            (e) *They are freemen, but I am banished.*

See Introduction, Vol. I, pp. 19–20, and Plate I. There are two possibilities in the reconstitution of the underlying copy for this text in which there is obvious inclusion of both original and corrected writing. We are not free to shuffle the lines as we please, in order to lose nothing, as do modern and recent editors.

(i) Lines (d) and (e) were deleted. Lines (a) and (b) were written in the margin to replace them, and the compositor printed them before, instead of after, 'But Romeo may not, he is banished', and printed the deleted lines also. This would give the reading:

> *But Romeo may not, he is banished.*
> *This may flies do, when I from this must fly,*
> *And sayest thou yet that exile is not death?*

Shakespeare thus cut out the conceit about flies and free-men and substituted lines giving a transition to the following lines about a 'mean of death'. He also changed the emphasis of the original line (d). '*This (kissing Juliet's hand) may flies do.*'

(ii) Lines (a) and (b) were deleted *currente calamo* and the thought postponed and modified to follow 'But Romeo may not, he is banished'. (I owe this suggestion to Miss R. A. Sisson.) The process was thus one of simple deletion, with no marginal writing and no compositor's error save

that of printing deleted matter. Shakespeare thus gave
emphasis to the line, 'But Romeo may not, he is banished'.
He rejected the thought, 'exile is not death', in favour of a
fuller treatment of the fly conceit, with its insistence on
banishment continued later. 'Flies are freemen' picks up
the 'more honourable state. . . . In carrion flies' (ll. 34–5).
Altogether this has superior probability.

> READ: *But Romeo may not, he is banished.*
> *Flies may do this, but I from this must fly;*
> *They are freemen, but I am banished.*

And relegate lines (*a*) and (*b*) to a footnote as deleted
during composition.[1]

3.85–6   *O wofull simpathy:*
           Pitious prediccament,

These words, attributed to Nurse, in the middle of a
speech, by Q2, Folio, and Q1 alike, have by the great
majority of editors been excised from it and given to
the Friar, against all available textual evidence and without
necessity. See Introduction, Vol. 1, p. 14. If editors were
right here, and the speaker's name omitted in the copy, we
should surely have had this reflected in print in broken lines.

> READ: as in Q2.

3.144 *Thou puts vp thy fortune and thy loue:*

Editors read *Thou pout'st upon.* But to read *pout'st* is
to go against the evidence, and is an unnecessary improvement of accidence. The copy clearly read *pouts vp̃*, which
the compositor misread as the familiar phrase *puts up*
('bears patiently'). Had the copy read *poutst* the error
would hardly have been possible.

> READ: *Thou pouts upon*

---

[1] The following are some of the principal readings of these lines: Q1, (*c*) (*d*);
F1, (*a*) (*b*) (*c*); *Globe*, (*c*) (*d*) (*e*) (*b*); *Oxford* (*d*) (*e*) (*b*); *Cambridge*, Furness,
Temple, Kittredge, Alexander, (*c*) (*a*) (*e*) (*b*). Of these only Q1 and F1 make
plausible copy.

5.127 *When the Sun sets, the earth doth drisle deaw,*

Editors read *air* for *earth*, from Q4, with no graphic plausibility, and with no improvement of sense. The thought is simply what happens on earth when the sun sets, as in *Lucrece* 1226:

> But as the *earth* doth weep, the sun being set,

READ: *the earth*

5.178–9 *Day, night, houre, tide, time, worke, play,*
        Alone in companie,

The reading of Q2 is in any case preferable to the clichés of Q1 followed by many editors, but should be re-punctuated.

READ: *Day, night, hour; tide, time; work, play;*
        Alone, in company;

5.182 *youthfull and nobly liand,*

Q1 reads *trainde*. Folio reads *Allied*, a manifestly editorial conjecture. The *liand* of Q2 was easily misread by an unintelligent compositor for *traind* in his copy.

READ: *nobly trained,*

ACT 4

1.84–5 *Or bid me go into a new made graue,*
        And hide me with a dead man in his,

Folio reads *in his grave*, for the incomplete *in his,*. Editors have preferred the Q4 reading *in his shroud*. I think it probable that the repetition of *grave* was in the copy, that the compositor of Q2 was led by the repetition to omit it, thinking 'in *his*' sufficient, and that Folio restored it. I see difficulties in hiding in an occupied shroud. Miss Husbands, however, reminds me of Trinculo in Caliban's gaberdine. It is a nice point. And *shroud* has undeniable attractions.

READ: *a dead man in his grave,*

1.99–100 *The roses in thy lips and cheekes shall fade:*
        Too many ashes,

Q4 reads *Too paly ashes,* followed by editors. *paly,* of course, cannot be derived from any possible copy underlying *many.* If, however, in the Q2 copy the word seemed to the compositor to be spelled *manie* he might well be misreading *waned.* In *Hamlet* 2.2.580 we have 'all his visage wanned'. (*Too* would naturally be read to accompany *many,* and the colon to precede it.)

READ: *shall fade*
        To waned ashes,

1.109–13 *Then as the manner of our countrie is,*
         Is thy best robes vncouered on the Beere,
         Be borne to buriall in thy kindreds graue:
         Thou shall be borne to that same auncient vault,
         Where all the kindred of the Capulets *lie,*

It seems plain that here again we have a deletion and correction *currente calamo,* l. 111 immediately rejected and deleted in favour of ll. 112–13 replacing it, and both printed by the compositor of Q2. *Is* in l. 110 is repeated from l. 109, for *In.*

2.41, 45 *helpe to decke vp her,* . . .*to prepare vp him*

Editors read *prepare him up.* But the precise order of the words, with the emphases upon *her* and *him,* is a kind of stage-direction for speaking the lines.

READ: as in Q2.

3.22 *Shall I be married then to morrow morning?*

Most editors prefer the reading of Q1, *Must I of force be married to the County?,* inexplicable unless Q1 is taken as authoritative, and clearly an improvisation.

3.29–30 *For he hath still bene tried a holy man.*
         How if when I am laid into the Tombe,

Editors, but not Alexander, insert the too-obvious line from Q 1, ' I will not entertain so bad a thought', between l. 29 and l. 30.

3.58 **Romeo, Romeo, Romeo,** *heeres drinke, I drinke to thee.*

Q 1, followed by all editors, reads, *Romeo I come, this doe I drinke to thee.* The reading of Q 2, however, cannot be ignored. It has not been generally realized that in this text what was a stage-direction in its copy has crept into the dialogue. What Shakespeare wrote was, *Romeo. Romeo. Romeo* (here drink), *I drink to thee.* There can surely be no question, apart from that of the comparative authority of the two Quartos, which reading is superior. Why 'Romeo, I come'? There is dramatic distraction in the Q 2 reading, compared with the cool logic of Q 1, which took the phrase *Romeo, I come* from earlier lines in this speech referring to Romeo's coming (ll. 32, 35).

READ: *Romeo! Romeo! Romeo! I drink to thee.*

4.20 *Twou shalt be loggerhead, good father tis day.*

Editors all read *Good faith,* for *good father.* It might seem certain that the original copy of Q 2 read *God Father* and should be retained. Capulet was not one for gingerbread oaths.

READ: *Thou shalt be logger-head. God Father, 'tis day.*
                              [*Exeunt servants.*

5.41 *Haue I thought loue to see this mornings face,*

Editors follow Q 1 and Folio, which read *long* for *love,* without any advantage over the Q 2 reading. Indeed *love* is preferable on all grounds. The period of the whole play is a week. Paris' passion for Juliet was evident. He is

looking upon Juliet now, as again at l. 58, 'O love, o life'.
No graphic confusion is possible.

READ: *Have I thought, love, to see*

5.80–1   *and as the custome is,*
            And in her best array

The compositor has carried over *and* from l. 80 to l. 81.
Q1 reads *In all*, followed by editors. But *All in* gives good
sense and is graphically more plausible.

READ: *All in*

5.82 *For though some nature bids vs all lament,*

F2 reads *fond* for *some*, and the reading is rightly accepted.
It is graphically likely for the compositor of Q2 to misread
fond as *some*.

READ: *fond nature*

5.143 *Because Musitions haue no gold for sounding:*

The Q1 reading, *such Fellowes as you haue sildome
gold for sounding*, may seem preferable, more pointed
and contemptuous, and justifying Catling's 'pestilent
knave'. But we are here in Q2 dealing with Shakespeare's
own copy, as evidenced by 'Enter Will Kemp' for 'Enter
Peter' at l. 101.

READ: as in Q2.

ACT 5

1.14–15 *How doth my Lady, is my Father well:*
            How doth my Lady Juliet? that I aske againe,

Both the repetition and the metrical derangement
indicate corruption in l. 15. The compositor has picked up
and repeated 'How doth my Lady' from l. 14 in place of
the copy before him. It is justifiable therefore to fill the
gap with the satisfactory reading of Q1.

READ: *How fares my Juliet? That I ask again,*
    Q1, it is to be noted, is exceptionally valuable in Act 5
for the restoration of the text.

1.24 *Is it in so? then I denie you starres.*

The Q1 reading, *defy* for *deny*, is irresistible on the
ground of sense, though no explanation can be offered for
misreading *defy* or *defie* as *deny* or *denie* (or for *pray* instead
of Q1 *pay* at l. 76). Romeo is not *denying* the influence of
the stars, he is admitting it (*Is it e'en so?*); he is *defying* their
omnipotence here as again at Sc. 3, ll. 111–12:

> And *shake the yoke* of inauspicious stars
> From this world-wearied flesh.

READ: *Then I defy you, stars.*

3.3 *Vnder yond young Trees*

Q1, and all editors, read *yew* for *young*, rightly. The
Q2 reading is a misreading of *yeugh* as *yongh*, hence *young*.
The error is repeated at l. 137.

3.68 *I do defie thy commiration,*

commiration is undoubtedly a graphic error for *coniura-
tion*, preserved in Q1 as *coniurations*; a mere matter of
minims.

READ: *conjurations,*

3.102–3 *Why art thou yet so faire? I will beleeue,*
        Shall I beleeue that vnsubstantiall death is amorous,

This is a further instance of correction and rewriting
currente calamo in 'foul paper' copy. *I will believe* has been
deleted and replaced, and the compositor has carried the
crowded words into the next line.

READ: *Why art thou yet so fair? Shall I believe*
      That unsubstantial Death is amorous,

3.107 ff. *And neuer from this pallat of dym night.*
        Depart againe, come lye thou in my arme,
        Heer's to thy health, where ere thou tumblest in.
        O true Appothecarie!
        Thy drugs are quicke. Thus with a kisse I die.
        Depart againe, here, here, will I remaine,

In l. 107 Folio corrected *pallat* to *Pallace*. The error
was the simple misreading of a *c* as a *t*. Q2 has here
preserved a passage of a first draft deleted by Shakespeare.
The lines between the first and last were deleted, and a
fresh start made with *Depart again* to include some new
and splendid writing in place of halting and puzzling lines,
the clue to which may be *tomb liest in* misread *tumblest in*.
Less probably the sense may be, as it stands, 'Here's to thy
health, where ere—[to himself] thou tumblest in', i.e. he
falls into the tomb, paying tribute to the immediate effect
of the Apothecary's drug. I feel sure that *thou, thy, thou,*
all refer to Juliet. Nowhere else in this scene does Romeo
apostrophize himself.

READ: *And never from this palace of dim night*
        Depart again. Here, here will I remain,

3.169–70   *O happy dagger*
        This is thy sheath, there rust and let me dye.

Some editors have preferred *rest* from Q1, perhaps to
make the dagger *happy*. But it is certainly spoken of a
dagger that will *rust* in its sheath, Juliet's body.

READ: *there rust,*

3.190 *What should it be that is so shrike abroad?*

Folio and Q4 read *that they so shriek abroad,* and most
editors have followed this obviously editorial emendation.
The compositor of Q2, however, has simply misread
shrikd as *shrike*, an easy error. Alexander agrees.

READ: *is so shrieked abroad?*

3.194 *What feare is this which startles in your eares?*

Editors, including Kittredge and Alexander, follow Johnson in emending to *our ears?* against all the evidence. It is not the Prince's ears that are offended. Lady Capulet has just been describing the outcry which has startled herself and Capulet. There is, at least, no necessity for emendation, and no graphic plausibility in such an error.

READ: *in your ears?*

TIMON OF ATHENS

The Folio list is clearly editorial as well as corrupt and incomplete. It seems absurd to follow it closely in a modern edition.

ACT 1

Sc. 1 *Stage-direction.* **Enter Poet, Painter, Ieweller, Merchant, and Mercer, at seuerall doores.**[1]

Editors follow Folio here. But there is no part for the *Mercer*, here or elsewhere. Moreover, at l. 8 the Painter's remark, 'I know them *both*', refers clearly to the Merchant and the Jeweller as the only tradesmen present. It would seem certain that the entrance for *Mercer* as well as *Merchant* is an error due to the abbreviation of *Merchant* to *Mer*. (The Folio list does not include a Mercer.) There are two parties, the artists and the tradesmen, entering severally.

READ: Enter Poet *and* Painter, *and* Jeweller *and* Merchant, *at several doors.*

1.40 **Poet.** *The Senators of Athens, happy men.*

Theobald, followed by all, reads *man* for *men*, referring to Timon instead of to the senators. But why should it not be *men*, and the senators? They are happy in their high rank, and in having free access on equality to Timon, which is very much to the point when the Poet is speaking.

READ: —*happy men!*

---

[1] The Folio text is basic for this play, and citations are from that text.

1.46–9   *but moues it selfe*
In a wide Sea of wax, no leuell'd malice
Infects one comma in the course I hold,
But flies an Eagle flight,

Editors find difficulty here, and Alexander follows one
of many emendations proposed, Staunton's *tax* for *wax*,
which is implausible and gives only a very forced sense.
a sea of wax surely bears its obvious sense as a piece of well-
known local colour in this play. (Shakespeare read
Golding's *Metamorphoses*.) 'My movements are not
restricted to the limits of a tablet of wax; I move freely in
a wide sea of wax; my drift is free of limits.' The sense of
the whole passage is made clear when we realize that *no
levelled malice . . . course I hold* is a parenthesis.

READ: *but moves itself*
In a wide sea of wax—no levelled malice
Infects one comma in the course I hold—
But flies an eagle flight,

1.87 *Euen on their knees and hand, let him sit downe,*

Rowe, followed by all, reads *slip* for *sit*. Alexander reads
thus, and *hands* for *hand*. *slip*, however, could only be
plausible if we assume dictation as the source of the error.
I suggest *fall*, which could easily be misread as *sitt*, and
gives better sense. The image is of a catastrophic, not a
gradual, *fall*, as is borne out by l. 94, 'the foot above the
head', a headlong tumble. As for *hand*, there is no need to
emend. One hand is likely enough to have something to
carry! It is not necessarily 'on all fours'.

READ: *Even on their knees and hand, let him fall down,*

1.128–9 Tim. *The man is honest.*
Oldm. *Therefore he will be* Timon,

This passage has given unnecessary difficulty, with great
variety of emendations. Recent editors agree upon the

Folio reading, with a comma before *Timon*. The Old Athenian replies to Timon, 'if he is honest, as you say he is, he will stay honest and not spoil his honesty by fortune-hunting'.

READ: *Therefore he will be, Timon.*

2.131–2 *There tast, touch all, pleas'd from thy table rise:*

Folio has the four preceding lines set as prose. All is obviously verse, however. And there is certainly corruption. Editors have emended on the assumption that *all* is a misprint for *smell*, which seems very unlikely. It is more probable that *smell* has been omitted by the compositor, whose eye was taken away from it by *all* following 'sm*ell*' in his copy. The omission of *all*, as in Alexander, ruins the metre. There can be no reasonable doubt of Warburton's *Th'ear* for *There*. There is no need to insert *and* after *touch*, as in Kittredge. The Folio reading and punctuation give an uneasy sense, obviously any port in a storm of difficult copy.

READ: *Th'ear,*
Taste, touch, smell, all, pleased from thy table rise.

2.142 *And spend our Flatteries, to drinke those men,*

There is no need for emendation of this line or others following. *to drink those men* simply means 'to drink (the health of) those men', which makes all clear.

2.167 *Else I should tell him well, yfaith I should;*

Rowe's version, *tell him—well yfaith*, is accepted by Alexander. The Folio punctuation represents more idiomatic Elizabethan English, and gives excellent sense.

READ: as in F.

ACT 2

Sc. 1. *Stage-direction*. The accepted stage-direction here seems to me misleading, 'Enter a Senator, with papers in his hand'. This is a typical 'study' scene, in which the Senator is 'discovered' sitting at his desk in the inner stage, which 'closes' at the end of this short scene.

READ: Enter *Senator* at his desk.

1.13 *Can sound his state in safety.*

Recent editors have rightly preserved the Folio reading, as against the unnecessary emendation of *found* for *sound*. *sound* means 'measure the depth or extent of his state.'

1.33–5 Ca. *I go sir.*
    Sen. *I go sir?*
    Take the Bonds along with you,
    And haue the dates in. Come.
    Ca. *I will sir.*
    Sen. *Go.*

Editors have taken the bit in their teeth here, and the extraordinary liberties they have taken, as recently also in Kittredge and Alexander, have killed a good comic scene. Alexander reads, for example:

    Caph. *I go, sir.*
    Sen.   *Take the bonds along with you,*
    And have the dates in compt.

But the Senator is fussy and agitated, as all the dialogue shows, and stage-business should indicate his confused haste. There is a full sequence from l. 13 onwards, 'Caphis ho! Caphis I say!', 'haste you', 'Get you gone', 'Get you gone', till Caphis gets a word in edgeways, 'I go sir.' The Senator echoes him, 'I go sir? (Why don't you get on—oh, the bonds?) Take the bonds with you. Come! (and take the bonds from me).' In the course of this, the

Senator recalls 'his fracted dates' (l. 22) but interrupts himself in saying *And have the dates in* (mind), to hurry Caphis' movements. As for the emendation *compt*, it seems impossible as a misreading of *Come*, as well as unnecessary.

> READ: Caph. *I go sir.*
> Sen. *I go sir?—Take the bonds along with you,*
> *And have the dates in—Come!* [Gives bonds.
> Caph. *I will sir.*
> Sen. *Go!*

2.38 *With clamorous demands of debt, broken Bonds,*

Editors unanimously read *date-broke* for *debt, broken*, without graphic plausibility or real necessity, even if the repetition of *debt* in l. 39 is awkward, and *date-broke* an improvement.

2.133 *You make me meruell wherefore ere this time*

Editors, except Alexander, read *marvel. Wherefore*, for no visible reason.

READ: as in F.

2.171–2 *I haue retyr'd me to a wastefull cocke,*
      And set mine eyes at flow.

Editors have run wild here, with *wakeful couch, lonely room, nook, cot, compt*, etc., until of late, when the Folio text has been restored, supported by Kittredge and Alexander. Flavius' whole speech is crystal clear, and ends, 'I have gone below to the cellar, next to a running barrel of wine, and I have added my tears to the waste of wine, my eyes flowing like its cock.'

2.205 ff. Tim. *Go you sir to the Senators;...*

Editors have invented an additional *Servant* (*Fourth Servant*) to whom Timon addresses this speech, along with instructions to 'Go to Ventidius' (l. 229) and remarks

about Ventidius (ll. 232ff.). So *Arden*, for instance.
Recent editors rightly address these speeches to Flavius.
They are spoken as Timon speaks to Flavius, not to a
Servant, as might well appear to be obvious.

ACT 3

4.111–12 *So fitly? Go, bid all my Friends againe,*
        Lucius, Lucullus, *and* Sempronius Vllorxa: *All,*

    This is a sweet problem. Recent editors all read l. 112
simply with the omission of the offending *Vllorxa*, and so
do I. But what justification is there for this? Some earlier
editors read *Sempronius, Valerius, all,* or *Sempronius,
Ventidius, all.* And indeed Ventidius is a notable absentee
from Timon's list, but there is no possibility of such misreadings of copy. Thistleton suggested that Shakespeare
interlined in his copy *All or xc* (i.e. *All or etc*) for the actor
to close the line with *all* or *etc* at his discretion (and that the
compositor read *Vllorxa* for *All or xc*), a fantastic suggestion.
But it was an attempt to face a problem which must be
faced. It is obvious that l. 112 is complete metrically
without *Vllorxa*, and that the *and* comes before *Sempronius*.
It would seem that *Vllorxa* is some kind of excrescence, as
well as a corruption. There are many possible misreadings
available for consideration, in particular *x* and the ampers-
and which resembles it. But I believe that the abbreviation
in Latin script for *us* gives the clue, together with the *x*, *&*
confusion, to this crux. If we envisage a seriously blotted
Lucullus and, and an interlineation rewriting the blotted
part, we have

                        ull₉ &
        Lucius, Luc⟨. . . . .⟩ Sempronius: *All*

The names, be it noted, are all in italics (not only *Vllorxa*
as stated in *Arden*). The compositor, finding the words

Lucullus and *and* in fact legible, took *ull₉ &* to be an additional name, and read the signs as *Vllorxa*, to be placed after *Sempronius*. The possibility would appear as a probability in a facsimile of the relevant contemporary writing.

READ: Lucius, Lucullus, *and* Sempronius; *all.*

5.14 *He is a Man (setting his Fate aside) of comely Vertues,*

Warburton's *fault* for *Fate* has been generally followed, unnecessarily and harmfully to the sense. It is extraordinary that classical scholars, of all people, should fail to understand the original, with medieval and Renaissance associations to fortify it.

READ: *his fate*

5.22 *He did behooue his anger ere 'twas spent,*

Rowe's *behave* is popular still for *behoove*, though Alexander rightly reads *behove*. The notion, 'he came at my behoof, i.e. for my benefit, and so at my command', leads naturally to this transitive verbal use, 'to control'.

READ: *behove*

Sc. 6 *Stage-direction and speaker's names.*

The initial Folio direction is simply *Enter diuers Friends at seuerall doores*, and the Lords speaking are marked as 1, 2, 3, 4. And so Alexander reads. But surely we should name the Lords in question, Timon's friends, as would be necessary in any production of the play. And it is clear enough which are which in this scene.

READ: *Music. Tables set out, Servants attending. Enter at several doors* Lucullus, Lucius, Sempronius, Ventidius, *and* Senators.

For 1. Lord, Lucullus; 2. Lord, Lucius; 3. Lord, Sempronius; 4. Lord, Ventidius.

At l. 115, Folio has an entrance, *Enter the Senators, with other Lords.* It is clear that this is a re-entry upon Timon's exit. They are driven out by Timon at l. 111.

L. 111. READ: [Drives them out.

L. 115. READ: [Exit *Timon*. Re-enter *Lords* and *Senators*.

6.88–90 *The rest of your Fees, O Gods, the Senators of Athens, together with the common legge of People,*

Hanmer's *foes* for *fees* is widely followed, e.g. by Kittredge and Alexander. *Arden* reads *fees* but in a note recommends *feces*, which is wild. The word *foes* would throw out of gear the whole movement of thought here. No *foes* have as yet been implied. The simple sense contained in the original text is far more telling, 'the rest of your property, possessions', a sense for which there is ample authority. Human kind is the property of the gods, all imperfect and amiss, fit for destruction. *legge* is certainly *lag* (not *tag*), 'what is left, what comes at the tail.'

READ: *The rest of your fees, o gods, . . . the common lag of people,*

ACT 4

1.21 *And yet Confusion liue:*

Hanmer's *let* for *yet* is generally accepted, as by Alexander. It is an unnecessary and implausible emendation, as Johnson saw and *Arden* agrees. The meaning of the original is far superior. It is simply, 'Down with Piety and Religion etc. But (*yet*) long live Confusion with Plagues and Fevers.' *let*, of course, is contained in the verb-form *live*.

READ: *And yet confusion live.*

3.12 *It is the Pastour Lards, the Brothers sides,*

On this line, see Introduction, pp. 11–12. Singer's-Collier's *rothers* for *Brothers* holds the field in recent editions. It is most implausible graphically. I arrived at *wethers* as the true reading by inspection of a Secretary transcript of the passage, and it is as certain as one could wish graphically, and in sense. The initial downstroke of a *w*, with its first minim, is very easily misread as *b*. I subsequently fell upon Warburton's early suggestion of the same emendation. 'Good pasture makes fat sheep', says Corin in *As You Like It* 3.2.28. Wethers and ewes were sold as well as cattle in the Rother Market at Stratford.

READ: *It is the pasture lards the wether's sides,*

3.120–1 *Thinke it a Bastard, whom the Oracle*
         Hath doubtfully pronounced, the throat shall cut,

Editors read *thy* for *the*, with no need. The oracle is doubtful, anyway. All it has pronounced is that the babe-bastard will cut somebody's throat, will be a cut-throat. Timon's strictures throughout the speech are general and not personal.

READ: *the throat*

3.122 *Sweare against Obiects,*

Various emendations have sought to remove a non-existent difficulty of sense, e.g. *weak objects* (*Arden*), or Farmer's *abjects*, adopted by Alexander. The sense of *objects* is simply 'objections (to cruelty) or accusations (of cruelty)'. 'Take an oath against all protests, and put on the armour of cruelty'. It is a quasi-legal use of the word, for which there is good authority in this sense.

READ: *Swear against objects,*

3.133–4 *Enough to make a Whore forsweare her Trade,*
         And to make Whores, a Bawd.

Emendation is unnecessary. The sense is plain. 'Enough to make a whore forswear her trade, and to make a bawd (forswear) making (*to make*) whores.'

READ: *And to make whores, a bawd.*

3.155–6   *Hoare the Flamen,*
        That scold'st against the quality of flesh,

There has been much curiously innocent misunderstanding of the sense throughout this scene. Here *Arden*
refers *flesh* to the sacrificial victim on the altar not giving
good omens. It is, of course, used in the familiar sense of
woman-flesh in reference to whores. Too many passages
have been unnecessarily emended to take note of all. Here
scold'st is rightly read *scolds* by editors, in view of the
following 'And not believes himself'.

3.223 *Will these moyst Trees,*

    Editors, except Alexander, read *mossed*. The emendation
is impossible graphically, and is not even an 'improvement'
in sense. Apemantus is describing the rigours of nature in
hard weather. The brook is cold, and the trees are moist,
in bleak air, wind and rain. *mossed* is irrelevant, and even
inconsistent with the true, profound thought here.
    R E A D : *will these moist trees,*

3.254 *To such as may the passiue drugges of it*
          Freely command'st:

    Editors read *drugs*, e.g. Kittredge and Alexander. But
the word is certainly *drudges* in modern English. *drugs* and
drudges were both generally spelled *drugges*, as were other
words of similar sounds, in Elizabethan English. *bedge* is
a Warwickshire spelling of *beg* in 1606 (St. Ch. 8. 212/12).
To read *drugs* is to ensure incomprehension.
    R E A D : *the passive drudges . . . command,*

3.271 *If thou wilt curse; thy Father (that poore ragge)*

    rag is a not impossible reading of a kind, and emendation
is perhaps not strictly necessary. Nevertheless it seems to
me that this is another instance of the concealment of the
word *rogue* in the Elizabethan spelling *roge*. *poor rogue* is

more probable than *poor rag*. And Timon continues the thought into the second generation with the words '*Poor rogue* hereditary' in l. 274. 'Thy father, a poor rogue, begat thee of a she-beggar, and thou art thus a hereditary rogue.'

READ: *thy father, that poor rogue,*

3.283 *First mend thy company, take away thy selfe.*

Editors all emend, reading *my company* for *thy company*. Having hitherto defended the reading *thy*, I am now inclined to accept *my*. Apemantus offers to 'mend thy feast'. Timon replies, 'First mend my company by leaving me', and Apemantus retorts, 'That will mend *my* own company, you being absent'. The compositor probably was misled by '*thy* feast' and *thy self*.

READ: *First mend my company,*

3.320 *Women neerest, but men: men are the things themselues.*

Editors read, e.g. as in Alexander,

Women nearest; but men, men are the things themselves.

This seems to me much less pointed than the Folio reading, and gives a different sense. The Folio punctuation should not be ignored. What things are *nearest* to being flatterers, asks Apemantus, and Timon replies, 'Apart from men, women are the nearest to being flatterers; but in fact men are not *near-flatterers*, they are the thing itself.'

READ: *Women nearest but men—men are the things themselues.*

3.397–8 Tim. *Long liue so, and so dye. I am quit.*
     Ape. *Mo things like men,*
      Eate Timon, *and abhorre then.*   Exit Apeman.
      Enter the Bandetti.

Alexander, following Hanmer's generally accepted version, reads

> Tim. *Long live so, and so die!* [Exit Apemantus.] *I
> am quit.*
> *Moe things like men? Eat, Timon, and abhor them.*
> Enter the *Banditti.*

This seems to be one of Hanmer's most officious inter-
ferences with a good original text to which there is no
intelligible objection. If Timon is a misanthrope, Apemantus is a cynic, and his speech is characteristic. The Folio
entry for the Banditti is marked at the place where they
first speak, instead of where they first enter and are seen.
They are seen entering at one door as Apemantus is on his
way out at the other. Timon's *I am quit* is not necessarily
held back until Apemantus has completed his exit. The
Folio version is far more effective, with this parting shot
from Timon's tormentor.

> READ: Tim. *Long live so, and so die. I am quit.*
> Enter *Bandits.*
>
> Apem. *Moe things like men! Eat Timon, and
> abhor them.* [Exit.

3.515–16 *Is not thy kindnesse subtle, couetous,*
> *If not a Vsuring kindnesse, and as rich men deale
> Guifts,*

Pope deleted *If not* in l. 516, and was generally followed,
and rightly. Of recent editors, however, Kittredge and
Alexander reject the emendation, and read as in Folio.
The compositor may well have caught up, from *Is not* in
l. 515, a picture in the mind leading to *If not* in l. 516. The
metre of l. 516 is obviously destroyed by the addition of
If not. Most conclusively, *If not* destroys the sense. Read
with *If not,* we have 'a kindness which is subtle and
covetous, nay I go so far as to say a usuring kindness (or
alternatively, though not a usuring kindness)'. But *subtle,
covetous,* is surely a description of *usuring,* and a further

description follows. The second alternative can be ruled out, with 'in return twenty for one' following in l. 517.

READ: *A usuring kindness, and as rich men deal gifts,*

ACT 5

1.150–1   *hath since withall*
         Of it owne fall,

The emendation *sense* for *since* is necessary to the intelligibility of this complex passage. Capell's *fail* for *fall*, though followed by recent editors, is unnecessary, and less satisfactory than the original. The Senate has *fallen* below its high standards in denying help to Timon. *it*, of course, is good Shakespearian English.

READ: *hath sense withal*
         Of it own fall,

2.8 *Yet our old loue made a particular force,*

Some editors now read *had* for *made*, seeing that *made* occurs in l. 9. No stronger case can be made for the change. The word gives good sense. Words are more frequently caught up from above to below than conversely, nor was one *made* directly above the other in this piece of copy. There is every reason for thinking that this part of the play had no final revision by Shakespeare. The repetition does not in fact affect the reader or speaker adversely.

READ: *made*

Sc. 3. *Stage-direction.* I suggest the following direction to make the contemporary setting clear, with its use of the inner stage and portable properties discovered by drawing the curtain:

         Before *Timon's* cave. At the cave mouth
                 a tombstone and mound.

3.4 *Some Beast reade this; There do's not liue a Man.*

The Folio *read* has been defended. The Soldier cannot read the inscription, and petulantly cries, *Some beast read this!* (I cannot). But this is extremely improbable, and contrary to the evident trend of the speech. The Soldier has not yet looked at the inscription, and when he does he takes a wax mould for his Captain to read. So far he has commented on the desolation of the place, in which no man lives. Warburton's *reared* (*reard*) for *reade* is plausible, gives perfect sense, and is irresistible to most editors.

READ: *Some beast reared this; there does not live a man.*

4.62 *But shall be remedied to your publique Lawes*

remedied by is no solution of the difficulty. Chedworth's emendation, *rendered* for *remedied*, is entirely plausible graphically, and is now accepted.

READ: *rendered*

4.70ff.   Alcibiades reades the Epitaph.
             Heere lies a wretched Coarse, of wretched Soule
                bereft,
             Seek not my name: A Plague consume you, wicked
                Caitifs left:
             Heere lye I Timon, who aliue, all liuing men did
                hate,
             Passe by, and curse thy fill, but passe and stay not
                here thy gate.

Editors print all four lines in their texts. But it may seem clear that here we have not one *epitaph* but two alternative epitaphs. The third line names Timon, where the second adjures us not to seek his name, which is decisive against one epitaph of four lines. Of the two, each in two lines, the second at any rate is metrically satisfactory as a seven-footer couplet. And it *is* the second. It is reasonable to conclude that Shakespeare rejected the first, deleted it, and wrote the second in its place, and that the compositor printed both. It is certain that the trend of Alcibiades' comment upon the epitaph refers to the second couplet, e.g. 'on faults forgiven' in parallel with 'who *alive* all living men did hate'. So also '(You bid us curse, not weep, and pass on), and indeed you scorned men's tears'. The first two lines should be relegated to a footnote, as deleted during composition.

> READ: Here lie I Timon, who alive all living men did hate,
>
> Pass by, and curse thy fill, but pass, and stay not here thy gait.

4.76–7 *Scornd'st our Braines flow, and those our droplets, which*
From niggard Nature fall;

The emendation *brine's* for *brain's* is officious, though Kittredge adopts it. There is ample authority for *brain's flow* in the sense of tears. *and those our droplets* is not a new or different thought but a variation of the same.

JULIUS CAESAR

ACT 1

1.16 Fla. *What Trade thou knaue?*[1]

Capell took this speech from Flavius and awarded it to
Marullus, with almost universal approval, including that of
Kittredge, *New Cambridge*, and Alexander, on the ground
apparently that Marullus at l. 12 has asked a similar
question. But Flavius and Marullus are both Tribunes,
and both are officers. Here Flavius reinforces Marullus,
who has asked the Cobbler for a direct answer and received
an indirect. Flavius reproves him and repeats the question,
whereupon the Cobbler replies of course to his original
questioner. Marullus similarly intervenes between Flavius
and the Carpenter earlier on. Theatrically, it is good to
keep both Tribunes busy. The emendation is unacceptable,
and damages the scene in the acting.

1.25–7 *I meddle with no Tradesmans matters, nor womens
matters; but withal I am indeed Sir, a Surgeon to old shooes:*

There has been much ado about the true reading of this
passage. It is obvious that there is a pun in the Cobbler's
withal, referring back to his previous *with the awl*. The
question is how far an editor should go to assist the reader
or the actor. Alexander reads *but with awl.*, making it
explicit, but at the cost of the apparent sense of the sentence
as a whole. It is, in effect, reading *but with awl* (=*all*)
instead of *but with all* (=*awl*). Alexander's reading is
probably intended to be interpreted as 'I do not meddle
with tradesmen's or women's matters except with my awl
(only as a cobbler)'. But Folio spells the word in l. 24
Aule, and why not here also? The sense is surely, 'I do not

[1] Citations are from the First Folio text, the basic authority for this play.

meddle specially with tradesmen or women, but with all', with the pun in *all*.

It is generally agreed that the Folio reading is mispunctuated and mis-read, and that *but withal*, i.e. *but with all*, closes a sentence. The Folio reading gives sense of a kind: 'I do not meddle with...matters, but nevertheless (*withal*) I am a surgeon to old shoes'; but it is poor sense, and overlays the pun, unless we think of it as, '*but with awl* I am a surgeon...shoes'. The actor would find it as difficult to point such a pun as it is easy to point it in the re-punctuated reading proposed by Capell and generally followed, as by Kittredge and *New Cambridge*.

READ: *I meddle...matters, but with all. I am indeed sir,...shoes;*

2.72 *Were I a common Laughter,*

Rowe's *laugher* for *laughter* has been generally followed, though to me it has a comic effect, and it is irrelevant in the context. Dover Wilson and Alexander read *laughter*, the former with an obelus as corrupt and with a note suggesting *loffer* ('lover'). *Laughter* seems to me to make good sense. 'If I were the sort of person that is generally contemned and ridiculed', the sort of person that Cassius goes on to describe as worthy of general, as of Brutus', contempt and ridicule.

READ: *a common laughter,*

2.255 *'Tis very like he hath the Falling sicknesse.*

Theobald's *'Tis very like. He hath* holds the field, as also in recent editions. It is a poor argument for so violent a change in the text that Caesar's defect must have been diagnosed and notorious, and therefore known to Brutus. It was obviously a surprise to Cassius, as to Casca, that Caesar swooned and fell. Why should Brutus know, and not they? And can one really believe that what Brutus said here was, 'Well, what did you expect? He is an epileptic'?

The Folio text gives far better sense in the context, 'It really sounds like epilepsy'.

READ: *'Tis very like he hath the falling sickness.*

3.20–1   *I met a Lyon,*
                Who glaz'd vpon me,

Rowe read *glared* for *glazed*, and many editors follow, including Kittredge. Yet a note of Kittredge vindicates *glazed* with ample instances in literature as well as dialect. The lion did not necessarily 'look angrily', as *glared* would suggest to moderns; it *glazed* (stared), as Alexander reads. As an emendation, *glared* is implausible, unless due to the 'foul case' suggested by Dover Wilson in a note.

READ: *Who glazed upon me,*

3.65 *Why Old men, Fooles, and Children calculate,*

Various unnecessary emendations clouded the plain sense of this line until recently. Kittredge, e.g., reads *Why old men fool and*, after Lettsom. Dover Wilson's interpretation of the line in a note in *New Cambridge* is decisive for the original text. 'It is a queer time when the portents are so plain that dotards, fools, and children can read them and foretell their significance'.

READ: as in F.

3.128–9 *And the Complexion of the Element*
        Is Fauors, like the Worke we haue in hand,

Johnson's *In favour's like* is most generally accepted as a correction of *Is favours, like*, in recent editions too. The Folio original has been painfully defended, but hopelessly. *In favour's like*, however, seems to me awkward, and I prefer Capell's *Is favoured like* for the run of the thought. Final *d* in *fauord*, and final *s* in *fauors*, are readily confused in Secretary, whereas final *n* in *In* could hardly be misread *Is*.

READ: *Is favoured like*

ACT 2

1.15 *Crowne him that,*

Rowe's *Crown him—that—* is typical of the general basis for emendation of these words, universal in variations, as in *New Cambridge* and Alexander too. (*Crown him!—* that!; crown him—that!) This version seems to me sophisticated and unnatural. I cannot focus the words except as 'Crown him *that*'. The words clearly refer back to l. 12, 'He would be crowned'. It seems to me that they may also be referred forward to l. 54, to Brutus' words on Tarquin, 'when he was *called a king*'. The horror of it for Brutus, even above other men (for he was descended from Lucius Junius Brutus), was to see a King again in Rome. 'Crown him *that*' means 'Crown him *King*' (the unspoken dreadful word, King). His thought and words now go straight on in logical sequence, 'and then I grant we put a sting in him'. I doubt if Shakespeare was aware that he had not used the word. But Brutus' horror of kings was familiar to him from the days of *The Rape of Lucrece*.

READ: *Crown him that,*

1.40 *Is not to morrow (Boy) the first of March?*

Theobald read *ides* for *first*, rightly, as l. 59 ('fifteen days') proves. But his conjecture that Shakespeare wrote j^s, misread 1st, is difficult, for j^s is not a possible abbreviation for *ides*. It is more probable that he wrote j^{de}, enough for a desperate compositor to read j^{st}, unlikely as this latter symbol would appear to him. But I think he merely took the *j* and ignored the rest as incomprehensible, or as a mere flourish.

1.83 *For if thou path thy natiue semblance on,*

Editors, after F 2, read *path, thy,* i.e. 'walk, (with) thy native semblance on', which is very forced and dubious in sense. I am satisfied that the true reading is *put* (*putt* mis-read as *path*, a misreading for which there is a very probable pattern of writing). I now find that Coleridge made the same suggestion, with a very close parallel to l. 225 in this scene, with Brutus again speaking, 'Let not our looks put on our purposes', a repetition of the same thought. *New Cambridge* reads *path*, but with an obelus.

READ: *For if thou put thy native semblance on,*

1.114 *No, not an Oath: if not the Face of men,*

Recent editors retain *face*, though *New Cambridge* marks it as corrupt and annotates it as 'almost certainly a corrup-tion of "faith"', as conjectured by Mason. But such a misreading is most implausible graphically. *Face*, where read, is very unsatisfactorily expounded. The sense seems clear, however, if we hark back to ll. 73–4, as Mrs V.K. Sisson suggested privately:

> No sir, their hats are plucked about their ears,
> And half their faces buried in their cloaks,

'Are not these motives enough, that our souls suffer, that we live in corrupt and evil days, that even men's faces dare not appear openly and men dare not be themselves?' The conspirators are muffled as Brutus speaks. 'monstrous visage' (l. 81), and 'dangerous brow' (l. 78) are further clues to this elliptic thought of Brutus. A gesture in acting would make the meaning clear.

READ: *if not the face of men,*

1.334 *That* Brutus *leads me on.*   Thunder
          Bru. *Follow me then.*   Exeunt
Sc. 2 *Stage-direction.*
                    Thunder & Lightning.
          Enter Iulius Cæsar in his Night-gowne.

Editors have retained the first direction *Thunder*, though it seems sudden and odd at the very end of a long scene without it. It is, in fact, irrelevant to Sc. 1 but very relevant to Sc. 2. It is a modern notion to interpret it as a prelude to Sc. 2. And it would reduce the dramatic effect of the storm breaking upon Caesar's appearance. I have no doubt that *New Cambridge* is right in omitting it, as a preliminary prompter's warning of the stage-effect due to follow.

2.46 *We heare two Lyons litter'd in one day,*

Upton's *are* for *heare* is read in recent editions, in preference to Theobald's *were*. I see no advantage for *are* over *were* in sense. On the contrary, *were* gives better sense. There is no plausibility in the suggestion of *are* being misread as *here* in any spelling. *weare* could well be misread as *heare* with an italic *h*, and in the 1620's there was much mixed Secretary-Italian writing, to which the compositor would be accustomed.

READ: *We were*

ACT 3

Sc. 1. *Stage-direction.* To reproduce the Folio stage-direction here, as in Kittredge and Alexander, is to leave the setting entirely to the imagination, and is inconsistent with heading the scene with indications not in Folio ('Rome. A street before the Capitol'). *New Cambridge*, on the other hand, offers complete suggestions for a modern production with a proscenium curtain. I suggest the essential indication only of the use here of the inner stage, and the order of the entry.

READ: Rome. Before the Capitol.
    Senators discovered sitting.
   Enter *Citizens, Artemidorus,* and *Soothsayer.*
   Flourish. Enter *Cæsar, Brutus . . .* and *Publius.*

1.31–2 Cæs. *Are we all ready? What is now amisse,*
That Cæsar *and his Senate must redresse?*

Only *New Cambridge* of recent editions, and that in a
note, shows any sympathy for Collier's suggestion that *Are
we all ready?*, which seems so obviously to lead up to what
follows in Caesar's speech, should be assigned to Casca. The
necessary stage-business of Caesar with the Senate requires
these words. And Folio does not confuse Caesar with
Casca elsewhere.

READ: as in F.

1.101–2 Cask. *Why he that cuts off twenty yeares of life,*
Cuts off so many yeares of fearing death.

Pope, diagnosing this speech as Stoic, assigned it to
Cassius, and Kittredge and Alexander, defying Folio,
follow. *New Cambridge* reads as in Folio, and surely
rightly. The words are entirely in Casca's vein, a sardonic
vein, and they are the last words he speaks in the play.

READ: as in F.

1.174 *Our Armes in strength of malice, and our Hearts*
Of Brothers temper, do receiue you in,

This is the most elaborately discussed passage in the play,
with a great variety of emendations, some fantastic in
improbability. *New Cambridge*, while reading as in Folio
with an obelus, favours in a note Singer's *amitie* for *malice*
as 'graphically easy' (which I think is going too far).
Kittredge and Alexander also read as in Folio, and Kittredge
in a note gives good reason why the reading should stand,
against emendations which destroy the sense of the original.
'Our swords are not aimed at you. We *are* armed, and
resolutely (against evil) and we are banded together by our
good cause. We will welcome you into this brotherhood of
hatred against evil.' It is *Brutus* speaking, be it remembered.
Malice, as Kittredge remarks, is simply 'enmity', and he

recalls Brutus' earlier antithesis between their 'cruel hands' and their 'pitiful hearts' (ll. 165–70).

READ: as in F.

ACT 4

1.37 *On Obiects, Arts, and Imitations.*

Earlier 'improvements' due to incomprehension, such as Theobald's *abjects, orts,* are now happily dismissed, except by Alexander, in favour of the original with its obvious sense, with a comma instead of the full stop, leading on to 'which...begin his fashion'.

1.44 *Our best Friends made, our meanes stretcht,*

To mark this as corrupt, as *New Cambridge* does, on purely metrical grounds, makes unwarranted assumptions, especially where it cannot be argued that the sense is not complete. Editors who have vamped up the syllables have merely watered the line down by their additions.

READ: as in F., as does Alexander.

Sc. 2. *Stage-direction.* I suggest the following as the true interpretation of the Folio direction indicated by the setting and action:

Before *Brutus'* tent, in the camp near Sardis.

Drum. Enter *Brutus* and *Lucius* from the tent. Enter *Lucilius* and *Soldiers* at one door, and *Titinius* and *Pindarus* at the other.

2.50–2 Lucillius, *do you the like, and let no man*
       Come to our Tent, till we haue done our Conference.
       Let Lucius *and* Titinius *guard our doore.*

Kittredge and Alexander retain the Folio reading. *New Cambridge* interchanges Lucius and Lucillius, rightly as I think and necessarily, and also deletes *Let* in l. 52 as caught

up from l. 50. Young Lucius, and not the notable soldier
Lucilius, is the right person to make a messenger, and not
the right person to stand guard, as Lucilius is. Pindarus has
already been a messenger from Cassius to Brutus. A stage-
direction is required. Confusion between abbreviations of
Lucius and Lucilius might be expected.

READ: *Lucius, do you the like, and let no man*

.   .   .   .   .

> *Lucilius and Titinius guard our door.*
> [Exeunt *Lucius* and *Pindarus* with *soldiers.*
> *Brutus* and *Cassius* enter the tent.*

3.28 Brutus, *baite not me,*

Theobald's popular emendation, *bay* for *bait*, is widely
followed still, because of Brutus' preceding 'bay the moon',
though *New Cambridge* in reading and vindicating *bay*
marks with an obelus. I see no reason for the change,
except to introduce this facile effect of echo. Brutus has
said, 'I had rather be a dog', and it is a natural sequence of
thought for Cassius to see himself as the bull *baited* by the
dog. If the copy read *bay* for *baite* in l. 28, why did the
compositor not make the same implausible misreading in
l. 27?

READ: *bait not me,*

3.181–95 *Had you your Letters from your wife, my Lord?*

.   .   .   .   .   .

> *But yet my Nature could not beare it so.*

Of recent editors, Kittredge and Alexander include
these lines in their text as they occur in Folio. Kittredge,
however, explains that they were deleted in revision, in
favour of an alternative treatment, and that the compositor
ignored marks of deletion. In this view he followed Resch,
as editors generally do now. There is obvious inconsistency
in Brutus informing Cassius at l. 147 that Portia is dead,

and at l. 182 denying any news of her. Attempts to reconcile the two on subtle grounds of character and behaviour are entirely unconvincing. The lines should be relegated to a footnote, as deleted in revision during composition. *New Cambridge* brackets them.

ACT 5

Sc. 4. The action of this scene requires consideration, and editors vary in their treatment of the movements of Brutus, as also of the speaker of ll. 7–8, for which Folio gives no prefix. Kittredge and Alexander follow the general practice, giving ll. 7–8 to Brutus, the obvious solution, where Folio reads as follows:

> Enter Souldiers, and fight.
> *And I am* Brutus, Marcus Brutus, *I,*
> Brutus *my Countries Friend: Know me for* Brutus.

Macmillan in *Arden*, however, attributed these lines to Lucilius, who in Folio speaks ll. 9–11 following, suggesting that the speaker's name was entered two lines late. The scene follows Plutarch closely, in whose account Lucilius personates Brutus in the battle. *New Cambridge* accepts this version, as I do without hesitation. (The want of a speaker's name for ll. 7–8 may perhaps be readily explained. The compositor found *Luc.* as speaker's name for lines beginning, 'And I am Brutus, Marcus Brutus, I', and understandably left a blank and entered the name where it might reasonably appear.) The conduct of the scene is then as follows:

> Brut. *Yet countrymen, o yet hold up your heads.*
> [Exit, fighting, followed by *Messala.*

Cato hears Brutus' words as he goes, and asks 'Who will go with *me*?' (as others have gone with Brutus).

Cato. *What bastard doth not? Who will go with me?*

I am the son of Marcus Cato, ho!
            Enter more *soldiers* fighting.

This stage-direction is from Folio and should not be
omitted, as by *New Cambridge*. Lucilius hears Cato's
challenge, and challenges the new entrants in the name of
Brutus, in a manner very alien to Brutus' character.

Lucil. *And I am Brutus, Marcus Brutus, I;*
Brutus my country's friend. Know me for Brutus!
                            [*Cato* is slain.
O young and noble Cato, are thou down?

The rest of the scene follows as in Folio. The alternative
version requires Brutus to utter a boastful and vociferous
challenge, and to make his exit at l. 8 precisely when Cato
falls slain, and also to delay Lucilius' impersonation of
Brutus until it becomes obvious at l. 14, when Lucilius
says, 'Kill Brutus, and be honoured in his death'. This
seems very lame and improbable.

MACBETH

ACT 1

1.1–2 *When shall we three meet againe?*
         In Thunder, Lightning, or in Raine?[1]

Hanmer omitted the question-mark in l. 1, and editors follow, except Alexander, and Muir in *New Arden*. The division of two parts of a question by an intermediate question-mark is frequent enough in Elizabethan printing. To retain it in l. 1 in a modern text is to make two questions, with the effect of turning l. 2 into a meteorological inquiry. It will hardly be argued that the answer comes in Sc. 3, when the Witches meet again, and the Folio direction is *Thunder* (not Lightning or Rain). Meetings of witches were always associated with elemental disturbances, not any one particular disturbance.

    READ: *When shall we three meet again*
          In thunder, lightning, or in rain?

Sc. 2 *Stage-direction.* a bleeding Captaine.

The eighteenth century reduced the *Captain* to a Sergeant's stripes, and some recent editors follow, e.g. Kittredge and Alexander. True, Malcolm calls him 'the sergeant' (l. 3), but rank and function were not so clearly distinguished in the Scottish Army List for 1605. The dialogue represents a man of gentleman's rank. The prefix to the speeches in Folio is also *Cap.*, and this ought to be decisive.

          [1] Citations are from the basic Folio text.

2.56 *Point against Point, rebellious Arme 'gainst Arme,*

Theobald, followed by many including Alexander, read *point rebellious*, with no reason for changing the Folio punctuation, and with damage to the sense.

READ: as in F.

3.97–8   *as thick as Tale*
        Can post with post,

Rowe's *hail* for *tale* is popular even in recent editions, though rejected by Kittredge and Alexander. The occurrence of 'thick as hail' elsewhere is no argument where the original gives more relevant sense. 'The posts came thronging, with tales thronging, to every tale a post, post after post, and tale after tale.' *Can* is clearly a slip for *Came*. *Tale* is inconceivable as a misreading of *hail*.

READ: *as thick as tale*

5.23ff. *Thould'st haue, great Glamys, that which cryes,...*

The debate here is what the 'cry' should include as a quotation: *New Cambridge* includes 'Thus thou must do, if thou have it', where Alexander and Muir include only 'Thus thou must do.' The debate seems unreal here.

READ: *Thou'dst have, great Glamis,*
       That which cries, thus must thou do—if thou have it;

5.31 *Stage-direction.* **Enter Messenger.**

It seems clear that we should read *Attendant* for *Messenger* here, and as prefix to his speeches. The 'messenger' from Macbeth gave the news to his fellow-servant (l. 36) who is in attendance and enters and speaks here. So Capell pointed out, and *New Cambridge* (if not Alexander and Muir) agrees.

READ: Attendant.

Sc. 6 *Stage-direction.* Hoboyes, and Torches.

New Cambridge omits *torches* as 'absurd' in a 'sunlit' scene. In the previous scene, however, we have 'Duncan comes here *tonight*'. The night is beginning, and it deepens to blackness, as is amply suggested in Sc. 5. There is, moreover, symbolic fitness in the torches. Finally, the Folio direction is specific here, as in Sc. 7, and is not to be dismissed.

READ: Hautboys. Torches.

7.5–6 *Might be the be all, and the end all. Heere,*
        But heere,

New Cambridge and Muir agree upon accepting, in effect, the Folio punctuation, rightly, as I think. 'Here, but here, which is only a shoal in the sea of eternity.' Alexander, however, follows Hanmer in reading *end-all here.* in defiance of Folio.

READ: *end-all—here, But here,...*

7.19 *Will pleade like Angels, Trumpet-tongu'd against*

Most editors inset a hurtful comma after *trumpet-tongued.* The point is that Duncan's virtues speak with a trumpet-tongue on this matter of his murder. His *murder* is condemned with trumpet-tongue. Virtues are not ordinarily *trumpet-tongued.* It is a fine point, but to me essential.

READ: *Angels, trumpet-tongued against*

7.27–8 *Vaulting Ambition, which ore-leapes it selfe,*
        And falles on th'other.   Enter Lady.
        How now? What Newes?

Difficulty is naturally felt with the phrase *falls on th'other*, which seems to require a concluding noun not readily 'understood'. It seems clear that this is an interrupted and incomplete sentence. Lady Macbeth enters as

Macbeth is speaking and he turns to her anxiously. He is, indeed, startled. And so *New Cambridge* and Muir read.

READ: *And falls on th'other—*

7.59 Macb. *If we should faile?*
      Lady. *We faile?*

Lady Macbeth's famous *We fail* has been printed and spoken as *We fail?*; *We fail!*; and *We fail.*, with obvious shades of significance. We may not ignore the Folio punctuation. It rules out the third of these, which is also inconsistent with Lady Macbeth's following words, '*But* screw your courage'. Folio punctuation often uses *?* for *!*, but most frequently where the exclamation is also a question, as in 'How now?' The indication of Folio is therefore for a question-mark. And this incredulity of failure is in character for Lady Macbeth, and in accordance with her continuing words: 'But screw your courage to the sticking-place, And we'll not fail.' The significance is clearly not, 'Well then we fail. But if you act resolutely we will not fail'; but, 'How can we fail? If only you act resolutely we cannot fail.' She is, as Macbeth says, 'undaunted', and had already given reasons why failure should be unthinkable, in her previous speech.

READ: as in F.

ACT 2

2.8   Enter Macbeth.
      Macb. *Who's there? what hoa?*

Attempts have been made to retain the Folio stage-direction. In them, Macbeth enters 'above', speaks this line, and exits, to re-enter below at l. 14. But it is manifest that Lady Macbeth cannot see the speaker and thinks the voice may be that of one of the grooms. The line is clearly spoken 'within', as Steevens read, and most editors follow.

The Folio direction here is simply to indicate Macbeth's entry into the dialogue, so that the prompter is ready for him.

READ: Macb. [within] *Who's there? What ho!*

2.35–6 *Me thought I heard a voyce cry, Sleep no more:*
    Macbeth *does murther Sleepe, the innocent Sleepe,*

Johnson's arrangement of these lines (as of ll. 41–3) is adopted almost universally, as by all recent editors. This includes in the 'cry', *Sleep no more; Macbeth does murder sleep.* (In ll. 41–3, the further report of the 'cry' is made to include the three lines, after 'Still it cried'.) Muir states that the Folio text does not instruct us. But l. 35 ends with a significant colon, which in Folio is frequently equivalent to a full stop, or to a dash. And so I think it was intended, as in Shakespeare's copy. These banshee cries are rather repetitive than extensive in good banshee circles. The 'cry' was, *Sleep no more,* in l. 35 as in l. 41, and what follows is Macbeth's appalled comment, in both cases. In the second instance, be it noted, we have a marked variation in the rest of the alleged 'cry', with *Glamis* for *Macbeth,* and *Cawdor* inserted. But it was entirely natural for Macbeth to vary his comment.

READ: *Methought I heard a voice cry, sleep no more.*
        Macbeth does murder sleep,...
        Still it cried, sleep no more, to all the house.
        Glamis hath murdered sleep,...

2.63 *Making the Greene one, Red.*

The obvious emendation for an editor thinking in a modern idiom instead of an Elizabethan is *making the green, one red,* and so Johnson read, followed by editors and, gratefully, by actors in search of dramatic emphasis. Kittredge interpreted it so. *New Cambridge* reads, *Making the green—one red,* and Muir agrees in a note though not in his reading. The only argument in support of the reading is the statement by Dr Simpson that in Folio punctuation a comma sometimes (Muir says 'often') follows a stressed word. But more often it *precedes* a stressed word, as here. Earlier editors dismissed the comma as a misprint to support this reading. The real trouble is the unfamiliarity to modern ears of *the green one*. There is a series of phrases in the passage, 'Neptune's *ocean*', 'multitudinous *seas*', followed by 'green *one*'. The nouns *ocean* and *seas* have been used, and the indeterminate pronoun for Neptune follows naturally. 'Green Neptune' is a familiar phrase (e.g. in *The Winter's Tale* 4.4.28). Davenant's version cited by Kittredge, 'and turn the green into a red' is neutral in the debate. The passage from *The Two Noble Kinsmen* 5.1.50, similarly cited, is certainly an echo from *Macbeth*. But 'Great Neptune into purple' does not contain the thought of *all* or *totally*, and is in fact a gloss of the undisturbed Folio reading, the more valuable therefore. No contemporary instance has been cited of the use of *one* to mean 'totally' (however familiar it may seem today) and we may not without authority gloss *one red* as meaning *total gules*. The stylistic parallel, with its exaggerated emphasis, is unfortunate to my mind. See Introduction, pp. 28–9. The Folio reading cannot, however, well be retained in a modern text. The absence of a comma or dash after *green* should suffice to ensure the true reading, and so Kittredge, Alexander and Muir in fact read.

READ: *Making the green one red.*

3. 7–8 *Come in time, haue Napkins enow about you, here you'le sweat for't.*

New Cambridge conjectures *time-server* for *time* (but not in the text, which is left with an obelus), and Muir follows in his text. There is no need for this improvement. *Come in time* is merely, and sufficiently, a phrase of welcome and approval. The farmer is a very fitting and proper arrival in hell. As for the napkins, they need no further explanation than that he will sweat in hell and will need all the napkins he can get to wipe himself.

READ: *Come in time! Have napkins*

3.85 *To countenance this horror. Ring the Bell.*
Bell rings. Enter Lady.

There is little real doubt that Theobald was right in reading *Ring the Bell* at the end of Macduff's speech as a stage-direction added by the stage-adapter marginally and more visibly than Shakespeare's direction in the original copy. There are many instances of such duplication in surviving MS. plays. The direction is imperative, as usual. And in Lady Macbeth's ensuing speech Macduff's line *To countenance this horror.* is completed metrically. Among recent editors, however, Kittredge and Alexander read as in Folio.

READ: *To countenance this horror.* [Bell rings.
Enter *Lady Macbeth.*

3.124 Lady. *Helpe me hence, hoa.*

Rowe interpreted Lady Macbeth's faint as only pretended, and so read with the stage-direction 'seeming to faint,' followed by *New Cambridge*, which supports the reading from Stewart's *Croniclis*, though the person concerned there is Donwald, and we do not know that Shakespeare used the book. Alexander and Muir give no stage-direction. Kittredge argues with cogency for the reality of the faint, which seems to me essential to action and character. There is no hint whatever of pretence in the Folio text. And Macbeth was doing very well, and in no need of a diversionary device. Finally, the only way such a difficult stage-effect could be produced and made intelligible to the audience would be by means more fitted to farce than to tragedy.

READ: Lady Macbeth. *Help me hence, ho!*   [Faints.

ACT 3

2.13 *We haue scorch'd the Snake, not kill'd it:*

Theobald's emendation, *scotched* for *scorched*, universally adopted, as recently also by Kittredge and Alexander, has made it almost impossible to restore the Folio reading against proverbial use. The word is, of course, a doublet of *scored*, and it occurs also in *The Comedy of Errors* 5.1.183. It is true that the word *scotch* occurs twice in Shakespeare. There is no evidence that the *scorched* spelling is compositor's spelling here or in *The Comedy of Errors*, any more than the *scotch* spelling elsewhere. On the whole, more would be lost than gained by preferring the less common spelling to the more common here.

READ: *scotched*

2.42 *The shard-borne Beetle,*

The debate is between *shard-born*, i.e. dung-born, and *shard-borne*, i.e. borne on scaly wings; and there is authority for both. The references here to the bat's *flight*, and to the crow *making wing*, are decisive to me, as to *New Cambridge* and Alexander, if not to Muir.

READ: *shard-borne*

4.37 *Stage-direction.* Enter the Ghost of Banquo, and sits in Macbeths place.

The Folio direction is plain, and is certain, at this place. The modern notion that the Ghost is a hallucination of Macbeth, like the earlier dagger, and that in producing the play no Ghost should appear, is bred of ignorance. A contemporary witness to the performance, Forman, records his appearance. And ghosts, as all Elizabethans knew, could decide to appear to one person only, while invisible to others, as is evident in *Hamlet*. So all recent editors agree, though with variation concerning the exact time of entry. It seems clear to me that the Ghost must be 'on' in time for Macbeth's invocation, at ll. 40–1, and not in sequence to his invocation.

READ: as in F.

4.105 *If trembling I inhabit then,*

This has generally been interpreted, as by *New Cambridge*, with *trembling* as the object of *inhabit*, 'if I harbour any tremors'. But *trembling* is surely a participle in agreement with *I*, as in Milton's 'Meanwhile inhabit lax' (*Paradise Lost*, vii. 162) and elsewhere.

4.134–6   *for now I am bent to know*
              By the worst meanes, the worst, for mine owne good,
              All causes shall giue way.

Johnson's reading is followed by recent editors:

> *By the worst means, the worst. For mine own good*
> *All causes shall give way.*

But sense and dramatic effect alike seem to tell against this. Macbeth is about to consult the Witches. By this evil means, he will learn the worst, but it will be for his own good. Johnson's reading destroys this effective antithesis. The whole trend of the speech is that Macbeth is seeking his own advantage by spies and by witchcraft, not that his own advantage will dictate his actions. The monumental phrase, *All causes shall give way*, now becomes fateful and impressive. From now on, 'evil be thou my good'.

READ: *By the worst means the worst, for mine own good.*
      All causes shall give way.

Sc. 5. There is no doubt that this scene is an interpolation, and it should so be marked in a modern edition. As for the action and setting, *New Cambridge* retains the Folio direction, 'Thunder. Enter the three Witches, meeting Hecat.', but in a note interprets this as a use of two traps,

one for the Witches and one for Hecate, on the ground
that thunder indicates the use of traps, which is doubtful.
It seems clear that while the Witches enter in the ordinary
way, Hecate descends from the heavens in a machine ('a
foggy cloud'), and ascends in it at the end of the scene, as
is indeed indicated in the dialogue,

> my little spirit, see,
> Sits in a foggy cloud, and stays for me.

READ: Thunder. Enter three *Witches*. *Hecate* descends.
l. 33. [Music and a song within. *Come away, come away*
&c. *Hecate* ascends.

ACT 4

1.39–43 This is a further passage of interpolated matter,
as all except Flatter agree. The stage-direction at l. 43
requires some expansion to make clear the action.

READ: [Music. The three other *Witches* sing, *Black*
Spirits &c. Exit *Hecate*.

1.97 *Rebellious dead, rise neuer*

Theobald's *Rebellion's head* for *Rebellious dead* has met
with general acceptance, as by Kittredge and Alexander,
but not now by *New Cambridge* (2nd ed. 1951), or by
Muir. I see no need for the emendation, nor is it plausible
graphically. As a reference to Banquo, the original makes
excellent sense, and links up with Macbeth's further
reference to him in ll. 100–3 below. Banquo stuck deep
in Macbeth's mind. And Banquo may rise yet again in
his son, his followers and supporters.

READ: *Rebellious dead,*

1.125–32 This further brief interpolation requires interpretation by a stage-direction. The Folio direction might
suggest that Shakespeare's Witches dance.

132 READ: [Music. The three other *Witches* dance.
All vanish.

2.21–2 *But floate vpon a wilde and violent Sea*
        Each way, and moue.

After many varied conjectural emendations, Aldis
Wright's *none* for *moue*, postulating a minim misprint, is at
least graphically plausible, and has been much followed, as
by recent editors except Muir. But there is no need for
emendation to change the good sense of the original. There
are clear indications of the true sense in Sir Humphrey
Gilbert's account of the seas in the North-West Passage.
There are two distinguishable motions of the sea, the wave
and the current, especially contrary in *a wild and violent
sea*, as indeed every seaman knows. 'we float, tossed by
contrary waves and currents'.

READ: *Each way and move.*

2.83 *Thou ly'st thou shagge-ear'd Villaine.*

Steevens' conjecture, *shag-haired*, has been widely
adopted, as by *New Cambridge* and Muir, though not by
Kittredge or Alexander. Dover Wilson's argument for
graphic plausibility is difficult, and assumes continuous
writing of the hyphened word. But there is no difficulty
in the Folio reading, as Kittredge amply demonstrates in a
note, 'with long hair over his ears like a shag-dog', which
seems perfectly natural as an image in the boy's mouth.

READ: *thou shag-eared villain.*

3.14–15   *I am yong, but something*
        You may discerne of him through me, and wisedome

Theobald's *deserve* for *discerne* seems to have led all
editors into adopting this facile corruption of the original
text and sense. The only defence of the Folio text, Upton's
quoted by Muir, is impossible. ('You may see something
to your advantage by betraying me.') The sense seems plain:
'you may appreciate (*discern*) something of Macbeth's
nature by his treatment of me (*through me*). (He has not

touched *you* yet, but he may—see what he has done to me, and learn wisdom.) The wisdom you may learn (*discern's* second object) may be to sacrifice me, a young victim, to the angry Macbeth, to save yourselves.'

READ: *I am young, but something*
            You may discern of him through me, and wisdom

3.107–8 *By his owne Interdiction stands accust,*
        And do's blaspheme his breed?

New Cambridge, followed by Muir, retains the Folio *accused*, against the *accursed* of F 2, hitherto accepted. Dover Wilson cites Grierson's instance of the use of *accused* in Scottish law, in relation to the 'voluntary interdiction' whereby a person might resign to another control of his estate. It is difficult to set up this piece of specialized Scottish lore, surely unknown to Shakespeare, against the normal and familiar use of *interdiction* in English, an ecclesiastical *curse*, more particularly with the relevant words following, 'And does *blaspheme* his breed'. The *interdiction* of an English King was familiar to English memory and thought. F 2 may not always be ignored.

READ: *accursed,*

ACT 5

3.20–1   *this push*
        Will cheere me euer, or dis-eate me now.

There is every reason for reading *dis-seat*, and none for reading *chair* in order to bring logic into imagery. The similarity of sound in Elizabethan English between *cheer* and *chair* may, of course, have led Shakespeare unconsciously to the image in *dis-seat*, assisted by *this push*. No one now follows the F 2 *disease*.

READ: *dis-seat*

3.44 *Cleanse the stufft bosome, of that perillous stuffe*

I can see no plausibility in any of the numerous emendations proposed for *stufft* or *stuffe*, except *slough* (spelled *sluffe*), nor any need for emendation or for the *New Cambridge* obelus to the line. The words *stuffed* and *stuff*, if not so far apart as *guilt* and *gilt*, are distinct enough to serve for a similar kind of punning use, which is intentional, and effective.

READ: as in F., without the comma.

4.11 *For where there is aduantage to be giuen,*

Among recent editors Kittredge and Alexander retain *given*, but *New Cambridge* (with an obelus) and Muir adopt Johnson's *gone* for *given*. *given* suggests a meaning in *advantage to be given*, though not in the context of the speech. But *gone* is plainly in accordance with the sense of Malcolm's words, and his final line here, 'whose hearts are *absent too*', is decisive for *gone*. *giun* could easily be misread for *gon* or *gonn*, especially with *giuen* in the next line.

READ: *advantage to be gone,*

5.27–8 *Told by an Ideot, full of sound and fury*
Signifying nothing.

Editors have agreed without discussion upon a comma after *fury*. Yet Folio, prodigal of commas in this text, has no comma here. The difference in sense and rhythm is considerable, and the Folio version to my mind is far superior. 'All the sound and fury of our words and passions are vain and empty, and the whole tale is an idiot's tale.'

READ: *Told by an idiot, full of sound and fury*
Signifying nothing.

5.42 *I pull in Resolution,*

Johnson's *pall* for *pull* has been followed by *New Cambridge* alone among recent editors. The original *pull in* has been fully vindicated by Kittredge as an image of reining back a restive horse.

READ: *pull in*

8.34 *Stage-direction.* **Exeunt fighting. Alarums.**
            Enter Fighting, and Macbeth slaine.

I suggest the following direction to meet the needs of the action, while preserving the indication of the Folio direction which is over-ridden by *New Cambridge*:

> Exeunt fighting, alarums, re-enter fighting, and exeunt. *Macbeth* exit falling.

To use the inner stage here, and close it with a curtain so that Macbeth's head could be brought on in the next scene, as proposed by Dover Wilson and Muir, would be an unnecessary strain upon *vraisemblance*, when a familiar device is available to take Macbeth off dying.

HAMLET

DRAMATIS PERSONAE

It is high time that the name *Barnardo* was generally restored (as in *New Cambridge*) in place of the usual *Bernardo*. It seems odd that the occasional *Bernardo* in Q1 should be followed in preference to the authoritative Q2 and Folio, both of which read *Barnardo*.

ACT 1

1.21 Hora. *What, ha's this thing appeard againe to night?*[1]

Both Folio and Q1 give this speech to Marcellus, and among recent editors Kittredge follows. The speech is quite inappropriate to Marcellus, and much is lost by taking its mockery from Horatio, who is 'a scholar', and has spoken of the Ghost as 'fantasy' (l. 23).

1.45 Mar. *Speake to it* Horatio.

Folio reads *Question it*, as does Q1. It might seem clear that the Q2 compositor has been led by 'speak to it Horatio', in l. 42, and 'It would be spoke to', in l. 45. But this is possibly one of the examples of revision by Shakespeare, of which there are undoubted instances in the Folio text. Horatio does in fact *question it*, as befits a 'scholar'. And so recent editors also agree.

    READ: *Question it*

1.93 *as by the same comart,*

Folio reads *Cou'nant*. Recent editors follow Q2 *comart*, glossed as a nonce-word improbably meaning 'joint

[1] Citations are from the Second Quarto, which is agreed to be from Shakespeare's autograph. Where supplemented from Folio, the citations are marked with an asterisk (*).

bargain', for which there is no other authority. The argument that *covenant* is pleonastic, as identical with *article* in l. 94, is erroneous. There are *articles* of agreement, to which *covenants* are attached. The compositor of Q2 seemed to be in rough water here, as evidenced by *desseigne* in the next line. *comart* is a plausible misreading of *counant*, which I believe to have been in the copy.

READ: *covenant*

1.121 *And euen the like precurse of feare euents*

Kittredge and *New Cambridge* read *fierce* for *feare*, after late Quartos. (Folio omits.) There seems no good reason for following this editorial corruption (Q2, *feare*; Q3, *fearce*; Q4, *fierce*). *feare* is an obvious misreading of *feard*, and *feared* gives a perfectly adequate and authorized reading. So Alexander reads.

READ: *feared*

1.117–25 *New Cambridge* reads these lines in the order 121–5 followed by 117–20, to improve the sense. I see no need for this change in the intelligible original text, nor does Kittredge or Alexander.

READ: as in Q.

1.126 *Stage-direction.* It spreads his armes.

New Cambridge and Kittredge follow Rowe in attributing the gesture to Horatio, despite the plain direction in Q. *his* is the normal Elizabethan equivalent of modern *its*. I cannot see much probability of *he* being misread as *yt*. The Ghost does not speak here, and there is the more need of a gesture. The gesture warns Horatio not to approach, and is the reason for his reply, 'I'll cross it, though it blast me'. As for the notion that Horatio *crosses* it by making a cross of himself, this seems improbable. The usual sign of the cross was familiar enough, as was the ordinary sense of *cross it*.

READ: *Ghost* spreads its arms.

2.17 *Now followes that you knowe young* **Fortinbrasse,**

This line is universally read with a stop after *know*, interpreting the line, 'Now follows what you already know; namely that Fortinbras'. But Claudius is instructing his Court, and reporting to them (as to the audience, incidentally), and this is the second main part of the information he supplies. If not, he is wasting nine lines in an already long speech. The sense, supported by the punctuation of Quarto and more plainly still by Folio (*Now followes, that you know young* Fortinbras,), and in accordance with the context, is 'Now the next point is, you must be told that young Fortinbras'. There is no difficulty in this Elizabethan syntax.

READ: *Now follows that you know young Fortinbras*

2.82 *Together with all formes, moodes, chapes of griefe*

The Folio *shewes* for *chapes* is editorial. *chapes* is a misprint for *shapes*. The digraphs *ch* and *sh* are easily confused with a tall *c* or a short *s*.

READ: *shapes*

2.129 *O that this too too sallied flesh would melt,*

The Folio *solid* for *sallied* is almost universally accepted, and rightly. *New Cambridge* reads *sullied*, and it is of course true that such a misprint would be easy to make. F. P. Wilson supports this reading. But *sullied* is artificial and false to the context. Hamlet is thinking of flesh in general as opposed to the spirit, and his own flesh is not here *sullied* in his thoughts. It is solid, substantial ('doth *grossly* close it in', as Lorenzo says in *The Merchant of Venice* 5.1). 'If only we could escape from this flesh of mortality by its own deliquescence (for we may not seek escape by suicide). But it is *too, too solid* for that wish.' Cf. 'solidity and compound mass' (3.4.49 below). The Quarto *sallied* probably derives from *sollid* in the copy.

READ: *solid*

2.198 *In the dead wast and middle of the night*

Folio also reads *waste*. Q1 reads *vast*, and we have the 'vast of night' in *The Tempest* 1.2.327. *v* and *w* are easily confusable. The adjective *dead* seems to me decisive if the authority of Q2 and Folio are questioned, and I see no reason for question.

READ: *waste*

2.229 **Ham.** *Then sawe you not his face.*

Folio reads with a question-mark, as do some recent editors. But Hamlet is stating a deduced fact, as he thinks, the Ghost being armed from top to toe. And it is important to him. But Horatio comments in obvious surprise, 'O yes we did'.

READ: as in Q.

3.21 *The safty and health of this whole state,*

Folio reads *sanctity*, and recent editors compound with Theobald's *sanity*, with what is surely undue insistence on the Ministry of Health in Denmark. It seems to me incredible as a revision by Shakespeare, and it is impossible to reconcile with the copy for Quarto. The *safety* of the state in Elizabethan thought was in the forefront, and dependent upon the Prince. Cf. the *Book of Common Prayer*, 'the safety, honour, and welfare of our Sovereign and her dominions'. Shakespeare went to church. (The argument for *sanity*, itself an unnecessary emendation, appears to be solely metrical.)

READ: *safety*

3.73-4 *And they in Fraunce of the best ranck and station,*
       Or of a most select and generous, chiefe in that:

'Corruption is indisputable', it is universally agreed. An infinity of emendation has been propounded, e.g. *Are* for *Or*, *choice* for *chiefe*, *often* (*ofn*) for *of a*, but the results are all unsatisfactory.

I do not believe that there is corruption. The text as it stands makes good sense, 'They in France who are of the best rank and station, or of a most select and generous (rank and station), being chief in (their gift for dressing as befits them)'. *generous*, of course, means 'of gentle birth', *generosus*. There is some apparent repetition of thought, to which Polonius is addicted if it produces a rounded statesmanlike sentence. But the highest rank is not always held by the most choice or by those with the longest pedigrees, and this was true of Shakespeare's England. There is no difficulty in the absolute construction. I once considered it necessary, on this reading, to emend *a most* to *the most*. I do not now, and it would alter the precise sense.

READ: *And they in France of the best rank and station,*
       Or of a most select and generous, chief in that.

3.108–9 *Or (not to crack the winde of the poore phrase*
         Wrong it thus) you'l tender me a foole.

Folio in desperation read *Roaming* for *Wrong*. *Running* is read in recent editions, and is applied to *the poor phrase*, 'running the phrase too hard'. I am convinced that the parenthesis is wrongly placed, as often, and should be closed after *phrase*. (Folio has no brackets.) Further, that Q 1 here yields the true reading *tendring*, strangely neglected by editors and in textual notes. For this there is some graphic plausibility in the misreading of *tēdring* as *wrong*, in copy with a tall initial stroke in the *w* resembling a *t*. The sense is then, 'Or—not to push the word too far—if you tender yourself less dearly you'll produce a baby for me'. This pursuit of *tender* and *tendering* to the last ditch is in Polonius' right vein. *it* (l. 109) is *yourself* (l. 107).

READ: *Or—not to crack the wind of the poor phrase—*
       Tend'ring it thus you'll tender me a fool.

3.130 *pious bonds*

Theobald's *bawds* for *bonds* has had an unholy attraction for editors. It is contrary to the sense which is obvious and relevant in the original, and it is now happily out of fashion.

READ: *bonds*

4.36–8   *the dram of eale*
                    Doth all the noble substance of a doubt
                    To his owne scandle.

This classical crux has been infinitely discussed. Yet Alexander reads as in Quarto. *New Cambridge* reads *evil* for *eale*, with a comma after *doubt*, and an obelus, but recommends in a note Collier's *often dout* for *of a doubt*, which is much followed, though it gives a sense contrary to the general sense of the speech. The general sense is that the defect of a man is observed and determines his reputation, despite his known good qualities. The emendation argues that the defect corrupts the whole and destroys the good qualities themselves. Mrs Nowottny privately suggests interpreting ll. 37–8 as 'Turns (*doth*) the noble substance all of a doubt, to the greater scandal (of evil).' I am sure that *doth* is thus to be interpreted, and that *evil* (*eule*) was the copy underlying the compositor's *eale*. I cannot accept as plausible the misreading of *often dout* (*ofn*, which I have never seen) as *of a doubt*.

I suggest a simple emendation, the transposition of *of* in l. 37 and *To* in l. 38, which gives admirable sense consonant with the whole of this complex thought. The Quarto reading in each case gives apparently a better immediate sense, *substance to a doubt; Of his own scandal*, and there are many instances of such interference by a compositor (or a reader). 'The modicum of evil in a man affects the reputation of all his noble qualities, creating the suspicion that all share in the scandal of the defect.' *Doth to a doubt* thus means 'subjects to a suspicion'. There is ample

evidence for this use of *do*, and frequently in conjunction
with *to*, surviving in 'do to death'. It is important to realize
that the whole speech is upon *reputation*.

READ: *The dram of evil*
              Doth all the noble substance to a doubt
              Of his own scandal.

4.49 *quietly interr'd*

So Q 1 also reads. Folio reads *enurn'd*, and editors silently
follow. It is possible for *interred* to be misread as *invrned*
(not *inurned*) or vice versa. *inurned*, of course, seemed a
certainty to the eighteenth century, as more 'poetical'. But
urn-burial was not a familiar process in England, and
kings were not *inurned* in sepulchres. The image here
offends, for it demands not only the sepulchre-gates rolling
back, but a further break-out. The bones, Hamlet says,
were *hearsed* (l. 47). Finally, if style is the sole criterion
for emendation of a text with authority and with a good
sense, we should need stronger argument than that Steevens
had a preference. The word *interred* was not too 'low' for
Antony in *Julius Caesar* 3.2.81.

READ: *interred,*

5.33 *That rootes it selfe in ease on* Lethe *wharffe,*

Q 2, Q 1 and Alexander read *roots*; Folio, Kittredge, and
New Cambridge, *rots*. Philologically, a reading *rootes* cannot plausibly be turned into *rots*, a long *o* into a short *o*, and
the words are sharply divided in spelling for that reason.
It is irrelevant that the word *rots* is used in relation to flags
in a stream in *Antony and Cleopatra*. The words *in ease* refer
more readily to *roots* than to *rots*, on the banks of Lethe.

READ: *roots*

5.110 *So Vncle, there you are, now to my word,*

New Cambridge reads *Word*, and I see no necessity to
give the word any esoteric meaning as a motto or watch-

word, other than the message Hamlet has received from the Ghost.

5.132 *I will goe pray.*

So also Q1, but Folio reads *Looke you, Ile goe pray.* followed by editors. It is no doubt another question of preference. Mine is strongly in favour of Quarto. The words are far more effective 'thrown away' than accompanied by the theatrical *Look you.*

ACT 2

2.137 *Or giuen my hart a working mute and dumbe,*

Folio reads *winking*, generally followed. But *New Cambridge* prefers the Quarto *working.* The whole phrase supports *winking*, 'making my heart *blind*, mute and dumb', opposed to 'idle *sight*' in l. 138. *working* is a plausible misprint for *winking*.

READ: *winking,*

2.167 *Stage-direction.* Enter Hamlet.

The earliest texts, Q1, Q2, and Folio alike, are unanimous upon the moment of Hamlet's entry, after Polonius has disclosed his plan to Claudius and Gertrude. Dover Wilson's emendation, giving an entry at l. 159 above, before the disclosure, to enable Hamlet to overhear it, has not met with acceptance by later editors, e.g. Kittredge and Alexander, and I am unable to see that it is either necessary or plausible. There is no question of the entry being postponed to the beginning of Hamlet's speaking, for he does not speak until l. 172. I do not see any reference to the disclosure in his first words, 'Well, God a mercy', in reply to Polonius' inquiry after his health. The words are common form.

READ: as in Q.

2.181–2 *For if the sunne breede maggots in a dead dogge, being a good kissing carrion. Haue you a daughter?*

This speech has afforded great scope for the most varied comment and emendation. Among many suggestions are Warburton's *god* for *good*, followed by most editors, and *New Cambridge*'s *good kissing carrion* in the sense 'carrion that is good for kissing', which Alexander appears to follow. The latter suggestion offers many difficulties, the former none. Dover Wilson's interpretation seems very improbable. Nor is a dead dog particularly good as carrion to be kissed, unless a dead dog were especially good material for experiments in natural history. But a maggotty dead dog was simply a sadly familiar object.

The reading *god* for *good* makes plain and understandable sense, for which there is an infinity of parallel instances in Shakespeare and elsewhere, as Malone amply demonstrates. The *kisses* of the sun, or of the god Titan, breeding maggots or with other functions, are a most familiar image to Elizabethans. There is no difficulty in the emendation on graphic grounds. *god* and *good* are frequently inter-read, and the spelling *godd*, which is frequent enough, makes this the easier.

The speech is cynical enough, especially if followed up in its afterthought, or background in Hamlet's thought. 'As the sun-god kisses carrion, breeding maggots, so a Prince might kiss Ophelia and breed of her.' The phrase *For if* is not indicating the sequel to a previous thought, it is pointing forward to a conclusion, here unspoken. But Hamlet's next words are, 'Haue you a daughter?', and next he speaks of her conceiving if she walk in the sun. The thought is tightly bound together.

READ: *being a god kissing carrion—have you a daughter?*

2.244–77 *Let me question more in particular:...I am most dreadfully attended;*

Q2 omits these lines. With their uncomplimentary references to Denmark, and to *bad dreams* in relation to royalty, they could not have passed the censor, when Q2 was printed in 1604, with Anne of Denmark sharing James' throne, and James haunted by the Gowry conspiracy among other *bad dreams*. We must not think solely in terms of stage-censorship. It may not be reasonably doubted that the lines formed part of the original copy.

2.287 *Any thing but to'th purpose: you were sent for,*

There is much support, e.g. in Kittredge and Alexander, for the Folio reading here,

Why any thing. But to the purpose; you were sent for;

which seems to alter the sense and tone for the worse. Hamlet is not treating Rosencrantz and Guildenstern so seriously. His reply to their question 'What should we say my Lord?' is a rapier-lunge, 'I know you will not give a straight answer'. And so *New Cambridge* reads. The Folio reading is editorial and too obvious. But its *Why* is irresistible as prefixed to the Quarto reading.

READ: *Why, anything but to the purpose. You were sent for,*

2.309–10 *it goes so heauily with my disposition, that this goodly frame*

The omission of the comma after *disposition*, as in many editions, changes the meaning. Folio reads *disposition;. it* is not antecedent to *that this goodly frame...;* it refers to Hamlet's want of his usual mirth and exercise in his preceding words.

READ: as in Q.

2.316–20 *What peece of worke is a man, how noble in reason, how infinit in faculties, in forme and moouing, how expresse and admirable in action, how like an Angell in apprehension, how like a God: the beautie of the world;*

This is an example of the all-importance of punctuation as between the Quarto text and the Folio. The Folio punctuation, mainly because of the prestige of the Folio in the eighteenth century, has predominated in editions, as also in Kittredge and Alexander. *New Cambridge*, however, asserts the Quarto reading, rightly to my mind on grounds both of authority and of sense.

Folio reads : *What a piece of worke is a man! how Noble in Reason? how infinite in faculty? in forme and mouing how expresse and admirable? in Action, how like an Angel? in apprehension, how like a God? the beauty of the world,* The text thus gives a series of brief explosions of thought, and not the slow linked meditations of a philosophic mind. I do not know in what sense man can resemble an angel in his *actions*, though it is plain enough how he may in his *apprehension*. Nor is *apprehension* a specific attribute of God, the omniscient. *how like a god* is the conclusion and climax. To reject the Quarto reading here unconsidered is unconscionable.

READ: *What a piece of work is a man, how noble in reason, how infinite in faculties, in form and moving, how express and admirable in action, how like an angel in apprehension, how like a god—the beauty of the world;*

2.388–9 *Gentlemen you are welcome to* Elsonoure, *your hands come then,*

Folio reads, *your hands, come:* editors generally read, in effect, *Your hands, come then.* But the stage-business is plain. Hamlet offers the intimate gesture of hand-shaking. The young men respectfully hesitate, and Hamlet reassures them. It is a mere fashion.

READ: *Gentlemen, you are welcome to Elsinore. Your hands. Come then,*

2.397 *I knowe a Hauke, from a hand saw.*

There has been much comment, some very far-fetched. I have no doubt that *handsaw* is *hernshaw* (heron). The underlying sense seems clear too, and the comma after *hawk* bears it out. 'I know a hawk', a hunter or enemy, 'and can distinguish him from a heron', his prey. 'You are my enemies and you do not delude me.' It is strange to dismiss this, as Kittredge does, as merely deliberate nonsense in a mad vein.

2.419–21 *Sceneca cannot be too heauy, nor* Plautus *too light for the lawe of writ, and the liberty: these are the only men.*

Quarto and Folio punctuate to the same effect, followed rightly by *New Cambridge*. The eighteenth century, followed also recently by Kittredge and Alexander, made a stop after *light* and read the rest as consecutive, with the whole speech referring to the actors. But does not Polonius' thought move here to the writers and to literary criticism? 'Whether you are writing according to classical rules or in the modern freer manner, Seneca and Plautus are good models; the heavy Seneca and the light Plautus are not too heavy or light for either way. In fact they are the only good models.' Polonius naturally ends with a pontifical pronouncement. *only* here means 'best of all'.

READ: *too light, for the law of writ and the liberty. These are the only men.*

2.616 *And fall a cursing like a very drabbe; a stallyon,*

New Cambridge alone reads as in Quarto, interpreting *stallion* as a male whore. Folio reads *Scullion* and Q1 *scalion*. The misreading of *sc* as *st* is one of the easiest to make. Drabs and scullions were proverbially foul-mouthed; male whores were not familiar enough to Elizabethan thought to be proverbial, and I have met the word in this sense only in literary use.

READ: *A scullion!*

ACT 3

1.1 *by no drift of conference*

Folio reads *circumstance*, and editors follow, until *New Cambridge* and Alexander, who rightly follow Quarto. *Conference* is obviously right. Rosencrantz and Guildenstern have just been 'conferring' with Hamlet to this very end.

READ: *conference,*

1.86 *of great pitch and moment,*

The Folio *pith* for *pitch* has become proverbial from its universal earlier adoption. But recent editors rightly follow Quarto, which gives perfect sense.

READ: *pitch*

1.164 *the honny of his musickt vowes;*

Editors follow the Folio *musicke* and read *music vows*, which I find more difficult than the Quarto *musickt*, as well as unnecessary. The *e* in F was surely a *d* in the copy.

READ: *musicked*

1.166 *Like sweet bells iangled out of time, and harsh,*

Folio reads *tune* for *time*, and editors are divided. I have no doubt that *tune*, easily misread as *time*, is the true reading. The question is not one of rhythm, but of harmony, in Ophelia's speech here.

READ: *jangled, out of tune and harsh;*

1.169 *Stage-direction.* Some copies of Quarto read *Exit.* at the end of Ophelia's speech. This may of course, be a

mere error, corrected in press. But it may suggest that the
ensuing lines, ll. 170–96, were an addition to the copy,
after Shakespeare had originally closed the scene with
Ophelia's exit here. She is certainly required to continue on
stage as the text stands.

2.68–70   *Since my deare soule was mistris of her choice,*
            And could of men distinguish her election,
            S'hath seald thee for herselfe,

  Folio reads *distinguish, her election Hath seal'd,* and this
seems to me to be clearly the true sense, though *New
Cambridge* and Alexander follow Quarto, apparently to
preserve the balance of *mistress of her choice* and *distinguish
her election.* But the true balance is *mistress of her choice* and
her election hath sealed thee.

  READ: *And could of men distinguish, her election*
            Hath sealed thee for herself,

2.94 ff. *Stage-directions.* There has been much discussion
concerning the settings for the Play-scene. Editors except
New Cambridge mostly are content to cite, or to paraphrase,
the Folio directions here. I suggest the following:
  L. 94. READ: [Trumpets and kettle-drums within.
    Ham. *They're coming to the play. I must be idle.*
  Get you a place.
    The state is set to one side. Enter to a Danish march
  Claudius, Gertrude,. . . Guards with torches. Flourish.
  Claudius and *Gertrude* take their place, on their left
  Polonius and *Ophelia; Lords* on the other side.
  L. 145. READ: Trumpets sound. The Dumb Show is
    discovered in the inner stage, and is there acted.
    Enter a King and a Queen very lovingly. . .but in
    the end accepts his love.   [The curtains close.
  Ll. 149–50. READ: Oph. *Belike this show imports the
    argument of the play.*
        Enter *Prologue* through the curtains.

2.176 ff. *Discomfort you my Lord it nothing must.*
For women feare too much, even as they loue,
And womens feare and loue hold quantitie,
Eyther none, in neither ought, or in extremitie,

Folio omits the second of these lines, reads *For* for *And* in the third, and omits *Eyther none* in the fourth. Editors, except *New Cambridge* and Alexander who omit only *Eyther none,* follow Folio. It would seem reasonably certain that Shakespeare improved the passage as he wrote it, deleting *women feare too much euen as they loue, And,* and made a fresh start after *For* with *womens feare . . . quantitie.* A second false start was made with *Eyther none,* which was also deleted, and the line completed as *in neither ought, or in extremitie.* Part of Shakespeare's difficulty was perhaps his inability to complete the distich with a line rhyming with *love.* The second attempt found its rhyme easily, and makes tight sense. The deleted line is obviously unnecessary, and lacks a rhyme. It is, moreover, in sense inconsequent with the rewritten line, as suggesting that women *all* fear and love *too much,* and not *either* too much *or* not at all. It should be relegated, along with *Eyther none,* to a footnote as deleted during composition.

READ: *Discomfort you my lord it nothing must.*
For women's fear and love hold quantity;
In neither ought, or in extremity.

2.262 *So you mistake your husbands.*

Folio reads *mistake Husbands.* Editors mostly follow Q1, *must take,* unnecessarily. *New Cambridge* and Alexander rightly read *mis-take,* which is entirely to the point here.

2.281 Pol. *Lights, lights, lights.*

Folio, in place of *Pol.,* prefixes *All* to this cry for lights, rightly as I think. This seems to me to be an instance of the direct result of the entry of *Hamlet* into rehearsal.

Polonius intervenes at l. 279, 'Give o'er the play'. The King calls for lights. In Shakespeare's first copy Polonius echoes that call. But in rehearsal it appeared to be good 'business' for all to echo that call, and not only Polonius. And so the Folio text records.

READ: All. *Lights, lights, lights.*

2.295 *A very very paiock.*

Recent editors offer *pajock* (Kittredge) and *paiock* (Alexander), while *New Cambridge* reads *peacock*, rightly to my mind. There is no evidence in favour of Dyce's suggestion that *pajock* is a Scots dialect word, or Kittredge's that *pajock* is a variant form of *peacock*. Dover Wilson conjectures a spelling *pacock*, misread as *paiock*. I find the spellings *Paicock* and *Paicocke*, among a variety of spellings of the name *Peacock*, in documents concerning a Yorkshire manor in *H.M.C. Various*, II, p. 66. Either could well be misread as here. The word *peacock* seems entirely appropriate in this context, and in Hamlet's thoughts, with his preceding 'a forest of feathers'.

READ: *A very, very—peacock.*

3.6–7 *Hazerd so neer's as doth hourely grow*
          Out of his browes.

Folio reads *Lunacies* for *browes*, followed by many editors, though Alexander retains the Quarto reading without gloss. The Folio reading appears to be an editorial escape from a difficulty. I arrived at the conjecture *braves* for *browes* as graphically most plausible, and apt in sense, and was confirmed in this by discovering the same suggestion in Dover Wilson's Additional Notes, p. 304, replacing his original emendation, *brawls*. Dover Wilson, however, informs me privately that he has abandoned the suggestion in the light of F. P. Wilson's defence of the original *brows* (*Studies in Retrospect*, 1945, pp. 124–5). I am nevertheless unsatisfied by *brows*, even with F. P. Wilson's defence, which seems forced. *Brows* alone do not imply threats, though 'threatening brows' do. Nor do I see any further difficulty in the Quarto reading, in preference to the editorial corruption of the Folio text here in both lines. The later words of Polonius, 'Tell him his *pranks* have been too broad to bear with' (3.4.2), are a parallel to *braves* here.

The King recognized the Play as a challenge, a *brave*.
READ: *Hazard so near us as doth hourly grow*
     Out of his braves.

3.69–70 *Art more ingaged; helpe Angels make assay,*
     Bowe stubborne knees,

All recent editors read *Help angels! Make assay:* without support from the punctuation of Quarto or Folio, and indeed without good reason. Claudius calls upon the angels to help him to make the attempt. He is a limed, struggling soul and needs angels' help *in the struggle*.
READ: *Help angels make assay.*
    Bow stubborn knees,

4.4 *Ile silence me euen heere,*

The persistence of Hanmer's *sconce* for *silence* is one of the puzzles of textual history, in the face of every conceivable reason for accepting the original reading in Quarto and Folio. No recent editor perpetuates it, though it has not yet vanished from the stage.
READ: *silence*

4.48–51   *heauens face dooes glowe*
    Ore this solidity and compound masse
    With heated visage, as against the doome
    Is thought sick at the act

The Folio reading is manifestly corrupt. *Yea, this solidity...is thought-sick* transfers the disgust from heaven's face to the visage of this *solidity*, i.e. the gross flesh which is the cause of the disgust. Yet editors follow Folio, including *New Cambridge*, with the interpretation of *solidity* as the moon and *thought sick* as in eclipse. The sense is surely, 'the face of heaven glows with shame above the grossness of the world of men, its face hot, as if the judgement day were near, and is thought-sick at the act'. The punctuation needs little alteration. And so Alexander too reads, with some early editors.

> READ: *With heated visage, as against the doom;*
> *Is thought-sick at the act.*

4.161–2 *That monster custome, who all sence doth eate*
       Of habits deuill, is angell yet in this

Editors who, like Alexander, retain the Quarto *devil*, are obliged to punctuate with a comma after *eat*, and interpret as 'custom which eats up all sense', without reference to *sense of habits*. It seems very difficult to justify this as intelligible, or the definition of the monster custom as also the devil of habits. Theobald's emendation, *evil* for *devil*, is graphically plausible, especially in Shakespearian spelling, and gives perfect sense. The compositor may well have been attracted to *devil* by *angel* following. But *monster* is sufficient antithesis to *angel*. 'The monster custom, which takes away all sense of the evil in habit, is yet angel in this way'.

> READ: as in Q., but *evil* for *deuill*.

4.168–70 *For vse almost can change the stamp of nature,*
       And either the deuill, or throwe him out
       With wonderous potency:

It is certain that some word is omitted in l. 169. Editors vary in the word supplied, e.g. *curb* (Alexander), *master* (Kittredge), or Dover Wilson's *exorcise* for *either*. Folio omits the lines. I think we should not seek a word meaning *control* or *oppose* the devil. The alternative is not the feeble dilemma of *partial* or *complete* mastery of the devil as the invariable result of use or custom. Use may habituate men to possession by the devil, or may make it easier to cast him out. *Use* can work both ways in changing nature. If custom dulls the sense of evil habits, it can also (*likewise*) help to resist evil. This sense is much more relevant to the trend of the whole speech and thought. The dilemma of ll. 161–5, in fact, is repeated here, and the words *wondrous potency* point the statement that use *can* have this unexpected effect also. I suggest *house*.

READ: *And either [house] the devil, or throw him out*

The Folio cut in this speech is very awkward, and suggests difficult copy. The *maister* of Q3 of 1611 has no authority.

ACT 4

1.40–1   *And whats vntimely doone,*
          Whose whisper ore the worlds dyameter,

The obvious lacuna in the Quarto text here, to which Folio offers no clue in its cut text, has been supplied by Capell to the satisfaction of all editors.

READ: *And what's untimely done; [so haply slander—]*

2.19 *he keepes them like an apple in the corner of his iaw,*

Folio reads *Ape* for *apple*, and Q1 *as an Ape doth nuts.* The common factor here, together with the obvious imagery of nut-eating (common in the theatres then), is decisive for the Folio reading, as in Kittredge, if not in *New Cambridge.* Alexander keeps both, *like an ape an apple.*

READ: *like an ape*

5.8–10   *doth moue*
          The hearers to collection, they yawne at it,
          And botch the words vp

Alexander reads *yawn*, Kittredge and *New Cambridge aim* as in Folio. Alexander glosses *yawn* as 'gape in surmise', for which no authority is given. It was apparently incomprehensible to contemporaries, to judge by Folio. I suspect the Quarto reader of a correction. If Quarto proof read *they aime*, printed *the yaime*, the correction becomes credible. Certainly the sense demands *aim*. *Collection*, i.e. inference or guessing, is not expressed by *yawning* in any sense.

    READ: *they aim at it,*

7.8 *As by your safetie, greatnes, wisdome, all things els*

Folio omits *greatness*, and editors follow, including apparently Alexander, but not *New Cambridge*. The argument for following Folio is that the line is metrically improved, though l. 9 is equally hypermetrical. But, apart from the authority of Quarto, *greatness* is as necessary an idea here as *safety* or *wisdom*.

    READ: as in Q.

7.22 *Too slightly tymberd for so loued Arm'd,*

Folio reads *so loud a Winde*, and editors rightly follow. Without guidance from Folio, the emendation might well have been reached on graphic grounds.

    READ: *so loud a wind,*

7.93 *Vppon my life* Lamord.

Folio reads *Lamound*, followed by Kittredge. *New Cambridge* and Alexander read *Lamord*. The Folio reading seems to me to point to *Lamond*, a known name (as *Lamord* is not), and easily misread by Quarto as *Lamord*.

    READ: *Lamond.*

7.160–1   *Ile haue prefard him*
           A Challice for the nonce,

Folio reads *prepar'd*, followed by most editors. *New Cambridge* and Alexander read *preferred*, which seems to offer difficulties of sense. The Quarto spelling is also most unlikely as a variant of *preferred*, but entirely credible as a variant of *prepared*, with a foul case *f* for *p*. The sense of *prepared* is obviously preferable, and is supported by the reading of Q1, 'I'le haue a potion *that shall ready stand*'.

READ: *prepared*

7.167 *ascaunt the Brooke*

Folio reads *aslant*, followed by most editors, including Alexander. But *askant* gives equally good, indeed the same, sense, and is read by *New Cambridge*. The same pattern of writing could well produce either reading.

READ: *askant*

7.172 *But our cull-cold maydes*

Folio reads *our cold Maids*, followed by all editors, and rightly. I have no doubt whatever that Shakespeare's copy here made a false start with *culd*, easily misread as *cull*, which was deleted but printed along with the correction *cold*.

7.178 *she chaunted snatches of old laudes,*

Folio and Q1 read *tunes* for *laudes*, followed by most editors. *New Cambridge* and Alexander, however, read *lauds*. There is no evidence of the popularity of *lauds* in England. The picture of Ophelia dying in songs of praise to God is not consistent with what we see in *Hamlet*, or hear from her in 4.5. The very next line describes her as 'incapable of her own distress', i.e. unaware or innocent of her plight. She did *not* 'make a good ending'. *tunes* could well be misread as *lauds*.

READ: *old tunes,*

7.192 *But that this folly drownes it.*

Folio reads *doubts*, and recent editors all read *douts*. The Quarto reading is entirely satisfactory and much more in character for Laertes, who like his father is given to pursuing a conceit to the last tasteless ditch, as here. It is an obvious sequel to 'Too much of water', and 'my tears'.

READ: *drowns it.*

ACT 5

1.109 *this madde knaue*

Folio reads *rude*, rightly followed by editors. The Quarto reading is a plausible misreading of *madd* for *rude*.

1.260 *To sing a Requiem*

The puzzling Folio reading *sing sage Requiem* suggests copy in which *saye* was first written, then deleted and *sing* interlined. The Folio compositor printed both, misreading *saye* as *sage*.

READ: as in Q.

1.321 *An houre of quiet thereby shall we see*

Folio reads *shortly* for *thereby*, rightly followed by editors. Unlikely as it may appear, *shortly* can well be misread as *thereby* in rapid writing.

2.114 *indeede to speake fellingly of him,*

Some copies of the Quarto read *sellingly*, followed by some editors, including *New Cambridge*. Folio omits. *sellingly*, 'as a salesman', is quite out of character for Osric, and is very forced here. The Q4 reading, *feelingly*, is entirely idiomatic, relevant and natural here, and gives the original copy misread easily by the compositor of Q2.

READ: *feelingly*

2.198 *and out of an habit of incounter,*

Folio reads *and outward habite*, followed by most editors, which certainly fits precisely into the train of thought—popular tune, outward fashion, surface tricks. *New Cambridge* follows Quarto, with an interpretation that seems very forced.

READ: *and outward habit*

2.201 *the most prophane and trennowed opinions,*

Folio reads *fond and winnowed* for *prophane and trennowed*, and clearly gives the true reading for *trennowed*, another example of the frequent confusion of *w* and *tr*. But *fond* is as irrelevant as the Quarto *prophane*. The sense requires an adjective to go with *winnowed*, 'choice and well-tested', in opposition to 'shallow'. Kittredge and Alexander, after Warburton, read *fanned*, which is tautological, and difficult to explain as a basis for *prophane* (though not for *fond*). *New Cambridge*, after Tschischwitz, reads *profound*, rightly as I think. The source of the error in Quarto is intelligible if Shakespeare wrote *pfound* or *pfund*, and the compositor read *profane* and spelled it *prophane*; and in Folio if the compositor simply omitted the *p* from similar MS. copy and read *fond*, which gave a kind of sense, and is a pointer to the copy.

READ: *the most profound and winnowed opinions;*

2.234–6 *since no man of ought he leaues, knowes what ist to leaue betimes, let be.*

This passage has offered great difficulty. Some editors follow the obviously editorial version of F1, *since no man ha's ought of what he leaues. What is't to leaue betimes?*, omitting *let be*. Kittredge reads *Since no man knows aught of what he leaves*, and Alexander (after Hanmer) *Since no man owes of aught he leaves*, both desperate conjectures. *New Cambridge* follows Quarto with a variation of punctuation, *Since no man, of aught he leaves, knows what is't to leave betimes, let be.* Dover Wilson's interpretation turns the *is't* of Quarto into *it is*, in effect, and presents other difficulties. I suggest the following reading, which makes good sense of the Quarto text:

> *Since no man of aught he leaves knows, what is't to leave betimes? Let be.*

'Since no man knows about (*of*) anything he is leaving, what does it matter if he leaves early? Let fate take its course.'

2.298 *Hee's fat and scant of breath.*

Steevens has a charming note upon *fat*. John Lowin, he suggests, was the original Falstaff, and his corpulence is again referred to here when playing Hamlet. *fat* ('corpulent') is now happily abandoned. Dover Wilson glosses as 'sweaty', Alexander as 'hot', and Kittredge, correctly, as 'out of condition', 'out of training.' The debate may perhaps be helped by the precise phrasing of evidence given in Chancery in 1578 (C 24/130/Nicholas v Nicholas): the black nag, 'but new taken vpp from gresse (grass)...is fatt and ffoggy', and therefore should not be put to hard work at once. 'fat and foggy' clearly has the sense of 'out of training and *scant of breath*'.

2.355 *O god* Horatio,

Folio, followed by many editors, reads *Oh good Horatio*. But the Folio reading is only one of many instances of the purging of profanity under the orders of the Master of the Revels. Malone rightly followed Q2, as *New Cambridge* and Alexander agree.

READ: *O God, Horatio,*

KING LEAR

ACT 1

1.85 *Although our last and least; to whose yong loue,*[1]

Q1 reads *Although the last, not least in our deere loue,*
with some irrelevance to the trend of the speech. The
reading has attracted many editors with its somewhat
sentimental appeal, though not Duthie, Alexander and
Muir. *last and least* is quite sufficiently opposed to *our
joy*, and emendation is unnecessary. Cordelia is plainly
conceived as of smaller stature than Regan and Goneril.

READ: *our last and least,*

1.151 *reserue thy state,*

Only Kittredge among recent editors adopts the Quarto
reading *reverse thy doom.* Kent's first concern is for Lear's
royalty and honour, imperilled by this *rashness* (l. 153).
His second is Lear's injustice to Cordelia, expressed in the
following sentence (ll. 153–6), to which *reverse thy doom*
might be appropriate, but not to the first.

READ: *Reserve thy state,*

1.158–9   *nere feare to loose it,*
         Thy safety being motiue.

Editors, including recent editors, follow Quarto in
reading *nor fear to lose it.* But the Folio reading is one more
example of the frequent *e : d* misprint, and should stand with
the obvious emendation *feared* (*feard*) for *fear* (*feare*),
which gives a sense far superior to that of the Quarto
reading.

READ: *ne'er feared*

[1] Citations are from the basic Folio text, except occasionally for lacunae in
Folio, when the text of the 1608 Quarto is cited, marked with an asterisk (*).

1.284 *Who couers faults, at last with shame derides:*

There is no need to emend the Folio text in any of the various ways proposed, e.g. the Quarto *shame them* for *with shame.* Alexander and Muir agree. 'Time' is the antecedent to *Who*: 'Time at first covers faults, but at last (unfolds them and) derides them with shame.'

READ: as in F.

2.20–1   Edmond *the base*
      Shall to' th' Legitimate:

Editors unanimously adopt Edwards' emendation, *top* for *to*, against the equally unanimous authority of all early texts in favour of *to*, or emend otherwise. But *the base shall to the legitimate* offers no difficulty. The base shall turn into the legitimate, shall usurp legitimacy, and so succeed to Edgar's land and position. There is ample authority for this use of *to*. *to* or *too*, as a misreading of *top*, is highly implausible.

READ: *Edmund the base*
      Shall to th' legitimate.

4.125 *when the Lady Brach may stand by' th' fire*

Many editors, including Alexander, follow Quarto *Ladie oth'e brach* in the variation *Lady the Brach.* *Lady the Brach* suggests *Lady* as the name of a bitch. Others rightly follow the Folio reading, which offers no difficulty, and is far more effective and relevant here. If we paraphrased it in a more modern idiom, *My Lady Brach*, the significance would be more obvious, with its plain hint at Goneril or Regan, braches of noble rank, and sycophantic.

READ: *the Lady Brach*

4.366 *Your are much more at task for want of wisedome,*

The variant Quarto readings *alapt*, and *attaskt*, the former readily misread for *ataxt* as Greg indicated, support each other, *tax* and *task* being practically interchangeable. The Folio reading is supported by Johnson and Kittredge on the ground that 'are taken to task' is equivalent to *are at task*. But the latter phrase has no authority in usage. Greg, Duthie and Alexander read *ataxt*, Muir *attax'd*, readings which confirmed my own independent conclusion from *alapt*.

    READ: *ataxed*

ACT 2

1.54 *latch'd mine arme;*

    Quarto, followed by most editors, reads *lancht*, i.e. 'pierced'. But the word *latch* can mean 'catch' in both modern senses, and offers no difficulty here as meaning 'struck'. And so Alexander and Duthie read, though Kittredge and Muir prefer the Quarto *lanched*.

    READ: *latched*

1.78–9 *Were very pregnant and potentiall spirits*
       To make thee seeke it.

    The Quarto reading *spurs*, for *spirits*, has attracted editors, e.g. Kittredge and Alexander, though not Muir, on the ground of sense, as 'incentives' to murder. But the sense and language of the whole speech points to *spirits*, with *pregnant* and *potential* as adjectives closely fitted to such evil spirits, incitements, or impulses, as move him, and referring back to *damned practice* in l. 75.

    READ: *spirits*

1.79 *O strange and fastned Villaine,*

    Editors, except Duthie and Muir, read with Quarto *strong* for *strange*. But *strong* is almost a synonym for *fastened*. And *strange* not only adds more to the sense; it is highly relevant here, when Edmund has been insisting on Edgar's '*unnatural* purpose' (l. 52), and Gloucester now contrasts Edgar with the '*natural* boy' Edmund (l. 86). If further argument were needed for the inclusion of the Quarto words in l. 80 (in place of the Folio *said he?*), *I neuer got him*, it is that they are a close sequel to the thought of *strange*, 'unnatural'.

READ: *strange*

2.65 *though they had bin but two yeares oth'trade.*

Quarto reads *houres* for *yeares*, and most editors follow, until recently. *hours* is surely ludicrous, in days when learning a trade was a serious matter and mastery gained after a seven years' apprenticeship. After two years one would still be a botcher in a world of craftsmen.

READ: *years*

2.119–20 *though I should win your displeasure to entreat me too't.*

The phrase has presented difficulty and doubts, e.g. in Muir, though hardly any emendations have been offered. Surely the sense is, 'even though I should win your displeasure if you entreated me to it, i.e. to be your flatterer—(for I wouldn't do it)'.

2.125 *When he compact, and flattering his displeasure*

Quarto reads *coniunct* for *compact*, followed by many editors. But *compact* gives far better sense, 'joined in a pact', 'in collusion with the King'. The Quarto reading might well be a misreading of *compact* as *conjunct*, printed *coniunct*.

READ: *compact,*

2.146–80 *Stage-directions.* I suggest that the conduct of this scene, as of Sc. 3 and Sc. 4 following, is best met if the stocks are not brought on and off, which offers difficulties, but if the stocks are set in the inner stage, to be discovered, closed off, discovered again, and finally closed off, as required in this and following scenes. This is not incompatible with the indications in the dialogue, the stocks being 'fetched forth' (ll. 132, 140) into the curtained inner stage. The Quarto text shows more clearly that Cornwall is shouting (to servants 'within').

L. 146 READ: [Stocks discovered in the inner stage.
L. 180 READ: [Sleeps. Curtains drawn.
Sc. 4 READ: *Kent* discovered in the stocks.

2.168–9 *Thou out of Heauens benediction com'st*
To the warme Sun.

The sense of this much-discussed passage is perhaps simple enough—'thou comest out of divine blessings into the ordinary chances of mortal life', an interpretation supported by 'under globe' in l. 170. There is no need to emend.

2.172–7   *Nothing almost sees miracles*
But miserie. I know 'tis from Cordelia,
Who hath most fortunately beene inform'd
Of my obscured course. And shall finde time
From this enormous State, seeking to giue
Losses their remedies.

This passage has offered great difficulty, and Greg roundly states, 'Nobody knows what lines 172–7 mean.' It is printed, however, as it stands in most editions, with an indication of Kent reading from a letter (but not so in Muir) the words, *And shall. . .remedies*, and rightly. The sense is, in fact, plain, as Mrs Nowottny confirmed privately and independently, with some minor variation. 'Miracles are hardly ever experienced save by the wretched. I know this letter is from Cordelia. She has by a stroke of fortune (a miracle) been informed of my attending the King in disguise. And (here she says in her letter that she) will find an opportunity for her intention to redress injuries, being out of this monstrous and corrupt State of Britain (where no one can do anything).' *From* means 'away from, out of'; *enormous* means 'full of enormities, monstrous', both in frequent senses of the word, the former indeed being still in common use, e.g. 'from home.'

READ: *Nothing almost sees miracles*
          But misery. I know 'tis from Cordelia,
          Who hath most fortunately been informed
          Of my obscured course—[reads] and shall find time
          From this enormous state, seeking to give
          Losses their remedies.—

4.103 *Would with his Daughter speake, commands, tends, seruice,*

Quarto reads, *commands her seruice* (edited from its earlier state, *come and tends seruise*), to the satisfaction of editors, including Kittredge, and Alexander (who reads *their* for *her* to include Cornwall as well as Regan. But surely Lear is still hopeful of Regan, turning to her from Goneril. And this is a pathetic note. Lear commands her service, being her King and father, and tenders his own courtesy to a Duchess, King though he be. He is the 'dear father' to his daughter (l. 102). The speech begins in tight control, though it ends in fury. This reading was indeed suggested by Greg in his *Variants* (with full support for this sense of *tends*) though without conviction, and for him it remains a crux. The earlier state of the Quarto reading bears out the Folio reading clearly, *come and* being an easy misreading of *command*. The later state is equally clearly editorial. *Tend* in the sense of 'attend, await' is weak and pleonastic after *commands*, and is unacceptable.

READ: *Would with his daughter speak, commands—tends—service.*

4.140–2   *I haue hope*
           You lesse know how to value her desert,
           Then she to scant her dutie.

Johnson and Greg argue that this passage states the
opposite of what is intended, and many agree. But the
meaning seems to me clear and relevant. 'I hope you will
find that you are more mistaken in your estimate of her
merit than she is deficient in her duty', i.e. you misjudge
Goneril. The construction is, 'You less know how to value
her desert than she (*little* knows how) to scant her duty.'

4.170–2 *To fall, and blister.*
              Reg. *O the blest Gods!*
           So will you wish on me, when the rash moode is on.
Quarto reads: *To fall and blast her pride.*
  Reg. *O the blest Gods, so will you wish on me,*
When the rash mood—
Editors select composite readings from Folio and Quarto,
with a preference (as in Kittredge and Alexander) for the
Quarto *and blast her pride.* I feel sure that *blister* is part
of the original copy, as does Muir. Lear is calling down
curses on Goneril's body, her *beauty* (l. 168), not her *pride*.
Sun-drawn fogs do not infect *pride*, but can strike her
young bones and blister her skin, as lightning could blind
her eyes. The Folio *when the rash mood is on*, on the other
hand, seems weak as well as unmetrical, and Lear is plainly
impetuous and breaks in upon Regan. The following
conflation of two imperfect texts is suggested:
  READ: *To fall and blister her.*
              Reg.   *O the blessed gods,*
           So will you wish on me when the rash mood—

ACT 3

4.130 Kent. *How fares your Grace?*

Editors follow Folio and Quarto in attributing this speech to Kent, and the question does not appear to have been raised. I am convinced, however, that the speaker is Gloucester. Gloucester has just entered, and knows that Lear is there. This speech links up with, 'What, hath your Grace no better company?' (l. 147). There is no reason why Kent at this moment should suddenly make this inquiry, but every reason why Gloucester should. Lear hears the strange voice (Kent's is familiar) and asks 'What's he?' Gloucester now hears voices, Lear's and Kent's, and naturally asks 'What are you there? Your names?' (l. 133). Finally, Gloucester's 'your Grace' seems to be clearly distinguished from Kent's 'my good lord' as a mode of address to Lear.

READ: Glou. *How fares your Grace?*

7.3–23 Stage-direction. Editors insert a stage-direction at l. 3, *Exeunt some servants*. But Cornwall is as yet only laying out his plans. At ll. 22–3 he gives his order, and a stage-direction is necessary, *Exeunt servants*. There is no need to despatch *two* expeditions in search of Gloucester, who is in the castle.

7.45–6   *To whose hands*
                    You haue sent the Lunaticke King:

Many editors read *Have you sent*, as a question. But obviously the Folio, Quarto reading is right. 'To *whose*' is in reference to *traitors* in the preceding line. The emendation is corruption.

7.63 that sterne time,

Quarto reads *dearne* for *sterne*, followed by Alexander and Muir on aesthetic grounds apparently, and with

support from use of the word in *Pericles*. Greg suggests
'sophistication' in the Folio text. I suggest, somewhat
timidly, revision in the course of rehearsal or for purposes
of euphony, as in l. 58. There Quarto reads 'In his
annoynted fle*sh* ra*sh* bori*sh* phangs', which is disastrous to
speak, and is made easier in the Folio by changing *rash* to
stick. So here 'hear*d* *that* *d*earne *t*ime' slips over more
easily with *stern* for *dearne*. In sense there is nothing to
choose.

READ: *stern*

7.64–5   *turne the Key:*
                 All Cruels else subscribe: but I shall see

Quarto reads *key, All cruels else subscrib'd but I shall see*,
increasing the difficulty felt strongly by editors. I do not
feel any difficulty in the Folio reading. *Cruels*, of course,
means 'cruel things, cruelties'. The difficulty felt is partly
in seeking too close a link with *wolves*. After the fancy
about the wolves, Gloucester starts afresh. The Folio colon
is a period. 'Humanity might have urged giving shelter
even to wolves on such a night (but *you* would not). You
will go on agreeing to all other cruelties (to Lear)—yet I
shall see vengeance for this strike such children.'

READ: *turn the key.*
         All cruels else subscribe—but I shall see

ACT 4

1.1–4 *Yet better thus, and knowne to be contemn'd,*
        Then still contemn'd and flatter'd, to be worst:
        The lowest, and most deiected thing of Fortune,
        Stands still in esperance,

Quarto agrees in punctuation, on the whole, and Muir
follows. Pope's full stop after *flattered*, however, is more

generally approved, rightly as I think, as giving far superior sense, where the Folio reading gives very doubtful sense. And so Kittredge and Alexander read. 'It is better to be openly contemned than to be secretly contemned and openly flattered. When things are at their very worst, in the lowest ebb of fortune, there remains hope, and fear is absent. Any change from the worst is for the better.'

READ: *Than still contemned and flattered. To be worst,*

1.10 *But who comes heere? My Father poorely led?*

This is a major crux. But I am inclined to believe that no difficulty would have been felt but for the perplexities of the Quarto readings, *poorlie, leed* (uncorrected); *parti, eyd,* (corrected). The reading of the uncorrected Quarto can readily be reconciled with that of Folio, for *ledd* could easily be read *leed. parti, eyd,* of course, suggests some bearing upon Gloucester's loss of his eyes, but I am convinced that it is a will-o'-the-wisp, and not, as Greg maintains, 'an emendation gone wrong' and concealing a true reading other than that of Folio. After many experiments with the possible patterns of writing, e.g. with *purblind* in mind among many, the only plausible confusion led back to *poorly led,* and to copy in which the corrector misread *porely* (or *porly*) *ledd* as *parti, eied,* the *y* read as *i* plus the usual straight comma.

The Folio reading seems to me entirely satisfactory. It is natural, for this is what Edgar would first observe. He would not see Gloucester's eyes at first, and his subsequent words refer to the effects of age. He learns that Gloucester is blind at l. 26 (or l. 20?). The phrase and the situation hark back to Lear's condition in 3.4.147, when Gloucester comments, in Edgar's hearing, 'What, hath your Grace *no better company?*'. Now Gloucester is in the same condition, poorly accompanied and led.

READ: *My father, poorly led?*

2.17 *I must change names at home,*

Quarto reads *armes* for *names*, and recent editors follow, seeking to link *arms* with *distaff* as insignia. But *names* gives at least as good sense, 'change the name of a woman for that of a man', and is far more natural in the context.

READ: *names*

2.55–7 **Wher's thy drum? France spreds his banners in our noyseles land,*
With plumed helme, thy state begins thereat

Folio omits. The uncorrected Quarto reads *thy slayer begin threats*. Editors mostly accept Jennens' emendation, *thy state begins to threat*, though Greg conjectures *his state begins therat*. It might seem evident that the compositor had very difficult copy here. If we assume the omission of *to*, and read *threat* for *thereat* from the uncorrected Quarto, both reasonable, the lines offer no difficulty, with a full stop after *helm*. 'Thy state begins to threaten with plumed helm' will not serve (as in editors' readings), for Goneril's complaint is precisely the opposite, that Albany is *not* fighting. *Our* land is 'noiseless', *our* drums are silent. The *plumed helm* is that of France. *Thy state begins to threat* means 'thy state begins to be in jeopardy,' 'to be threatening' in that sense. (Miss Husbands suggests that the phrase simply means, '(France) begins to threaten thy state'.)

READ: *Where's thy drum?*
France spreads his banners in our noiseless land
With plumed helm. Thy state begins to threat,

3.31–3 *   *there she shooke,*
The holy water from her heauenly eyes,
And clamour moystened her, then away she started,

The Quarto *her* in l. 33 is certainly hypermetrical, and denies sense to a passage which becomes clear with its deletion. It was surely caught up from l. 32, or even

inserted to give some crazy sense to l. 33 by itself. The
sense is apparent with a change into a more familiar order of
words, 'from her heavenly and clamour-moistened eyes'.
But the original order is common enough in such highly-
wrought poetic language as that of the Gentleman here.
The *clamour* of Cordelia's grief is described by him fully
in the preceding lines.

READ: *And clamour-moistened; then away she started*

6.80 *Stage-direction.* Enter Lear.

Quarto reads *Enter Lear mad.* The accepted direction
in editions is taken from Theobald, generally in the form
Enter Lear, fantastically dressed with weeds, and Lear
appears on the stage bare-headed but with garlands of
weeds as a head-dress. The reference is, of course, to
4.4.3–6, 'Crowned with rank fumiter' etc.

It is, however, much too readily accepted that Lear
'runs unbonneted' throughout this Act, and not only in
the storm-scenes. The point at issue has been fully discussed above in the Introduction, pp. 31–3.

READ: Enter *Lear*, his hat bedecked with weeds and
flowers.

6.161–3 *And the Creature run from the Cur: there thou
might'st behold the great image of Authoritie, a Dogg's obey'd
in Office.*

Editors read without question, *run from the cur? There.*
It does not seem necessary for Lear to pursue his question,
to which Gloucester has answered, 'Ay sir'. There is no
question-mark here in Folio, though they are numerous
on this page, and Quarto reads *cur,.* Lear is drawing
conclusions here from what Gloucester agrees he has seen.
And, of course, frequently has the sense of *if*, and is con-
veniently represented by *an.* '(You have seen a farmer's
dog bark at a beggar; well) if the human being run from

the cur, there you might well think you see the image of authority—for a dog in office is obeyed.'

READ: *An the creature run from the cur, there thou mightst behold*

6.184 *I will preach to thee: Marke.*
6.187–9   *This a good blocke:*
        It were a delicate stratagem to shoo
        A Troope of Horse with Felt:

Ingenuity has run wild in the attempt to keep Lear hatless here. *block* has been interpreted as a mounting-block, and a tree-stump introduced as a stage-property to that end. Booth, seeing a hat to be necessary, made Lear borrow a hat in order to comment thus upon it. But the sequence of word and action is close and logical. Lear is about to preach. 'Every man praying, or prophesying', says St Paul, 'having his head covered, dishonoureth his head' (*1 Cor.* xi. 4). The custom indeed survives, though the Puritans rejected it, as did Cranmer (*Confutation of Unwritten Verities, 1582*). Lear therefore takes off his hat, looks at it, and his mind wanders from the preaching he has barely begun in consideration of the block and of the material, felt, into a crazed logic of strategy for revenge.

READ: L. 184 [Lear takes off his hat.

Sc. 7 *Stage-directions.* The scene is 'Before a tent in the French camp', the tent being the inner stage. The indications are all contrary to the Folio stage-direction at l. 20 (not in Quarto), 'Enter Lear in a chaire carried by Seruants', though Kittredge and Muir retain it. This may have been an additional direction inserted upon performance on a stage without a 'study'. And so Alexander appears to conceive the matter.

READ: L. 25 [Music. *Doctor* draws curtains. *Lear* discovered on a couch.

7.31-2   *Was this a face*
To be oppos'd against the iarring windes?

Quarto reads *warring*, and it may well be that *iarring* was a misreading of the copy for *warring*. Shakespeare uses an *a* with a preliminary ascender. And so editors read.

READ: *warring*

ACT 5

3.81 **Reg.** *Let the Drum strike, and proue my title thine.*

Quarto attributes the speech to *Bast.* (Edmund) and reads *proue my title good.* Most editors follow Folio, with every good reason. For one, Regan has a *title*, Edmund none. The Quarto reading suggests editorial incomprehension.

READ: as in F.

3.108-18 Editors have conflated Folio with Quarto here, unnecessarily as I see it. At l. 108 where Folio reads *And read out this*, Quarto adds, *Cap. Sound trumpet?*, which I take to be a stage-direction, eked out in error with a speaker. Folio here has the stage-direction, *A Tumpet sounds*, confirming this view. Again, at the end of the Herald's speech, where Folio gives the direction *1 Trumpet.*, Quarto inserts the speech, *Bast. Sound?* followed after a long space in the line by *Againe?* It is reasonably clear that *Bast. Sound?* is again a stage-direction, *Sound*, with a prefix, though Kittredge includes it; Muir attributes it to the Herald, and Alexander makes the Herald say *Sound, trumpet.* For this there seems to be no need, nor reason to depart from Folio. The signal for the trumpet's first sounding is the end of the Herald's challenge, and possibly a gesture. But he must notify the second and the third sounding with *Again*, and *Again*. (Certainly for Edmund to give the order for the trumpet would be unthinkable to

Shakespeare or his audience, as against all laws of chivalry. Quarto is very untrustworthy here.)

READ: *And read out this.*   [A trumpet sounds.

      Her. [reads]. If any man of quality...bold in his defence.   [First trumpet.

      Her. *Again!*   [Second trumpet.

      Again!   [Third trumpet.

            [Trumpet answers within.

3.251 **Edg.** *Hast thee for thy life.*

Quarto reads *Duke* (Albany) for Edgar. It may seem clear that Albany is the speaker, having already, in l. 247, bidden Edgar 'Run, run, o run', and that Edgar exits here. And so Kittredge and Alexander read. Muir reads as in Folio, with an exit for an Officer. But this was no task for an Officer, and Edgar shows that it was he whom Albany ordered to 'run'. He re-enters with Lear and Cordelia at l. 256.

READ: Alb. *Haste thee for thy life.*   [Exit *Edgar.*

OTHELLO

The names of the characters in this play merit curious attention. As is known, Shakespeare's source contained one name only, that of Desdemona, in the form *Disdemona*. Othello was Il Moro. There is no known original for this name in Italian history or fiction, though sources have been invented in later fiction. Othello was a Moor, but a Christian, and a servant of the Republic of Venice. The usual, well-known, names of Moors in contemporary history or on the contemporary stage would not serve here, e.g. Abd-el-Melec or Muly Mahamet or the like. Othello is a sworn enemy to the 'malignant and turbaned' Turks who were a menace to Venice and to Christian Europe. A Musulman name would be inappropriate. Othello, finally, is descended from 'men of royal siege'.

I suggest that he is, by name, descended from two Roman emperors. Shakespeare knew his North's *Plutarch* well, and was much engaged with the book before and after writing *Othello*. In it, he would find the name of the emperor Otho, and near it, on the same page, that of his successor Vitellius. The union of these two names, with an Italian termination, gave Shakespeare a name of Roman dignity and exotic colour, *Othello* (not unlike the Italian name Ottilio). He too was an emperor among men, and an *imperator*, a general.

The name *Iago*, the Spanish form of James, is odd for a Florentine and a villain, and one might wonder what King James thought of it. His pro-Spanish policy was, of course, highly unpopular. But Spaniards were noted for pride and cruelty, where Italians were noted for dissimulation. They were, moreover, the hereditary enemies of the Moors, and were at this time engaged in a cruel and ruthless expulsion of the Moors from Spain, as was well known to English seamen engaged in the transport of exiled Moors to North Africa. This might well be in Shakespeare's mind. In *Cymbeline* a similar character, *Iachimo*, bears the Italian form of James, *Giacomo*. *Cassio* seems at a far remove from Shakespeare's earlier *Cassius*.

ACT 1

1.21 (*A Fellow almost damn'd in a faire Wife*)[1]

An amazing amount of conjecture has been attracted, from Hanmer to Greg, to what seems a clear and intelligible line, supported by the Quarto reading. The Quarto spelling *dambd* recurs in 4.1.192, in the undoubted sense of *damned*, and should not encourage emendation. The trouble seems to be that Cassio is not, in fact, married. But the word *almost*, taken to refer only to *damned*, refers to *damned in a fair wife*, i.e. 'practically married and damned therefore'. Iago's words in 4.1.126, '*the cry goes* that you marry her', are significant. (The 'cry' begins in Sc. 1.) So are Cassio's words there, 'She is persuaded I will marry her'.

Iago is alleging reasons against Cassio's promotion, as a theoretical soldier only. And incidentally he is given to women, practically married and likely therefore to be uxorious and distracted from soldierly virtue. It is a point to make. In 3.4.195, Cassio tells Bianca he has no wish to have Othello 'see me womaned'. And Othello himself feels it necessary to promise that Desdemona's presence in Cyprus will not be allowed to interfere with his duty as a general. Finally, Iago is speaking, and we need not assume that he is speaking literal truth, nor need we be too much concerned with time-tables. There is no indication that Cassio had *not* been to Cyprus before, or Bianca to

---

[1] Citations are from the basic text of the First Folio.

Venice. Iago slips in this slur upon Cassio, as the Folio brackets indicate, in the middle of his attack. Recent editors follow the Folio reading, though with misgivings about its meaning and about Bianca.

READ: *A fellow almost damned in a fair wife,*

1.25 *the Tongued Consuls*

Quarto reads *toged*, and is certainly right. The Folio compositor read *toged* as *tŏged*, i.e. *tonged*. The contrast is between soldier-arms and consul-toga. 'Mere prattle' (l. 26) should not tempt us to *tongued*.

READ: *toged*

1.65 *For Dawes to pecke at; I am not what I am.*

Editors read with a full stop after *at*, thus breaking the sequence of thought from preceding lines. '*When* I appear outwardly what I am inwardly, so that I come to wear my heart upon my sleeve, why—*then* I am not what I am (a dissimulator).' There is nothing enigmatic in this famous phrase. Quarto has a comma after *at*.

READ: *For daws to peck at; I am not what I am.*

1.119 *You are a Senator.*

Editors import explosive irony into Iago's reply to Brabantio's 'you are a villain', and read *You are—a senator!*, which seems to me sophisticated and pointless. *You are a senator* is a sufficient reply. 'You are a man in high place, and it is our duty to tell you. (Why call me a villain, when I am doing the right thing?)'

READ: *You are a senator.*

2.23 *May speake (vnbonnetted)*

There is no need to emend. *unbonneted* simply means 'though with due modesty' (though Alexander and others interpret in the opposite sense).

3.44 Marcus Luccicos

Alexander, following attempts to rationalize this name as Italian, adopts Capell's *Lucchese* for *Luccicos*, i.e. 'Marcus from Lucca'. But Cyprus had a Greek and not an Italian population, and a Greek form of name is quite appropriate here. No process of misreading copy could turn *Lucchese* or *Luccese* into the *Luccicos* of Folio and Quarto. If the name *must* be rationalized, in the absence of any other source for it, I make the brazen suggestion that Shakespeare simply turned *Mark* and *Luke* into some sort of Greek form as *Marcus Luccicos*, not without amusement.

READ: *Marcus Luccicos,*

3.235 *This present Warres*

Alexander retains the Folio *This*, supported by Quarto. Most editors read *These*, rightly I think. *thes* (for *these*) is easily misread as *this*, and the phrase *this present* is familiarly misleading. The sense points clearly to *These*.

READ: *These present wars*

3.258 *The Rites for why I loue him,*

Alexander retains *why*, against the Quarto *which*, in what seems to me an excess of purism. It is a common thing in MS. copy to use *wh* for *why* or for *which* indiscriminately.

READ: *for which*

3.264–5 *Nor to comply with heat the yong affects*
In my defunct, and proper satisfaction.

Quarto also reads *In my defunct*, and attempts have been made to justify the original text, with *defunct* in the sense of 'deferred, laid aside' as in Hart (*Arden*). Mrs Nowottny in support suggests privately that *young affects* means 'passion new-born (for Desdemona)'. Upton's emendation, *me* for *my*, is generally accepted, as by Kittredge,

Alexander, and Walker, inevitably to my mind, unless insuperable difficulties of sense are to be ignored. The words do not mean that sexual passion is extinct in Othello, but that he is beyond the uncontrollable form it takes in youth (*the young affects*, in close relation to *heat*).

READ: *Nor to comply with heat—the young affects*
        In me defunct—and proper satisfaction;

3.356-9 *She must change for youth: when she is sated with his body she will find the errors of her choice. Therefore, put Money in thy purse.*

Quarto omits *She must change for youth*, and inserts after *choice, shee must haue change, shee must,* and most editors follow. With Alexander, I find the Folio reading incomparably better. The Quarto reading seems to me a typical improvisation, and the repetition of *she must* a false note in this tight close-lipped speech.

READ: as in F.

3.384ff. Iago. *Go too, farewell. Do you heare* Rodorigo?
          Rod. *Ile sell all my Land.*   Exit.

It is not to be doubted that there is an awkward lacuna here, which is supplied by Quarto, though Quarto too is clearly incomplete:

Iago. *Go to, farewell:—doe you heare* Roderigo?
Rod. *what say you?*
Iag. *No more of drowning, doe you heare?*
Rod. *I am chang'd.*   Exit Roderigo.
Iag. *Goe to, farewell, put money enough in your purse:*

The Folio compositor, one guesses, jumped from *Go too, farewell*, opening l. 384, to the later line which also opens with *Go to, farewell*, and omitted the intervening words. A conflation of Folio and Quarto is necessary to restore the original text.

READ: Iago. *Go to, farewell. Do you hear, Roderigo?*
Rod. *What say you?*
Iago. *No more of drowning, do you hear?*
Rod. *I am changed.*
Iago. *Go to, farewell. Put money enough in your purse.*
Rod. *I'll sell all my land.*   [Exit.

So Alexander also reads. Kittredge omits the penultimate line.

ACT 2

I.12 *The chidden Billow*

Quarto reads *chiding*, preferred by some editors. But the sea is *chidden* by the wind which has 'ruffianed so' upon it (l. 7).

READ: *chidden*

I.13 *with high & monstrous Maine*

Quarto reads *mayne*. All editors since Knight follow his emendation *mane*, generally without comment as self-evident. The image assumed is, of course, the 'white horses' of the sea. But the image seems to me sudden, forced, and irrelevant. I boggle at the sea-horse seeming 'to cast water on the burning Bear' (l. 14), and I do not think Shakespeare capable of this tactlessness. A *monstrous mane* is almost equally absurd. Nowhere else, moreover, do we find *mane* spelled otherwise than *mane* in Shakespeare's original texts, and the spelling is reserved for *mane*. *main, maine, mayne*, on the other hand, is frequent in Shakespeare in the various senses of *main*, as in this play, with this compositor—*the Heauen, and the Maine*, a few lines earlier (2.1.3), and a few lines later, *till we make the Maine* (l. 39). The sense of *main* is as in 'with might and main', and is frequent. *N.E.D.* quotes Spenser's 'huge force and insupportable main' (*Faerie Queene* I.vii.11), for example. The force of the sea is *monstrous*, 'portentous'.

READ: *with high and monstrous main,*

1.64–5 *And in th'essentiall Vesture of Creation,*
        Do's tyre the Ingeniuer.

Quarto reads, at l. 65, *Does beare all excellency:*, which appears to be an editorial evasion of a difficulty which modern editors have felt in the Folio text. Kittredge, who reads *Does tire the ingener*, explains as 'tires out the most skilful contriver of compliments'. Alexander, with the same reading, glosses *ingener* as *engineer*, 'an inventive mind in words or devices of war', and leaves *tire* unglossed, which suggests Kittredge's interpretation. This seems very forced and inadequate, especially in relation to the sense and imagery of l. 64. *Vesture* inevitably suggests *attire* as the sense of *tyre*. The word *tire* or *tireman* is familiar. *essential*, as often, has the sense of *real* as distinct from *imaginary*, and the phrase means, with transferred epithet, 'the vesture of real creation'. *ingener* can well mean artist or poet. The whole sentence means therefore, 'Desdemona incarnating the imagination of the poet dresses the inventive poet praising her in the garment of real creation; his ideal picture is reality'. I owe something of this to a private suggestion from Mrs Nowottny.

READ: *And in th'essential vesture of creation*
        Does tire the ingener.

1.290 *I will do this, if you can bring it to any opportunity.*

Quarto reads *if I can*, followed by Kittredge. But the preceding dialogue, with Iago's reply here, 'I warrant thee', shows that Roderigo is dependent on Iago.

READ: *if you can*

1.312–13 *If this poore Trash of Venice, whom I trace*
          For his quicke hunting,

Quarto reads *crush* for *trace*, and with its easy misreading of *t* as *c* and *a* as *u* gives *trash* as the true reading corrupted in Folio *trace*. Roderigo must be *trashed*, 'weighted', to keep him from hunting wildly, so that Iago can keep him on the right scent for his own purposes. So recent editors read.

READ: *trash*

3.164 Mon. *I bleed still, I am hurt to th'death. He dies.*

Quarto reads *Zouns, I bleed still, I am hurt, to the death:* Editors mostly conflate Folio and Quarto, but taking the Folio *He dies* as a stage-direction, in the form *He faints.* But Montano is at once addressed by Iago, and can neither have *died* nor *fainted*. It is plain that Montano speaks the words in anger, 'I will kill Cassio (wounded though I am)'. It is Othello who parts them, 'Hold for your liues' (l. 165) and 'When you yourself did part them' (l. 239). As for *Zounds*, Folio eliminated strong oaths, and Quarto here records the original copy. Alexander also includes *He dies* in the speech. I suggest a stage-direction to make the point clear.

READ: *Zounds, I bleed still; I am hurt to the death.*
      He dies.   [Thrusts at *Cassio.*

ACT 3

3.66 *Out of her best,*

Quarto also reads *her*, and Alexander follows. Rowe's *their* for *her*, however, seems necessary to me to make sense. *her* is easily misread for *ther*, an *h*, *th* misprint being frequent and understandable. 'Even our best men at war must be subject to the discipline of war-time.'

READ: *Out of their best—*

3.74 *Trust me, I could do much.*

Alexander has preferred the Quarto *Birlady* to Folio *Trust me*. But *Trust me* is entirely appropriate, a much more lady-like oath than *Birlady*, which is more in Falstaff's vein, and is not, incidentally, censored in the Folio, so that we may not assume expurgation here.

R E A D : *Trust me,*

3.123 *They're close dilations,*

Quarto reads *denotements*. Editors mostly read *dilations*, with the sense of 'postponements', or as Kittredge glosses, 'swellings (of the heart)'. But Othello has moved further than in his previous speech. And *close*, 'secret, safe', points clearly in the direction of Steevens' suggestion, *delations*, which gives admirable and relevant sense here if interpreted as 'spyings, laying information'. Alexander, after early editors, glosses as 'accusations', which is less satisfactory.

R E A D : *delations,*

3.166–7 *It is the greene-ey'd Monster, which doth mocke*
        The meate it feeds on.

Theobald's *make* for the Folio and Quarto *mock* has been widely adopted, giving the sense that 'jealousy invents its own causes', with Iago arguing against himself for an imaginary cause. Graphically, of course, it is most plausible, given the frequent *oc* form of *a*, but in every other respect unacceptable. 'Jealousy feeds on the jealous man, playing cat and mouse with him', as the rest of Iago's speech shows.

R E A D : as in F.

3.170 *Suspects, yet soundly loues?*

Quarto reads *strongly*. There is much support among editors both for the Folio *soundly* and for its emendation *fondly*. *soundly*, though not impossible, seems to contradict the sense. To *suspect* is inconsistent with *sound* love, true and hearty love. As for *fondly*, it is repetitive of 'Who *dotes*' in the same line. The Quarto reading, on the contrary, is entirely apt here. And so recent editors read. The Folio reading offers no difficulty as a misreading of *strongly*, except in respect of *d* for *g*. Alliteration, as Miss Husbands points out to me, supports *dotes—doubts*, *suspects—strongly*.

READ: *strongly*

3.340 *I slept the next night well, fed well, was free, and merrie.*

Quarto omits *fed well*, and many editors, e.g. Kittredge, follow (not Alexander). The only support for the omission is metrical. But alexandrines occur in Shakespeare, and this one is unobtrusive. *fed well* is relevant, for the Elizabethans even more so, though Collier thought it 'absurd'.

READ: as in F.

3.361 *Or by the worth of mine eternall Soule,*

Quarto reads *mans* for *mine*, followed by most editors, including Kittredge and Alexander, possibly in contrast with 'born a dog' (l. 362). But this seems to me forced. *My love, my soul*, and *my wrath* (l. 363) seem nearer to Othello's vein than this touch of abstract theology, to which he was less given than editors. There is more in it. For Othello's own immortal soul *is* in question; in due course 'chaos is come again'; and his vision of himself in hell (5.2.274 ff.) harks back to this.

READ: *mine eternal soul,*

3.429 *'Tis a shrew'd doubt, though it be but a Dreame.*

In Folio this concludes a speech of Othello; in Quarto it opens a speech of Iago. Editors disagree, though most read with Folio. Alexander, following Warburton, reads with Quarto, rightly as I think. It is natural for Iago to follow up his previous line, 'this was but his dream' and give it force. Othello is beyond 'shrewd doubts' by now, capable only of thoughts of certainties, of his 'foregone conclusion' in the preceding line, a contradiction of 'shrewd doubts'. He does not entangle himself; he is entangled.

READ: Iago. *'Tis a shrewd doubt, though it be but a dream,*

3.453-6 *Neuer* Iago. *Like to the Ponticke Sea,*
          Whose Icie Current, and compulsiue course,
          Neu'r keepes retyring ebbe, but keepes due on
          To the Proponticke, and the Hellespont:

Quarto omits, but later Quartos read *feels* for the first *keeps* in l. 455, followed by practically all editors, who think the repetition of *keeps* to be an indication of corruption. I think so too, but not as a substitute for the true word. I suggest that the word *keeps* was anticipated by the poet in his copy from the second half of the line, then deleted, and that the compositor retained it. It could also be a scribal anticipation. No substitute word is required if we simply delete the first *keeps*, and read *ebbs* for *ebb*, no difficult misreading. No substitute, e.g. *feels, knows, makes, brooks*, has satisfied commentators even when admitting it into their texts. A similar verbal use of *ebb* occurs in l. 458, in close parallel to this thought, 'my bloody thoughts.. shall...ne'er ebb to humble love'.

READ: *Never retiring ebbs, but keeps due on*

3.468 *And to obey shall be in me remorse,*

The meaning of *remorse* here is surely its common meaning of 'pity' (not 'solemn obligation', as glossed in Onions and *N.E.D.*). 'To obey Othello in any command shall take the place of pity in me, shall exclude or overcome pity.'

ACT 4

1.78 (*A passion most resulting such a man*)

Quarto reads *vnsuting*, which is surely right. And so Theobald read, though many editors have followed *unfitting* from later Quartos, e.g. Kittredge.

READ: *unsuiting*

1.108 *Now, if this Suit lay in* Bianca's *dowre,*

Quarto reads *power*. The Folio *d* does not appear to be, as Collier argued, a turned letter, but a genuine variant. *dower* seems more in Iago's vein than the simplicity of *power*, and he has her marriage to Cassio in mind (l. 116).

READ: *dower,*

1.125 *they laugh, that winnes.*

Quarto reads *laugh that wins.*, and I have no doubt that the Quarto reading should be followed, as the compressed proverbial form of words. Recent editors are divided.

READ: *laugh that wins.*

1.227–8 *I warrant something from Venice,*
        'Tis Lodouico *this, comes from the Duke.*
        See, your wife's with him.

Quarto reads:
    Something from Venice *sure, tis* Lodouico,
    Come from the Duke, and see your wife is with him.
Editors are divided between the Folio and the Quarto readings. There can be no reason, other than a general preference for Quarto over Folio, for rejecting the Folio reading. The Quarto reading, moreover, sounds improvised and uncharacteristic.

READ: *I warrant, something from Venice.*
        Enter *Lodovico, Desdemona,* and *Attendants.*
        'Tis Lodovico—this comes from the Duke.
        See, your wife's with him.

2.64 *I heere looke grim as hell.*

Quarto also reads *I here.* Theobald's *there* for *here* is generally read. Alexander, however, retains *here*, which seems difficult, especially in view of 'Turn thy complexion *there*' (l. 62). The misreading of *h* for *th*, and vice-versa, is easy and frequent.

READ: *Ay, there look grim as hell.*

2.183–4 *I haue heard too much: and your words and*
      Performances are no kin together.

Quarto reads: *Faith I haue heard too much, for your words,*
      And performance are no kin together.

The almost incredible variant in some copies of Folio (corrected as above in later copies) is:

> *And hell gnaw his bones,*
> *Performances are no kin together.*

It occurs at the top of a page, and is inconsistent with the catchword '*Rodori. I*'. The compositor has repeated *And hell gnaw his bones* from l. 136 above. The correction in proof, however, seems to have left *and your words* in error for *for your words*. The Quarto *Faith* was evidently expurgated as profanity in Folio.

READ: *Faith I have heard too much, for your words and performances are no kin together.*

ACT 5

1.105 *Stay you good Gentlemen.*

Quarto reads *Gentlewoman*, and some editors follow. But it is plain that Iago wants Lodovico and Gratiano to remain to be witnesses to Bianca's 'guilt' as a party to Cassio's injury, as appears in the rest of this speech and in ll. 85–6 above.

READ: *gentlemen.*

2.15 *Ile smell thee on the Tree*.

Quarto reads *it* for *thee*, and Johnson and most editors follow. Alexander rightly reads *thee*. Desdemona is the fragrant rose. *it* is painfully prosaic here.

READ: *thee*

2.110 *She comes more neerer Earth*

Quarto reads *more neere the earth*, but only acceptance of Quarto as the basic authority can justify departing from Folio, which is also more idiomatic.

READ: *more nearer earth*

2.281 *Oh* Desdemon! *dead* Desdemon: *dead. Oh, oh!*

Quarto reads: *O Desdemona, Desdemona dead, O, o, o.* The Folio reading seems to be both imperfect and editorial. The spelling *Desdemon* suggests an attempt to make metre out of intractable material. The repetition of *dead* seems out of place. The Quarto reading at all points seems preferable, with Desdemona first in Othello's desperate apostrophe and *dead* second only. Alexander retains Folio

O Desdemona! Dead! Desdemona! Dead! O! O!,

changing the spelling, and with metrical difficulty. But this seems to me too much of a diagnosis, as compared with an outcry above all of love and of guilt.

READ: *O Desdemona! Desdemona! Dead!*
        O, o, o!

2.317 *But that (belike)* Iago *in the interim*

Quarto reads *nicke* for *interim*. It can hardly be doubted that *interim* is editorial, and destructive to the true sense, which is precisely given by *nick*. *interim* is also unmetrical. *nick* was perhaps too 'low' for the Folio reader as for most editors, of whose preference for more 'official' language there are other instances. Alexander reads *nick*.

READ: *nick*

ANTONY AND CLEOPATRA

DRAMATIS PERSONAE

Kittredge and Alexander (not *New Cambridge*) continue
to read Hanmer's correction, *Thyreus*, for the Folio name
Thidias, on the ground doubtless that this is his name in
North's *Plutarch* (though Plutarch reads *Thyrsus*). Shakespeare's spelling of the name cannot but be deliberate. It
occurs in this spelling not only in stage-directions or
prefixes, but also in dialogue, e.g. 'My name is Thidias'
(3.13.73). And the copy for the play was Shakespeare's
autograph.

I do not agree with *New Cambridge*, however, in
reading *Dercetus*, the majority of indications being in
favour of *Dercetas*, for we cannot ignore the spelling
Decretas which occurs twice to one *Dercetus*. The same
termination occurs in Thidias, Alexas, Menas, and
Maecenas. And so Kittredge and Alexander read. There
is no authority in the play for the name *Euphronius*, which
occurs only in Plutarch. As far as the play is concerned,
this character is clearly thought of simply as *Schoolmaster to
Antony*, and he should be thus described in the *Dramatis
Personae*, and as *Schoolmaster* in prefixes.

ACT 1

2.5 *this Husband, which you say, must change his Hornes with
Garlands.*[1]

Theobald's *charge* for *change* has rightly been accepted
by most later editors (though there is much support for
change, with ingenious interpretations). The emendation is

[1] Citations are from the First Folio.

graphically plausible. But there is debate on the meaning of the phrase. Surely the husband, a destined cuckold, is to be like an ox led to the slaughter, with garlands on his horns, a familiar image of a prize beast.

READ: *charge*

2.29 *Finde me to marrie me with* Octauius Cæsar,

Editors, including Dover Wilson but not Alexander, delete the second *me*, causelessly, for the phrase is the more idiomatic and natural as in Folio.

READ: as in F.

2.101 *Things that are past, are done, with me. 'Tis thus,*

My independent conclusion upon reading with a full stop after *done*, followed by *With me, 'tis thus*, is confirmed by a similar conclusion in *New Cambridge*, though Alexander retains the Folio reading. In the Folio reading *'Tis thus* is left in the air, and is lame. Antony's contrast of himself with 'the fool and coward' requires this emendation. 'With *me*, 'tis thus.'

READ: *Things that are past, are done. With me, 'tis thus,*

2.114 *When our quicke windes lye still,*

Editors, including recent editors, follow Warburton's *minds* for *winds*, unnecessarily as I think. The Folio *winds* gives better sense, literally and metaphorically. The *winds* and the *earing* are both valuable to the earth and its fruit, and hostile to weeds. Cf. *3 Henry VI* 2.6.21, 'For what doth cherish weeds but gentle air?' *Wind* is, moreover, rumour, gossip, criticism. So Jaques in *As You Like It* 2.7.48–9, 'as large a charter as the *wind*, To blow on whom I please'. Rumour, in *2 Henry IV* Prologue, speaks of 'Making the *wind* my post-horse', and Ulysses, in *Troilus and Cressida* 1.3.144, of Achilles as 'Having his ear full of his *airy* fame'. I owe these instances to Mrs Nowottny. 'We are like soil that needs quickening winds and ploughing, and criticism is good for us.' This sense links up closely with Antony's previous words in this speech, 'Speak to me home', with instances of the salutary home-truths available.

READ: *our quick winds*

2.117 *From* Scicion *how the newes? Speake there.*

Late and recent editors except Ridley follow Dyce's *ho!* for *how*, for which I see no need or advantage. The question is more natural than the demand. And it is a question in Folio. This compressed speaking is frequent in Antony's idiom, e.g. 'Grates me. The sum?'

READ: *From Sicyon how the news?*

3.11 *Tempt him not so too farre. I wish forbeare,*

Kittredge and Alexander, like most editors, retain the Folio reading, which seems to me quite improbable and unnatural. My reading *ywis* is supported by a conjecture recorded in *Variorum* and by *New Cambridge* which reads *iwis. ywis* is a typical 'lady's' expletive, like 'trust me' or 'in sooth' (not that Charmian is always mealy-mouthed, being an Elizabethan Egyptian lady).

READ: *ywis*

3.20 *What sayes the married woman you may goe?*

The accepted reading, as with Kittredge and Alexander, is

What says the married woman? You may go?

New Cambridge confirms my reading of the line nearer to the Folio original, which is much more biting and relevant. The opposition is clear, moreover, between *says . . . you may go* and 'given you leave to come' in the following line.

READ: *What, says the married woman you may go?*

4.43-4 *And the ebb'd man,*
        Ne're lou'd, till ne're worth loue,
        Comes fear'd, by being lack'd.

Recent editors follow Theobald's accepted *deared* for *feared*, for which I see neither need nor probability. Octavius is clearly referring back to the Messenger's words in l. 38, 'those That only have *feared* Caesar'. Pompey has come to be feared as well as loved, has grown in stature and is a greater danger. The emendation *deared* for *feared* has no graphic plausibility.

READ: *Comes feared by being lacked.*

4.46 *lacking the varrying tyde*

On this famous crux see Introduction, pp. 3-4. One may well be tempted to retain with Rowe the Folio reading, and to resist the brilliance and success of Theobald's *lackeying*, for *lacking* makes sense. 'The mob, in the absence of the firm influence of the regular variations of the tide, moves to and fro aimlessly. The flags in a tideless stream move in eddies aimlessly, not bending all in one direction, as they would obey a tide. The influence of a leader is like that of the compelling tide.' The tide, be it noted, does not 'go to and fro' irregularly; it goes *to* for twelve hours, and *fro* for twelve hours; it does not vary aimlessly. The metaphor is suggested by *ebbed* and *lacked* in ll. 43-4. Emendation is not necessary.

But, on the other side, the metaphor is clearly of the mob seeing men in ebb and flow, in rise and fall, without judgement of their real merits or stable quality, and of its subservience to tidal variations, to which metaphor the word *lackeying* is most apt and relevant. I remember long ago, in the park of Charlecote House, finding a brook-fed pool with flags swaying aimlessly in eddies, and wondering whether Shakespeare had passed that way. If so, the picture may well have become associated in his mind with the mob of lackeys who served Sir Thomas Lucy there, subservient to his wishes and his whims. The word was certainly caught up in Shakespeare's mind from *lacked* in l. 44. There is no graphic implausibility. The spelling *lackijng* could well yield *lacking* to the compositor, or, as Miss Husbands suggests privately, *lackying* could well yield *lackyng* (printed *lacking*), a mere minim error.

On the whole, the Folio reading appears to be inadequate and accidental. The emendation *lackeying* is superior to it, as to all alternatives, and is perhaps too good *not* to be true for once.

READ: *lackeying*

5.3 Cleo. *Ha, ha, giue me to drinke* **Mandragora.**

New Cambridge again anticipates my own reading, with the necessary stage-direction. Cleopatra is bored, and desires a sleeping potion to 'sleep out this great gap of time', Antony's absence.

READ: Cleo. [Yawns] *Ha—ha.*

5.48 *an Arme-gaunt Steede,*

Many conjectures for emendation have been offered, in the belief that *arm-gaunt* is unacceptable here. *New Cambridge* marks with an obelus as corrupt, and records with approval the suggestion of *armigerent*. I find no difficulty in the Folio word, which is entirely apt in the context, in the sense of 'battle-worn', or 'trained in battle', a war-horse, fit for a soldier. He is to be mounted 'soberly', not for caracoling or other shows. And he neighs, scenting the battle when Antony mounts him. There is no need to interpret, as editors do, as a starved Rosinante. It is the opposite of 'fat and scant of breath'.

READ: *an arm-gaunt steed,*

5.50 *What was he sad, or merry?*

New Cambridge reads *What was he, sad or merry?* which seems to be in a modern idiom rather than Elizabethan, and ignores the Folio punctuation.

READ: *What, was he sad, or merry?*

5.61 *So do's it no mans else.*

Editors emend to *no man else*, from F 2. The reading seems to me to be editorial, more obvious than the original, which is to be defended, in the sense 'So does it become no other man's *violence*; no other man's violence of sadness or merriment so becomes him', a more elliptical, but also more subtle and significant expression than the emended version.

READ: *So does it no man's else.*

ACT 2

1.2–3, 5–8 Mene. *Know worthy* Pompey, . . . *not deny.*
        Mene. *We ignorant of our selues*, . . . *our Prayers.*

The prefix *Mene.* is invariable in this scene in Folio, whether the speaker be Menecrates or Menas. *New Cambridge* attributes all to Menas, as against Malone's attribution of the first two speeches to Menecrates and the rest to Menas. Kittredge and Alexander, rightly as I think, follow Malone. There seems to me to be a difference in character, the first two speeches being of a philosophic turn of thought, the rest those of a man concerned with facts and soldiering. It is true that Menecrates does not speak elsewhere in the play, but this would be no unique instance in Shakespeare.

READ: as above (*Mene.* for Menecrates).

1.23 *Tye vp the Libertine in a field of Feasts,*

New Cambridge comments, 'Unexplained', and conjectures in a note *file* for *field*. But the sense seems plain.

Pompey's imagery is that of a soldier, and the *field* is a field
of battle or of tournament, or should be; but Antony is
restricted to competing only in eating and drinking. It is
a close parallel in thought to Pompey's previous, 'Antony...
will make No wars without doors', i.e. all his 'wars' now
are indoor exercises. No emendation is required.

READ: as in F.

1.41 *His Brother wan'd vpon him,*

waned upon might well bear the sense of 'made defection
from'. But the F 2 reading *warred upon* is more natural
and apt, and is supported by, 'Your wife and brother Made
wars upon me' (2.2.42–3). The misreading *wand* for *ward*
is entirely plausible. Recent editors read accordingly.

READ: *warred*

2.43–4   *and their contestation*
          Was Theame for you, you were the word of warre.

Various emendations offer to improve the sense of these
lines, marked as corrupt in *New Cambridge*. But the sense
seems plain in the original text. 'Their contestation was a
debate in your behalf (*for you*); it had your cause for theme
or purpose.'

READ: as in F.

2.52–4   *If you'l patch a quarrell,*
          As matter whole you haue to make it with,
          It must not be with this.

Rowe's emendation, *you have not,* with comma after *not,*
for *you have*, is generally accepted, as by recent editors, the
attraction being the contrast between *patch* and *matter
whole*. 'If you would patch up a quarrel, since (*as*) you
have not a complete quarrel'. But *as* can no less readily
mean 'as if, as though' (e.g. as in *Othello* 2.1.71, 'As having
sense of beauty', as Mrs Nowottny privately pointed out
to me) and this gives good sense here, without violence to

the Folio text. Mrs Nowottny interprets 'as though you had a real (*whole*) ground for quarrel'. My inclination is, however, to read *you'll* or *you'd* for *you* in l. 53 (in parallel with *you'll* in l. 52), with the sense, 'as though you wanted to show complete cause for quarrelling', which seems to me to be natural in the context. This emendation is less violent, and avoids the ugly metrical effect of the inserted *not*.

READ: *As matter whole you'd have to make it with,*

3.7–8   *good night deere Lady:*
        Good night Sir.

No editor now questions the F 2 attribution of *Good night Sir* to Octavia, instead of its Folio place at the end of Antony's speech. He has already said 'Good night Sir' to Octavius, and Octavia replies to his salutation to her.

READ: Octa. *Good night Sir.*

5.37–9 *But there's no goodnesse in thy face if* Anthony
        Be free and healthfull; so tart a fauour
        To trumpet such good tidings.

Editors, including recent editors, follow Rowe in reading *in thy face. If Antony*. Kittredge and Alexander, moreover, follow Capell in reading *why so tart* for *so tart*, apparently on metrical grounds chiefly, though the medial pause in the line gives admirable Shakespearian dramatic metre. The Folio reading, however, should stand. Cleopatra is speaking, and this is Cleopatra's characteristic logic. 'You have the wrong kind of face for bringing news that Antony is well—*what* a miserable face for such good news! (I suspect that face of bad news.)' The whole speech is quite intelligible (to Cleopatra): 'You have the wrong face, though human, for good news of Antony. If you bring bad news of Antony, you should be a Fury, not even human.'

READ: *But there's no goodness in thy face, if Antony*
        Be free and healthful—so tart a favour
        To trumpet such good tidings.

5.43-4 *Yet if thou say* Anthony *liues, 'tis well,*
     Or friends with Cæsar, *or not Captiue to him,*

I agree with recent editors, following Tyrwhitt, in
reading *is well* for *'tis well*. *'tis well* is awkward here and
in the air. And Cleopatra is curiously insistent on Antony's
health in her inquiries. The Messenger, moreover, replies,
'Madam, he's well', and continues with, 'And friends with
Cæsar'.

READ: *is well*,

7.117 *The holding euery man shall beate as loud,*

Editors all follow Theobald's *bear* for *beat*. No doubt
one can *bear* a burden to a song, but one can also *beat* the
rhythm and emphasize it by singing it loudly. A misreading of *beare* as *beate* is not at all self-evident graphically.

READ: *beat*

ACT 3

6.61 *Being an abstract 'tweene his Lust, and him.*

Kittredge and *New Cambridge* retain the Folio *abstract*
as recommended by Delius and others, giving it the sense
of 'summary, précis', hence 'short cut', which seems to
me an acrobatic leap in sense. There is no other instance
of such a use, nor does it seem likely that there could be.
Theobald's *obstruct* seems to me, as to Alexander, a
necessary and plausible emendation, giving plain and
relevant sense. *N.E.D.*, it is true, does not record the word
elsewhere, but it seems an easy and probable formation to
suit the metre here.

READ: *obstruct*

6.72 *King* Mauchus *of Arabia,*

Editors are divided between *Manchus*, from North, and
Malchus, from Plutarch, but united in rejecting *Mauchus*.

But *Mauchus* would be a phonetic spelling of an English *Malchus* (a name known from the Bible), with parallels in *malkin*, *mawkin*, or *malgré*, *maugre*. *Malchus* is an 'improvement' of Shakespeare, not of his compositor.

READ: *Mauchus*

6.87–9   *and the high Gods*
            To do you Iustice, makes his Ministers
            Of vs,

Editors, following F 2, all read *make* for *makes*, and most, following Capell, read *them* for *his*, or Theobald's *their*. Neither is necessary. *the high Gods* is a collective phrase, the equivalent of *God*. Shakespeare is not writing 'grammar', he is writing his kind of English. This, moreover, removes the difficulty of *his*, interpreted by *New Cambridge* as 'Justice's', for Justice is a feminine deity in Shakespeare as elsewhere (cf. 'persuade Justice to break *her* sword'. *Othello* 5.2.16–17), and in any case is not personified here. Neither *them* nor *their* could conceivably be misread as *his*.

READ: *makes his ministers*

7.57–8 *Can he be there in person? 'Tis impossible*
            Strange, that his power should be.

Editors, including recent editors, all follow Pope without question, in placing a full stop, colon, or dash after *impossible*, thus distorting the sense. Antony has already allowed for the possibility of *Octavius* arriving, in this scene. What seems 'impossible' is that his whole *army*, and not only an advance-guard, should have arrived. The Folio punctuation is not to be ignored, and *impossible strange* offers no difficulty of sense, on the contrary.

READ: *Can he be there in person? 'Tis impossible*
            Strange that his power should be.

10.10 *Yon ribaudred Nagge of Egypt,*

Among recent editors, Kittredge and *New Cambridge* follow Steevens' *ribald-rid*, with a very difficult interpretation, 'a nag ridden by ribalds, e.g. by Antony'. It is also out of character for Scarus, whose insults are aimed at Cleopatra, not at his own general. I see no difficulty in the Folio original, *ribaudred—ribaudered—ribaldered*, i.e. rotted by ribaldry and licence. Alexander reads as in Folio, and glosses 'harlot'.

READ: *Yon ribaldered nag of Egypt*

12.13 *He Lessons his Requests,*

Recent editors read *lessens* from F 2, without any need to emend the original, which gives excellent, and better, sense. 'If his first demands are not met, Antony schools, disciplines, his requests, and sues to you...'. It seems particularly relevant from his *Schoolmaster*, but in any case is a familiar use of the word *lessons*.

READ: *He lessons his requests,*

13.74–5 *Say to great* Cæsar *this in disputation,*
          I kisse his conqu'ring hand:

Most editors, including Kittredge and Alexander, follow Warburton's *deputation* for *disputation*, with a colon after *this*. *New Cambridge*, however, retains the Folio reading, interpreting as, 'I fight him by kissing his hand', which seems extremely forced, and out of key for Cleopatra here. 'Not know me yet?' (l. 157).

READ: *Say to great Caesar this: in deputation*
          I kiss his conquering hand.

ACT 4

4.3 *Come good Fellow, put thine Iron on,*

Kittredge and Alexander (not *New Cambridge*) follow
Hanmer's *mine* for *thine*, an officious emendation. *thine*, of
course, is a familiar colloquialism for 'the armour you have
ready for me'. It is clearly deliberate, with *mine Armour*
in the preceding line. The word *iron* for *armour* invites the
familiar touch of *thine*.

READ: *thine iron*

10.1–9 Ant. *Their preparation is to day by Sea,*
       We please them not by Land.
        Scar. *For both, my Lord.*
        Ant. *I would they'ld fight i'th' Fire, or i'th' Ayre,*
        Wee'ld fight there too. But this it is, our Foote
        Vpon the hilles adioyning to the Citty
        Shall stay with vs. Order for Sea is giuen,
        They haue put forth the Hauen:
        Where their appointment we may best discouer,
        And looke on their endeuour.

The Folio text offers serious difficulties, as all editors
feel. Most suggest a missing line or phrase after *the haven*.
It seems to me clear that the compositor had a complicated
piece of copy here, with six regular lines revised by two
marginal additions, *order for sea . . . the haven* for Scarus at
l. 2 (the words are surely a part of Scarus' report), and
where their . . . discover for Antony at l. 6. The compositor
read both consecutively and inserted all into Antony's
speech. This may seem deep surgery. But the consequent
rearrangement of the order of the lines, without verbal
change or addition, gives perfect sense and improves the
metre. It brings the scene into the sequence of its source
in Plutarch. And it readily permits a reasonable reconstruction of the underlying copy in Shakespeare's 'foul

PLATE II

Antony and Cleopatra (act 4, sc. 10)

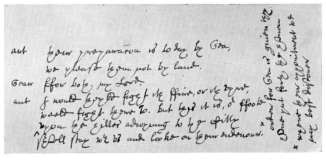

(*a*) Shakespeare's MS. reconstructed

Enter *Anthony and Scarrus*, with their *Army*.

Ant. Their preparation is to day by Sea,
We pleafe them not by Land.

Scar. For both, my Lord.

Ant. I would they'ld fight i'th'Fire, or i'th'Ayre,
Wee'ld fight there too. But this it is, our Foote
Vpon the hilles adioyning to the Citty
Shall ftay with vs. Order for Sea is giuen,
They haue put forth the Hauen :
Where their appointment we may beft difcouer,
And looke on their endeuour.   *exeunt*

Enter *Cafɣr*, and his *Army*.

(*b*) The Folio version of 1623, p. 361

papers' which gave birth to the confused Folio text here
(Plate II). Scarus, be it noted, is Antony's co-general and
is reporting on his fleet, the practical man of war. Antony is
on the heights of optimism.

READ:

Ant. *Their preparation is to-day by sea,*
We please them not by land.
Scar. *For both, my lord. Order for sea is given,*
They have put forth the haven.
Ant. *I would they'd fight i' th' fire, or i' th' air,*
We'd fight there too. But this it is, our foot
Upon the hills adjoining to the city,
Where their appointment we may best discover,
Shall stay with us and look on their endeavour.

12.37 *For poor'st Diminitiues, for Dolts,*

Kittredge and Alexander follow Thirlby's *doits* for
dolts, i.e. 'farthings', with *diminutives* in much the same
sense, 'small coins'. *New Cambridge* reads *dolts,* but finds
the reading difficult. The Folio reading, in fact, offers no
difficulty. The metaphor is clearly of shows of 'monsters'.
'Cleopatra', says Antony, 'will be put on show as monsters
are shown, in place of (*for*) dwarfs and idiots'.

READ: *For poor'st diminutives, for dolts,*

13.10 *And bring me how he takes my death to' th' Monument.*

Editors read, *takes my death. To th' monument!* for which
violent change in punctuation and sense I see no need. The
Folio text has clear sense, 'Bring (the news) to me to the
monument how he takes my death'. This use of *brings* is
familiar. A repetition of *To th' monument!* seems to me
transpontine. And Cleopatra does not order *twice.*

READ: as in F.

14.35 *Vnarme* Eros, *the long dayes taske is done,*

It may seem incredible that any editor should interfere
with this line. But Rowe's *Unarm me, Eros,* has survived

even into Kittredge's recent edition, in the erroneous belief that *Unarm, Eros*, must mean, 'Unarm yourself, Eros'. And there is frequent support elsewhere.

READ: as in F.

14.112–13 *This sword but shewne to* Cæsar *with this tydings,*
          Shall enter me with him.

A stage-direction seems to be needed for clarity here, in the light of Act 5, Sc. 1.

READ: *Shall enter me with him.* [Takes up *Antony's* sword.

15.12 *Helpe* Charmian, *helpe* Iras *helpe:*

New Cambridge stigmatizes this as certainly interpolated and unnecessary in view of later lines, 'Help me my women'. But this is a laying of plans, a preparation, interrupted by Antony who, apparently dead, now speaks. Other editors find no difficulty here.

15.22–3 *Deere my Lord pardon: I dare not,*
         Least I be taken:

New Cambridge marks as corrupt and supplies *open* after *not* to complete the sense and metre, following Malone's comment on the line. This may well seem to be mere 'improvement', and to me is ruinous to the passage. Cleopatra is not reporting the situation to Antony, who is dying. She is speaking her own thoughts. She cannot leave the monument and go to him. He must be lifted to her.

READ: as in F.

15.28–9   *shall acquire no Honour*
             Demuring vpon me:

New Cambridge, following Furness in *Variorum*, reads *demurring* for *demuring*. But for Shakespeare, or any

Elizabethan, the normal and familiar meaning of *demur* was to object to a Bill in a Court of Law on grounds of insufficiency or uncertainty, generally in 'evasive action'. No *honour* could be acquired by *demurring*. Nor does one *demur upon*, one *demurs to*. *Demuring upon* is similar in formation to 'frowning upon', and *demuring* bears its obvious and effective sense of 'looking demurely upon', with her 'married woman' look, protected, honoured, and supercilious (upon Cleopatra led in triumph, a captive in Rome). It is no argument to allege that the word was not apparently used elsewhere. Shakespeare creates words for his needs.

READ: *demuring upon me.*

15.38–9   *Dye when thou hast liu'd,*
                  Quicken with kissing:

New Cambridge retains the Folio *when*, against the general acceptance of Pope's *where*, as did also my text as a result of the same misprint which occurred, as I believe, in Folio. 'Die *when* thou hast lived' seems a tasteless conceit and out of key. 'Die *where* thou hast lived' is profoundly true to Cleopatra's thought, and is moving. *Quicken with kissing* follows naturally enough. 'If kissing you could keep you alive a little longer....'

READ: *Die where thou hast lived.*

ACT 5

1.52–3 *A poore Egyptian yet, the Queen my mistris*
          Confin'd in all, she has her Monument

Theobald, and many editors including Kittredge, read *yet. The Queen.* But this is a misunderstanding, as also is the suggestion that *A poor Egyptian* means Cleopatra. Caesar has asked 'Whence are you?' and the Messenger replies, '*I* am a poor Egyptian (I am from Egypt), *yet* I come from a Queene, my mistress, with her message'. (The *yet* is important, and not to be deleted, as by Capell.) It was not for a Messenger to humble Cleopatra to Caesar, nor probable that Cleopatra would bid him describe her as 'a poor Egyptian'.

READ: *A poor Egyptian, yet the Queen my mistress, Confined in all she has, her monument,*

Sc. 2. *Stage-directions*. There is much debate upon the conduct of this scene. I suggest the following directions, using the upper stage and the inner stage as well as the main stage, in place of the *New Cambridge* directions:

Enter above *Cleopatra, Charmian*, and *Iras*.

L. 8 Enter to the gates of the monument *Proculeius, Gallus*, and *Soldiers*.

L. 11 [*Cleopatra, Charmian*, and *Iras* exeunt above, and re-enter below behind the bars of the gates.

L. 34 [Meanwhile, *Gallus* and *Soldiers* ascend the monument by a ladder, exeunt above, and re-enter below behind the bars.

L. 35 [*Soldiers* open the gates.

2.7–8 *Which sleepes, and neuer pallates more the dung, The begger's Nurse, and Cæsars.*

There is much to be said on behalf of the Folio *dung*, and much for Warburton's emendation, *dug*. Among recent editors, Kittredge and *New Cambridge* read *dung*, and Alexander *dug*. The only real parallel offered in support of *dung* is Antony's 'Our dungy earth alike Feeds beast as man' (1.1.35–6), but it is close. 'Suicide', to paraphrase Johnson, 'produces a state in which there is no need more for the earthly nutriment (the *nurse*), which is, in life, necessary equally to Caesar and the beggar'. Cleopatra is expressing, in this language, *contemptus mundi*, as in 'Tis paltry to be Caesar' (l. 2), and 'death . . . That rids our dogs of languish' (ll. 41–2).

On the other hand, the word is *sleeps*, not *dies*, and the metaphor is of a *Nurse*. The whole image suggests a baby which drops off from life into sleep, from the nurse's breast into an eternal sleep, and will never again be greedy for the breast which feeds Caesar and beggar alike. Between *dung* and *dug* there is only the presence or absence of a nunnation mark over the *u*, and there is no easier misreading. It is, moreover, not the *dung*, but 'the dungy *earth*' that feeds man and beast in Antony's words. *Dug* is a woman's image, as *dung* is not.

It is a torturing decision. But one cannot be certain of reading Shakespeare's mind here. And all canons of textual criticism are in favour of the Folio *dung*, which gives good and relevant sense. The more probable spellings of *dug* and *dung*, *dugge* and *dunge*, are less likely to be confused. Finally, *dung* is the *durior lectio* here.

READ: *Which sleeps, and never palates more the dung,*

CYMBELINE

DRAMATIS PERSONAE

For *Imogen*, see Introduction, Vol. 1, pp. 15–16.

ACT 1

3.8–10   *for so long*
   As he could make me with his eye, or eare,
   Distinguish him from others,[1]

Warburton's *this* for *his* in l. 9 is widely followed, as by Kittredge, and other emendations, e.g. *or*, have been proposed. None is necessary, and the suggestion that Pisanio points in turn to his own eye and ear is ludicrous. Pisanio has imagination enough to see the matter from Posthumus' point of view: 'for so long as he could believe me (*make me*) to distinguish him, as his own eye or ear led him to judge from what he could see and hear'. (Alexander's *care* for *ear* is apparently a mere misprint.)

READ: *for so long*
   As he could make me with his eye or ear
   Distinguish him from others,

4.22–4 *which else an easie battery might lay flat, for taking a Begger without lesse quality.*

Rowe's facile *more* for *less* has been frequently followed (though not recently) on the ground that the Folio reading contradicts the obvious sense intended. But this is another example of a kind of double negative reinforcing itself. The sense is 'for taking a beggar—unless he had some extraordinary quality.' There is, as often, a coalescence of two

---

[1] Citations are from the basic Folio text.

constructions, 'without quality', and 'if he had less quality'. Emendation is unnecessary.

READ: as in F.

4.80 *I could not beleeue she excelled many:*

There seems to me to be no escape from Malone's *could not but believe*, and so Kittredge and Alexander read. (The trend of Iachimo's speech will not permit the acceptance of such forced sense as can be read into the Folio text.) 'If she outshines others I have seen, as your diamond outshines many I have seen, I must admit that she excels many. But I have not seen the perfect diamond, nor you the perfect lady.'

READ: *I could not but believe*

4.90–1 *the one may be solde or giuen, or if there were wealth enough for the purchases, or merite for the guift.*

Rowe omitted *or* in *or if*, an emendation rebutted by Collier. But most editors follow Rowe, including recent editors. *or if* clearly is *either if*, in apposition to the following *or* (if there were) *merit*.

READ: as in F.

4.146 *You are a Friend, and there in the wiser:*

Theobald's *afraid* for *a friend* is generally accepted, though not by Alexander. There is no need for emendation. Iachimo is referring back to the distinction between a *friend* and an *adorer* (l. 74). 'You are, I see, a *friend* after all, not an *adorer* (for an *adorer* would not accept a wager), and you are the wiser therefore. (*Adorers* are beyond reason)'.

READ: *You are a friend, and therein the wiser.*

6.36 *Vpon the number'd Beach,*

Of many wild conjectures, Theobald's *unnumbered* for *numbered* has met with most acceptance. The Folio reading, however, makes far better and more pregnant sense. 'Nature has given men such eyes that they can not only distinguish between stars and stones, but if put to it can even number the stones on the beach. (The beach is *numbered* in respect of the stones on it.)'

    READ: *Upon the numbered beach,*

6.102–4   *This obiect, which*
      Takes prisoner the wild motion of mine eye,
      Fiering it onely heere,

Later Folios read *Fixing* for *Fiering*, and many follow, including Kittredge and Alexander. The emendation bears all the signs of editorial interference in the direction of a more obvious reading, to give logical sequence after *Takes prisoner...mine eye*. The F1 reading is thereby made inexplicable. *Fixing* could not be misread by a compositor as *Fiering*, nor would a compositor start aside from the obvious to the unexpected. *Firing*, moreover, makes good sense, if unexpected. The style of *Cymbeline* is in the extreme of Shakespeare's latest manner, with complex sequences of thought. Here the pattern of the speech is 'cheek...lips (to kiss); hand...hand (to touch); eyes... eye (to look into)'. *This object*, generally interpreted as Imogen, is Imogen's *eyes*, and perhaps a stage-direction is required to make this clear. The sense, therefore, is 'Your eyes which alone can give fire to mine, and imprison my wandering eyes'. The thought is continued and illustrated in the following lines, by contrast with kissing common lips, holding hard hands, and looking into eyes of no fire or lustre ('Base and *illustrous* as the *smoky* light').

    READ: *this object* [looks in her eyes], *which*
           Takes prisoner the wild motion of mine eye,
           Firing it only here:

ACT 2

1.15 *Whorson dog: I gaue him satisfaction?*

Editors follow F 2 with *give* for *gave* and retaining the question-mark. I see no need to emend otherwise than to use an exclamation-mark for the mixed question-exclamation Folio mark. Cloten *had* broken the jackanapes' pate with his bowl. He had paid him out, and 'given him satisfaction' enough for a 'dog'. The emended version seems to me inexplicable.

READ: *Whoreson dog, I gave him satisfaction!*

2.48–9   *that dawning*
     May beare the Rauens eye:

The emendation *bare* for *beare* is accepted now, and rightly. The raven is not a night-bird to general knowledge. The phrase simply means, 'that the dawn may waken the raven'.

READ: *bare*

3.48   *some more time*
   Must weare the print of his remembrance on't,

Kittredge and Alexander follow Rowe's *out* for *on't*, as do most editors. There is no need to emend, and the sense is better with the Folio reading. *on't* means 'on some more time'. 'More time must elapse which will still bear the impress of his memory.'

READ: as in F.

3.52 *To orderly solicity,*

Alexander reads *solicity*, without gloss, a very improbable coinage. Other editors read *soliciting*, or *solicits* (F 2). *solicits* is the more plausible, with a form of final *s* easily confused with *y*, and with ample authority for the word and its use here.

READ: *solicits,*

4.23–4   *Their discipline,*
           (Now wing-led with their courages)

F 2 reads *mingled,* with general agreement, rightly as I think. The misprint was easy to make. *wing-led* has had much support, however, as suggesting Roman eagles, and hence Roman discipline. But this is opposed to the sense of the speech. The British are now more disciplined and skilled in war than when Julius Caesar fought them, and have the same courage as then. 'Their discipline is now allied to their courage' (and this not by Roman teaching). Other emendations, such as *winged,* are less plausible. The hyphen in *wing-led* is not necessarily significant. Once the compositor read *w* for *m,* the hyphen followed.

READ: *mingled*

ACT 3

2.2. *What Monsters her accuse?*

Capell's *monster's her accuser?* has been strangely popular, unnecessary as it is. Alexander rightly follows Folio.

READ: as in F.

2.69 *How many store of Miles may we well rid*
      Twixt houre, and houre?

store is, of course, a clear instance of a *c : t* misprint for *score. rid* has been strongly supported as meaning 'dispose of, cover', with instances of proverbial use. But it seems to me forced here. F 2 reads *ride.* Imogen's next speech harps upon *riding,* 'one that *rode* to's execution', '*riding* wagers', 'a *riding* suit'. Most editors agree.

READ: *How many score of miles may we well ride*

3.2–3   *Sleepe Boyes, this gate*
    Instructs you how t'adore the Heauens; and bowes you

Various emendations, e.g. *See, Sweet,* '*Sleep, boys?,* arose out of resistance to Hanmer's *Stoop* as having no resemblance to the Folio *Sleep,* however apparently necessary to the sense. But the misreading in fact is graphically most plausible.

READ: *Stoop boys,*

3.23 *Richer, then doing nothing for a Babe:*

Hanmer's *bribe* for *babe* cannot well be resisted in the context, and recent editors agree. Graphically, the emendation is easy enough, for *bri* in cursive writing could well be read as *ba*. The Folio *babe* cannot be justified by improbable interpretation as a wealthy ward.

READ: *bribe,*

3.25 *Such gaine the Cap of him, that makes him fine,*

Rowe's *them* for the second *him*, or the equivalent, is universally accepted (except by Alexander). But *him* offers no difficulty. The relation of *such* to the second *him* is clear. 'Your parasite is respected by the man who contributes to his finery but is not paid what he owes him.' Shakespeare was not careful about 'agreements'.

READ: as in F.

4.104 *Ile wake mine eye-balles first.*

Johnson's *out first* for *first* is widely accepted, and rightly to my mind. One must be wary of metrical arguments, but the metre halts, and moves happily with *out*. The sense also requires *out*. 'I have not slept one wink', says Pisanio, and Imogen bids him carry out his orders and go to bed. To reply, '*I'll wake my eyeballs first*', can at best mean merely 'I would sooner watch'. But what is required is, 'I would sooner blind myself with staying awake at all costs', as Imogen clearly understands his extravagant protest.

READ: *I'll wake mine eyeballs out first.*

5.9 *Madam, all ioy befall your Grace, and you.*

There has been much pother over this line, mostly on grounds of protocol, and various emendations seek to improve Lucius' manners. But Lucius owes no greetings to Cymbeline, whom he has just declared his Emperor's enemy. He desires only his right, a safe-conduct. But with due courtesy he greets the Queen and the Prince, Cloten. A stage-direction is desirable.

READ: *Madam, all joy befall your Grace*, [to *Cloten*] *and you.*

5.32–4   *She looke vs like*
              A thing more made of malice, then of duty,
              We haue noted it.

Recent editors have rightly followed Folio in reading *looks us*, against emendations proposed. (The Folio *looke* is an easy misprint for *lookes*.) The accepted interpretation, however, 'seems to us' (*looks to us*), is not only awkward; it is erroneous. The meaning is 'she looks *at us, upon us,* as a thing of malice, not duty, would look at us.' Cymbeline's *We have noted it* is decisive.

READ: *She looks us*

5.44 *to' th' lowd of noise, we make.*

Editors, following Capell and others, read *the loudest noise* or *the loud'st of noise*. Alexander rightly follows Folio (1951: later revision unauthorized). There is no difficulty in the Folio reading, *loud* being 'loudness', a use of the word as a noun-adjective that Shakespeare would not hesitate to make. *loudest noise* seems forced here. And *lowd of* could not be confused in copy with *lowdst*.

READ: *to th' loud of noise we make.*

6.75–6   *'Mongst Friends?*
              If Brothers: would it had bin so,

Most recent editors read with Rowe, *'Mongst friends, If brothers* (ignoring the Folio *?*), unnecessarily. Imogen

is replying to Arviragus and echoes his words, 'you fall
'mongst friends'. *If brothers* is surely an afterthought.

READ: *'Mongst friends?*
     If brothers—[aside] *would it had been so,*

ACT 4

2.57–8 *That greefe and patience rooted in them both,*
     Mingle their spurres together.

Editors, including recent editors, follow Pope in reading
him for *them*, with the sense 'both grief and patience rooted
in him (Imogen)'. But there is no need for an emendation
which in fact diminishes the pregnancy and subtlety of the
speech. Arviragus has just spoken of Imogen's 'smiles'
and 'sighs' yoked together in her, Guiderius now completes
his image. 'Grief and patience are rooted in both her sighs
and her smiles'. *him* is a facile 'correction' of the true text.

READ: as in F.

2.111–12   *For defect of iudgement*
     Is oft the cause of Feare.

Among many emendations of *cause*, e.g., *cure*, *loss*,
cease, *cease* has been thought the most probable, and
Alexander so reads. Kittredge rightly retains the Folio
cause. The sentence is closely bound up with preceding
lines and with indications earlier in the play. The essential
thought is that 'defect of judgement in *others* led them to
fear *him* (and so he was never opposed)'. This is why
Cloten had no 'apprehension of terrors'. He had no reason
to know terrors, for all feared him, not understanding what
a poor creature he was. Indeed Cloten tells us, 'they dare
not fight with me', and so he can never be matched
(2.1.20–4).

READ: *Is oft the cause of fear.*

2.170 *thou thy selfe thou blazon'st*

Pope's officious *how thyself* for *thou thyself* is generally read (not by Alexander), apparently to reduce the number of *thou*'s. The sense of the Folio reading is clear, and it is good English usage.

READ: as in F.

ACT 5

1.1–2   *for I am wisht*
            Thou should'st be colour'd thus.

Pope's *wished* for *am wisht* must be right, as editors agree. The only plausible explanation of the Folio reading is that Shakespeare's copy made a false start, *for I am*, and that the *am* was deleted but printed by the compositor.

READ: *for I wished*

1.14–15 *To second illes with illes, each elder worse,*
            And make them dread it, to the dooers thrift.

This line, widely accepted as corrupt, is perfectly plain and just in expression and meaning. *elder* means *later*, the deeds of an elder man. 'The Gods permit some men to heap evil upon evil, until the very mass of evil makes the sinners afraid of it, so that they repent, to their spiritual advantage or benefit.'

READ: as in F.

3.46–8   *heauens, how they wound,*
            Some slaine before some dying; some their Friends
            Ore-borne i' th' former waue,

Capell's reading, *how they wound! Some slaine before, some dying,* is generally accepted. But the construction and sense of the passage is much less clumsy and odd. The comma after *wound* in Folio should be deleted.

READ: *heavens, how they wound*
            Some slain before, some dying, some their friends
            O'erborne i' th' former wave.

'In the confusion they strike indiscriminately, at dead bodies, at dying men, and some of these their own friends struck down in a previous assault.'

5.228–9 *Thou scornfull Page, there lye thy part.*

Editors give the stage-direction, 'Strikes her. She falls.' But this is inconsistent with the indications of ll. 261–3 below, from which it is evident that Imogen seeks to embrace Posthumus, and he throws her from him to the ground. The direction should read accordingly.

READ: [*Throws her down.*

5.261–3 *Why did you throw your wedded Lady fro you?*
   Thinke that you are vpon a Rocke, and now
   Throw me againe.

Editors, including recent editors, read as in Folio, interpreting *rock* as 'cliff' or 'precipice', which yields very difficult sense in the context; and the alternatives, 'on a firm rock' or 'shipwrecked on a rock', are no better. Dowden's brilliant suggestion, *lock* for *rock* (though he did not read it in the text), is irresistible and to my mind certain. The phrase 'upon a lock' is most amply instanced elsewhere. The whole picture is of Imogen embracing Posthumus, and using the language of wrestling. She is referring back to Posthumus' words and action at ll. 228–9, 'Thou scornful page, There lie thy part. [*Throws her down.*' So here she says, 'Think you are (not embracing me but) wrestling with me, and now throw me again, as you did just now'. It is difficult to allege graphic plausibility. Foul case is a last resort. Perhaps the compositor, no wrestler (nor were Malone and his predecessors), made an 'intelligent' correction of his copy. I know of no wrestling 'hold' known as a 'rock'.

READ: *upon a lock,*

PERICLES

DRAMATIS PERSONAE

The name *Pericles* is taken from Plutarch's *Life* of Pericles
of Athens, along with something of his character, as
Dr Tompkins has demonstrated (*R.E.S.* Oct. 1952).

THE TEXT

It is generally agreed at present that of the two Quartos of
1609 that which reads *Enter Gower.* at Sig. A 2 is prior to
that which reads *Eneer Gower.* Citations here are from the
Malone copy in Bodley of Q 1, reproduced in the Oxford
facsimile of 1905 and the Shakespeare Association facsimile of 1940, for ease of reference. Collation with other
copies reveals unobserved variants indicating correction in
press, e.g. in the Flower copy at Stratford, the B.M. copy,
and the White copy in Folger which Dr McManaway has
kindly examined for me. Variants of significance are sig-
nalled in the following notes. It is unfortunate that both
Lee and Greg decided upon the Malone copy for their
respective facsimiles of Q 1. A full collation of all extant
copies of Q 1 and Q 2 is needed, with detailed biblio-
graphical analysis, e.g. of running titles, to establish the
history of the text. Q 2 appears to have been set up from
an uncorrected copy of Q 1, with editorial interventions
which are analysed in part in Lee's Introduction to his
facsimile.

ACT 1

Chorus, l. 21 *This King vnto him tooke a Peere,*

Recent editors read *fere*, as do earlier editors. But I see
no difficulty in the Quarto reading. 'The King married a
wife of royal birth', his 'equal' in birth. There is no need

to out-Gower Shakespeare's Gower. *Peere* and *fere* could not be confused in copy.

READ: *took a peer*,

1.33 *all the whole heape must die:*

Editors read *thy* or *this* for *the*, unnecessarily. It is tempting to suggest *hope* for *heape*, the spelling *hoape* making the misreading plausible, and the sense being, 'Only desert can gain the prize, and if desert is lacking, all hope must be lost.' But there is a closer sense indicated which points to the original reading. 'Because your eye (a part of you) presumes without desert to look upon her face, the whole of you must die for the fault of the part.' This use of *heap*, meaning 'the whole mass', is perhaps more unfamiliar to modern readers than to Shakespeare who was nearer to the wider uses of the word in mediaeval English or in Anglo-Saxon. (Kittredge glosses, 'crowd, throng, band', giving a different sense.)

READ: *heap*

2.1 *why shold this chãge of thoughts*

Editors mostly read *charge*. The F 3 text, and Alexander, rightly read *change*. *chãge* could not be an abbreviation of *charge*. Pericles' speech proceeds to explain in what sense his thoughts have *changed* ('and so with me', l. 16).

READ: *this change of thoughts*,

2.29-30 *Which care of them, not pittie of my selfe,*
        Who once no more but as the tops of trees,

Editors all read *am* for *once*, without troubling about graphic plausibility. And *am* is a very weak improvisation here. I suggest *care*, with more plausibility, giving a fuller sense, and referring back to *Which care of them* in l. 29. 'My care for my subjects, not pity for myself (for I care only as do tree-tops which defend the roots they grow from) troubles me.'

READ: *Who care no more*

2.40–1   *but a sparke,*
        To which that sparke giues heate, and stronger
        Glowing,

The second *sparke* is obviously an error, repeated from the first. Recent editors read *blast*, though *breath* and *wind* have also been proposed, and all seem odd to me. It seems more reasonable to be guided less by the preceding image of 'the bellows', and more by the probability of the compositor's source of error. I therefore suggest *spur* (*spurre*) which could more readily lead him to repeat *sparke*. Shifts of metaphor are frequent enough, especially in the later Shakespeare. 'Flattery is a spur to sin.'

READ: *that spur*

2.48–9   *let your cares ore-looke,*
        What shipping, and what ladings in our hauen,

The accepted *lading's* seems much less idiomatic in Elizabethan English than *ladings*. *What* means 'such (as are)'.

READ: *let your cares o'erlook*
        What shipping and what ladings in our haven,

2.86 *And should he doo't, as no doubt he doth,*

do it makes no sense here. I prefer *doubt* for *doo't* to the accepted *doubt it*, on grounds of graphic probability, even if the metre suffers. There has been much editorial patching of metre in this play.

READ: *should he doubt,*

3.22 *and doubting lest hee had err'de or sinn'de,*

Editors all insert *that* after *lest* to improve the metre, unconscionably, though encouraged by the F 3 text.

READ: as in Q.

3.28–9 *the Kings seas must please: hee scap'te the Land to*
perish at the Sea,

Editors read *at the seas* (Alexander) or *on the seas*, to
perfect a rhyme with *please* in an unrhymed speech. The
sense enforces a change in punctuation. 'It must be the
pleasure of the King's seas (that) he should escape by land
to perish at sea'. *at the sea* is alternative with the more
familiar modern *at sea*.

   READ: *the King's seas must please*
                 He 'scaped the land to perish at the sea.

4.13–14 *Our toungs and sorrowes to sound deepe:*
           Our woes into the aire, our eyes to weepe.

Editors (except Alexander) read *do* for *to* in both lines.
But the construction of the whole passage rests upon 'Who
wanteth' in l. 11. 'Who wants, or can conceal, his
hunger, tongues to speak, eyes to weep.'

   READ: *Our tongues and sorrows to sound deep our woes*
            Into the air, our eyes to weep, till tongues

ACT 2

Chorus, ll. 23–4 *How* Thaliart *came full bent with sinne,*
                And hid in Tent to murdred him;

The reading cited is agreed by the Malone and Flower
copies. The B.M. and White copies, however, read

           And had intent to murder him;

at l. 24. The compositor of Q1 apparently rationalized *hid*
intent in his copy to *hid in Tent,* and the press-corrector
improved this to *had intent.* The compositor of Q2,
working on an uncorrected copy of Q1, arrived at what

seems likely to be the true original text, and the three copies collated, B.M., Folger 1, and Folger 2, read

> *And hid intent to murder him;*

which is also the reading of Q 3 of 1611. Recent editors, including Alexander, follow the reading of Q 4 of 1619, F 3, and later Quartos:

> *And had intent to murder him;*

hid intent means 'concealed his purpose to kill him', i.e. 'with a concealed purpose'. Q 2 also corrects *Thaliart* to *Thaliard*.

> READ: *How Thaliard came full bent with sin,*
>   *And hid intent to murder him;*

1.57–9 *Honest good fellow what's that, if it be a day fits you Search out of the Kalender, and no body looke after it?*

The following reading is accepted, as in recent editions:

> *Honest—good fellow! What's that? If it be a day fits you, scratch't out of the calendar, and nobody look after it.*

Apart from the liberties taken with the text, this does not seem to be the sense of the passage, as I see it. The sense is, 'What does honesty matter, if it is a day that fits your job? Look *elsewhere than in* (*out of*) the calendar, and seek no advice of anyone (or, let no one ask any questions)'.

These fishermen have odd ways of thinking, as appears throughout, but this is practical, if unconventional, good sense.

> READ: *Honest, good fellow? What's that, if it be a day fits you? Search out of the calendar, and nobody look after it.*

1.60 *May see the Sea hath cast vpon your coast:*

With all zeal for retaining the original text, I cannot think that *May* (presumably 'You may'), as read by editors, is genuine. Malone's *Nay* seems irresistible to me, and plausible. Pericles is impatient, not without cause, to get his story told to these interrupting fishermen.

READ: *Nay, see the sea hath cast upon your coast—*

1.82–4 *Die, ke-tha; now Gods forbid't, and I haue a Gowne heere, come put it on, keepe thee warme:*

Editors read *forbid't! And I have a gown here!* which seems very improbable in the Fisherman. Miss Husbands suggests privately that *and* is here 'if', and this seems to me certain. The modern convention of using *an* for *and* ('if') has concealed the clear sense.

READ: *Die quotha? Now gods forbid't, an I have a gown here; come put it on, keep thee warm.*

1.94 *Why, are you Beggers whipt then?*

Editors all read *all your beggars,* doubtless because of 'O not all' in l. 95. *your* for *you* is undoubtedly right, but *all* is unnecessary. *your beggars* means 'beggars as a class' or 'beggars, in your experience'. Pilch answers with precision, 'Not all'.

READ: *Why, are your beggars whipped then?*

1.140 *Since I haue heere my Father gaue in his Will.*

Editors all follow the F 3 reading *my father's gift in's will,* which I take to be editorial and without authority. The Quarto reading, awkward to modern ears, yet presents no difficulty. It is an elliptical phrase, '(what) my father gave', to which there are many parallels. This speech has just offered, 'the rough seas...Took it in rage, though calmed have given't again', which is no less elliptical.

READ: *Since I have here my father gave in his will.*

1.152 *Why di'e take it:*

Editors read *do'ee* or *do'e,* suggesting dialect in the Fisherman's speech suddenly. But it is clearly the familiar *d'ye* of ordinary speech, with the same sense.

READ: *Why, d'ye take it,*

1.161 *And spight of all the rupture of the Sea,*

Editors emend to *rapture*, interpreted as 'robbery, forcible seizure'. It seems to me that the Quarto *rupture* may well stand unemended, in the sense of 'the breaches of the sea, the breaking seas'. Pilch has just spoken of the *rough...waters*. The phrase might alternatively mean 'the damage done by the sea'.

R E A D : *the rupture of the sea,*

Sc. 2. **Stage-direction.** I suggest that the upper stage represents a pavilion or gallery for the King and his Court. The lists are behind the stage, unseen. The gallery looks out one way upon the Knights passing over the main stage, and the other way to the lists. There is no need for the erection of a pavilion on the main stage, as in most editors' stage-directions.

R E A D : Pentapolis. Before the Lists.

Enter above *Simonides, Thaisa, Lords,* and *Attendants.*

2.14–15 *T'is now your honour (Daughter) to entertaine*
The labour of each Knight, in his deuice.

Editors read *explain* for *entertaine*, a violent emendation, and unexplained. Simonides in fact does all the 'explaining' of the devices, in his replies to Thaisa. *Entertain* means, in effect, 'receive' the shields presented by the Squires with each Knight's device. There is no need for emendation.

R E A D : *to entertain*

3.24–6 *Contend not sir, for we are Gentlemen,*
Haue neither in our hearts, nor outward eyes,
Enuies the great, nor shall the low despise.

Editors follow F 3, and read *That neither* in l. 25, and *Envy* in l. 26. The Folio reading, however, has no more than editorial validity, if any. Here a plausible error on the part of the Quarto compositor is *enuies* for *envied*. The sense, moreover, is superior with this simpler emendation of Quarto. Logic is with the sequence of thought, 'we have not envied the great, nor shall we despise the low'. The elliptical construction, omitting the relative pronoun *that* in l. 25, is familiar in Elizabethan English, e.g. 'You cannot name the persons bring this danger' (*Bloody Brother* 4.2).

READ: *Have neither in our hearts, nor outward eyes,*
     Envied

3.64 *Therefore to make his entraunce more sweet,*

Having read *explain* for *entertain* in Sc. 2, l. 14, editors here read *entertain* for *entraunce*, with no more probability or necessity. *Entrance* surely gives good sense, and refers back to 'every one *that comes* To honour them' above (ll. 60–1). Metrically, *entrance* can well be a trisyllable.

READ: as in Q.

4.34–7 *Whose death in deed, the strongest in our sensure,*
     And knowing this Kingdome is without a head,
     Like goodly Buyldings left without a Roofe,
     Soone fall to ruine: your noble selfe,

Editors emend: *death's* for *death*, *if* for *is*. But emendation is unnecessary if the construction of the original text be understood. Lines 34 and 35 are absolute constructions, which are frequent in the style of this play elsewhere. The Lords *knew* the kingdom to be without a head, judging Pericles' death to be certain. In l. 36 *Like*, as often, means *as*, as in modern colloquial English. The colon after *ruin* points to a break in the construction, and is best represented by a dash.

READ: as in Q., ending with
     Soon fall to ruin—your noble self,

ACT 3

Chorus, l. 6 *Now coutches from the Mouses hole;*

Editors all read *fore* for *from*. But perhaps Shakespeare knew better how cats catch mice. No mouse would run out straight into a cat's mouth. *from* means 'near but not immediately in front, at a little distance', and is exact.

READ: *from*

Chorus, l. 8 *Are the blyther for their drouth:*

Editors read *E'er* or *Aye* for *Are*, unnecessarily. The text as it stands is a disjunctive sentence with good sense, 'they sing because they are drouthy'. The construction is familiar and frequent.

READ: *Are*

Chorus, l. 46 *but fortune mou'd,*

Editors read *fortune's mood*, presumably to perfect the rhyme with *flood* in l. 45. The original text gives good sense, and Shakespeare-Gower permits some poor rhymes which editors pass unemended, e.g. *oppress—Pericles*, *moons—dooms*, in this same *Chorus*.

READ: as in Q.

1.26 *Vse honour with you.*

Most editors read *vie* for *use*. But *vie* gives a wrong sense. The sense of the Quarto text is clear, and the phrase 'use honour' quite normal. 'We behave in an honourable way with you gods, not taking back our gifts to you'. (Not so the gods; there is no question of *vying* in honour with them.)

READ: *Use honour with you.*

1.53 *And we are strong in easterne,*

Boswell's conjecture, *custom* for *easterne*, is fully justified in sense, and is entirely plausible graphically, as other conjectures are not.

READ: *strong in custom.*

1.61–3 *Must cast thee scarcly Coffind, in oare,*
       Where for a monument vpon thy bones,
       The ayre remayning lampes,

There is evident corruption here. In l. 63, *The* must be an error for *And*. 'In place of a monument and of lamps or torches ever kept burning on it'. *in oare* offers great difficulty. P. Edwards (*Shakespeare Survey* 5, p. 35) calls it 'unguessable'. *wave* might seem plausible graphically, with *the* omitted. But the accepted conjecture *ooze* answers the sense better, for Pericles is clearly thinking of the coffin falling upon the *bed* of the sea, 'lying with simple shells' (l. 65), to which *ooze* is appropriate. In a mixed hand, with the modern italic form of z used in place of the long Secretary form, *z* and *r* could well be confused, as could *oo* with *oa*. (Possibly, however, in damaged copy, the descender of the z was torn or obliterated, and the letter thus read as *r*. In 4.1.27 the compositor's *marre it* for *margent* suggests the similar loss of the descender of the *g*.)

READ: *in the ooze;...*
       And aye-remaining lamps,

2.41 *Tie my pleasure vp in silken Bagges,*

Editors, except Ridley, accept the facile emendation *treasure* for *pleasure*, without plausibility or need. The sense is, 'set my pleasure in money tied up in silken bags', with a clear recurrence of the thought 'in course of true *delight*' (l. 39).

READ: *tie my pleasure up*

2.48 *Such strong renowne, as time shall neuer.*

F 3 reads, editorially, *renown, as never shall decay.*
Editors all read with the guess *never raze* or *ne'er decay.* But
it is reasonable to consider that the speech is interrupted by
the entry of servants with the coffer, a dramatic moment,
upon which Cerimon cries, 'What's that?'

READ: *as time shall never—*

3.36 *to the mask'd* Neptune,

Recent editors rightly reject emendation. *the masked
Neptune* means 'the sea whose fury is masked'. Cf. 'the
gentlest winds of heaven'.

READ: *the masked Neptune,*

ACT 4

1.4–8 *let not conscience which is but cold, in flaming, thy loue
bosome, enflame too nicelie, nor let pittie which euen women
haue cast off, melt thee, but be a souldier to thy purpose.*

Editors have found inevitable difficulty in arranging
these words into metre and sense, and have resorted to
emendation, e.g. Knight's *inflaming love in thy bosom* for *in
flaming, thy loue bosome,* But we have surely 'foul papers'
for copy here, with corrections *currente calamo* in line and
margin, all printed by a baffled compositor. I suggest that
the copy read as follows: *Let not conscience which is but
cold,* [*inflaming*] *thy* ∧ ⌐*love*⌐ [*bosom*] with marginal *enflame
too nicely.*[1] The sense is clear: 'Let not thy love enflame thy
conscience (which is but cold) too nicely'.

READ: *Let not conscience,*
          Which is but cold, thy love inflame too nicely;
          Nor let pity, which even women have cast off,
          Melt thee, but be a soldier to thy purpose.

The metrical pattern of l. 6 is very similar to that of l. 11,
'She comes weeping for her only mistress' death'.

---

[1] Square brackets indicate deleted words, broken brackets a word interlined.

2.22 *Thou sayest true, ther's two vnwholesome a conscience,*

Editors read *They are too unwholesome,* I cannot conceive why. The Pandar is precise in reply to the Bawd. 'You are quite right; there are two of them that are really badly diseased (*unwholesome a conscience*), and the little one actually killed the Transylvanian.'

READ: *there's two unwholesome a conscience.*

2.108 *there was a Spaniards mouth watred, and he went to bed to her verie description.*

Editors follow Q4 of 1619, and read *mouth so watered, that he.* Kittredge reads *so* also, but *and he* for *that he.* There is no need to emend the much more idiomatic and characteristic original text, which offers no difficulty of sense or syntax, except to pedantic grammar.

READ: as in Q.

3.27–8 *he did not flow from honourable courses.*

Recent editors read *sources* for *courses,* despite Malone's just defence of *courses. sources* has no graphic plausibility. And *courses,* as in the familiar word 'water-courses', is relevant here in relation to *flow.*

READ: *courses.*

4.1 *Thus time we waste, & long leagues make short,*

Editors improve Shakespeare-Gower's metre by reading *longest.* But here as elsewhere Shakespeare is consciously archaizing, and Gower, like Chaucer, was then held to be metrically uncertain, as is well known. There is no other point in reading *longest.*

READ: *long*

6.43 *it giues a good report to a number to be chaste.*

Various emendations, e.g. *member, wanton,* have been proposed for *number.* Recent editors read as in Quarto, though *New Temple* thinks it colourless and therefore corrupt. The sense is plain, and pregnant. 'Modesty (in speech) gives a reputation for chastity to many (who are unchaste in act).'

READ: as in Q.

ACT 5

Chorus, l. 20 *with former hyes,*

In the Flower and White copies *former* is corrected to *feruor*, as in Q2 also.

READ: *with fervour hies.*

1.84 **Per.** *Hum, ha.*

A stage-direction is required to interpret this inarticulate growl, and is indicated in l. 127 ('Didst thou not say, when I did push thee back') as also in Shakespeare's sources.

READ: Per. [thrusts her aside]. *Hum, ha.*

1.155–6 *Haue you a working pulse, and are no Fairie?*
　　　Motion well, speake on, where were you borne?

Here Folio gives the true reading, *Motion? Well speak on.* Kittredge emends *No motion?* as does *New Temple.* Alexander reads *Motion!*, presumably with Pericles observing that Marina does in fact move. I cannot doubt that *motion* here is used in the sense of 'puppet', as a sequel to *fairy*, and presumably Kittredge and Ridley read in this sense. While *No motion* improves the metre, it is not essential to the sense or a necessary emendation.

READ: *Motion? Well, speak on,*

1.164–5 *This cannot be my daughter, buried,*

Editors emend to, *This cannot be. My daughter's buried.* The speech is, however, disjointed, and Pericles is speaking

aside here, a close reflection of thought. Folio conveys the
true reading, as I think, *daughter; buried!*

READ: *This cannot be*
         My daughter—buried!—Well, where were you
         bred?

1.168 *You scorne, beleeue me twere best I did giue ore.*

Malone proposed *You'll scarce believe me*, but among
recent editors only Kittredge and Ridley find corruption
in the Quarto text. Marina naturally feels that her story
is difficult to believe. And Pericles is questioning her
closely. He has just said, 'O stop there a little'. It is all
quite natural and intelligible.

READ: *You scorn. Believe me 'twere best I did give o'er.*

1.209 *And an other like to* Pericles *thy father.*

Mason's *life* for *like* is certain, and graphically plausible.
Pericles is restored to life from his melancholy. Cf. 'Thou
that beget'st him that did thee beget' (l. 197).

READ: *life*

1.233 Lys. *Musicke my Lord? I heare.*

Most editors, including Alexander, take *Musicke* as a
stage-direction, and read, Lys. *My lord, I hear.* [Music.]
New Temple reads, Lys. *Music, my lord?* Per. *I hear.* It
does not appear to be understood that this heavenly music
is audible only to Pericles, even as a ghost may appear to
one person only, invisible to others. The stage-direction is
therefore out of place. Lysimachus has just said that
Pericles must be humoured, 'It is not good to cross him,
give him way', and now humours him by saying that he
does hear the music. The F 3 editor seems to have understood this.

READ: *Music, my lord, I hear.*

1.262 *I haue another sleight.*

Editors rightly emend to *another suit,* and the emendation is plausible, with *suit* spelled *shoote* as often, misread *sleite* (printed *sleight*).

READ: *suit.*

2.2 *More a little, and then dum.*

Editors, including recent editors, read *dumb.* But the spelling *dum* for *dumb* is very unusual, nor could *dumb* be misread as *dum.* Gower, moreover, is not *dumb* hereafter; he speaks again. The rhyme is weak. I suggest that the true reading is *done,* possibly spelled *dun* for eye-rhyme. (Cf. *mum* for *nun* below.) So Rowe and Steevens read.

READ: *More a little, and then done.*

3.15 *What meanes the mum?*

Some editors, with Q4 and F3, read *woman* for *mum,* a bad editorial guess. *nun* is certain, and so recent editors agree. Thaisa is High Priestess here.

READ: *What means the nun?*

3.69–70 *Pure* Dian *blesse thee for thy vision, and will offer night oblations to thee* Thaisa,

Editors follow F3 in reading *Pure Dian, bless thee for thy vision, I will offer.* There is no v⸺⸺ editorial in Folio, however. And *I* could h⸺ as *and.* A much more probable error of⸺ was the simple omission of *I* before *bless,* a⸺ suggested privately, which gives a far more⸺ And so *New Temple* reads also.

READ: *Pure Dian, I bless thee for thy* ⸺
      Will offer night-oblations to thee ⸺

NEW
READINGS
in
Shakespeare

C. J. Sisson

VOL. II

❦

Cambridge